INTRODUCTION TO LEGAL METHOD

AUSTRALIA
The Law Book Company
Sydney

CANADA
The Carswell Company
Toronto, Ontario

INDIA
N. M. Tripathi (Private) Ltd.
Bombay
and
Eastern Law House (Private) Ltd.
Calcutta

M.P.P. House
Bangalore

Universal Book Traders
Delhi

ISRAEL
Steimatzky's Agency Ltd.
Tel-Aviv

PAKISTAN
Pakistan Law House
Karachi

INTRODUCTION TO
LEGAL METHOD

Third Edition

by

JOHN H. FARRAR, LL.M., Ph.D.

Barrister of the High Court of New Zealand; Professor of Law at the University of Canterbury, New Zealand and formerly at University College, Cardiff.

and

ANTHONY M. DUGDALE, B.A., B.C.L.

Professor of Law in the University of Keele

LONDON
SWEET & MAXWELL
1990

First edition 1977
Second impression 1978
Third impression 1981
Second edition 1984
Third edition 1990
Second impression 1992

Published by Sweet & Maxwell Limited of
South Quay Plaza, 183 Marsh Wall, London E14 9FT
Phototypeset by LBJ Enterprises Limited, Chilcompton, Somerset
Printed by Richard Clay Limited, Bungay, Suffolk

British Library Cataloguing in Publication Data
Farrah, John H. (John Hynes), 1941–
    Introduction to legal method.—3rd ed. *by J. H. Farrar,*
A. M. Dugdale
1. England. Law
I. Title   II. Dugdale, Anthony M.
344.2

ISBN 0–421–42770–1

To
Susannah, Sarah, Nicholas
and
Rebecca

PREFACE TO THE THIRD EDITION

WE had two goals in undertaking a third edition of *Legal Method*. The first was to update our illustrative material. Our method of encouraging students to reflect on theoretical issues has been to provide plenty of examples in the text and we have striven to keep these as fresh and interesting as possible. As a result, the Case Law in Operation chapter has been entirely rewritten and many other chapters have been substantially revised.

Our second aim was to reflect changes in thinking about legal method. Hence, in this edition we have made reference to recent developments in the legal literature. We have also noted writings which examine method from a comparative and cultural perspective. We have had more to say about the contribution of Professor Ronald Dworkin to everyone's thinking about legal method. Legal Method does not stand still. In this edition we have treated the single market due for completion in 1992 as an example of how the E.E.C. works. By the next edition it may be the dominating theme of the book. It is this dynamic nature of the subject which makes it so fascinating to teach and, we hope, to study.

Once again we are indebted to Clive Ward for his advice in relation to the Law Library appendix. Our thanks also go to Jackie Williams for wordprocessing much of the text.

July 1989
John Farrar
Anthony Dugdale

PREFACE TO THE SECOND EDITION

THE first edition of this book received a general welcome. In one instance criticism of the book appeared somewhat gratuitously destructive but for the most part the critics were constructive in their approach and we hope that this edition has benefited from at least some of their comments. The second edition is written by both of us. We have together revised the whole but Tony Dugdale has taken specific responsibility for Chapters 3, 4, 6, 13 and 14, and has written Chapters 5, 8 and 10. John Farrar has taken specific responsibility for Chapters 1, 2, 7, 10 and 11, and has written Chapters 15 and 16. Ann Farrar has revised Chapter 9. The result is a substantially re-written second edition. The book has been revised to accommodate case law and statutory developments, the authors' experiences using the book for both law and liberal studies and to meet some of the criticisms made by others. There is new material (including in some cases new chapters) on

(1) legal classification
(2) law and fact
(3) dispute resolution including dispute resolution in the welfare state
(4) precedent
(5) interpretation of statutes
(6) the role of the European Convention on Human Rights and the legislative powers of the EEC with particular reference to problems of sex discrimination
(7) law reform and the pattern of legal change
(8) comparative legal cultures
(9) justice and policy.

Other new features include extended treatment of case law, legislation and codification in operation. Overall an effort has been made to use more examples from the substantive law to illustrate the 'method' themes of the book.

We hope that these changes improve the book and help it to fulfil its aims of liberalising introductory law courses, showing how lawyers think, helping students to think for themselves about legal issues, and supplementing books on the legal system. In spite of appearances writing a book of this kind is not easy. We are especially grateful for the criticism and advice of colleagues, in particular David Feldman, Keith Stanton, Brenda Sufrin, Harold Wilkinson and Clive Ward. We would also like to thank Julie Smith for wordprocessing our manuscript.

February 1984   *John Farrar*
Anthony Dugdale

PREFACE TO THE FIRST EDITION

THE aim of this book is to introduce the reader to law and legal method and to stimulate thought about law and society. Part I of the book introduces law by discussing the nature and functions of law, the classification of law and the basic techniques of social control used in the legal system. Part II introduces legal method more specifically by discussing the general problems of law and fact, legal categorisation and reasoning, the particular data and ground rules relating to case law, legislation, codification, legal literature and the impact of membership of the EEC. This Part is supplemented by three appendices which set out specimen legal sources, give instruction in legal bibliography and provide a detailed study of the case law process. Throughout Parts I and II there is an attempt to relate law to its social background and this is the special focus of Part III of the book which deals with socio-economic change, the limits of law and the underlying questions of policy and values. The book does not deal in any detail with the institutions of the legal system which are already adequately dealt with elsewhere and it is hoped that, together with works on the institutions, it can be used in a first-year course on the legal system in the universities and polytechnics. I have used the bulk of the material for that purpose in the LL.B. course at the University of Bristol. The main problem I encountered was the lack of a suitable accompanying text on legal method—a gap which this book attempts to fill. It is hoped that it will, therefore, be of some use to first-year law students in helping them to acquire a basic knowledge of legal rules, an understanding of the relationship of law to the social and economic environment in which it operates and the ability to handle facts and apply abstract concepts to them, which the Ormrod Report identified as the objectives of the academic stage of legal education. At the same time it is hoped that it will assist others (such as social scientists) who are keen to learn something of the lawyer's viewpoint and some basic detail about legal sources. Lastly it is hoped that it might be of some use to continental lawyers who need to be familiar with

English legal method. The book reflects some experience which I have had in teaching EEC officials on courses held at the University of Bath from which, in all honesty, I probably learned as much as I taught about the differences between the various systems.

Although footnotes are used in the text I have tried to keep them to a minimum, and have added a bibliography of further reading at the end. I apologise for the table which appears on pages 205 *et seq.* Ideally, I would have liked to have inserted details of abbreviations, but there was insufficient space. As it is, there is a lot of detail crammed into a relatively small space. I only hope its utility will outweigh its unattractiveness.

The genesis of this book owes a great deal to Professor Glanville Williams' *Learning the Law.* It differs from that book, which is and will remain a guide, philosopher and friend to the aspiring law student, in the following respects. It is less didactic in style. It concentrates on legal method in more detail, and it attempts to give a prologue to a social view of law in the way described above. It makes frequent comparisons with Scots law and other systems. In some of these respects it owes something to Pollock's *A First Book of Jurisprudence*, Derham, Maher and Waller's *Introduction to Law*; and Levi's *Introduction to Legal Reasoning*. The late Professor Friedmann's *Law in a Changing Society*, Sir Rupert Cross, *Precedent in English Law* and Professor Robert Summers' *Law: its Nature, Functions and Limits* and his recent articles on legal techniques and process values have all been drawn upon for useful comment and examples. I have also profited from attending a seminar given by Professor Summers on the limits of law.

Despite its relative brevity this has not been an easy book to write. Whatever merit (if any) it has is due in some measure to students and colleagues who have discussed things with me. Amongst these I would particularly thank Neil Johnson, Dorothy Nelson, Hugh Beale, Stephen Jones, Brenda Sufrin, Tony Dugdale, and David and Carolyn Yates.

Last, for those sceptical academics who might think that to use this kind of material at the beginning of the first year is expecting too much too soon—all I can say is that it has been shown to work in the past with what I think was a moderate degree of success. I found student response on the whole to be enthusiastic. They seemed to use the training to advantage in other subjects, and Jurisprudence was not such an alien subject to them in the third year.

January 1977   *John Farrar*

ACKNOWLEDGMENTS

THE extract from *Essays in Jurisprudence and the Common Law* is reproduced by kind permission of Professor A. L. Goodhart and Cambridge University Press (© Cambridge University Press 1931).

Extracts from "The Ratio of the Ratio Decidendi" (1959) 22 M.L.R. 597 are reproduced by kind permission of Professor Julius Stone and The Modern Law Review Ltd.

The Human Organ Transplants Act 1989 and Statutory Instrument 1974 No. 654 are reproduced by kind permission of Her Majesty's Stationery Office.

The extract from [1976] 1 Q.B. is reproduced by kind permission of The Incorporated Council of Law Reporting for England and Wales.

CONTENTS

Book I

Introduction to Law

Book II

Sources of Law and Methods of Legal Reasoning

Book III

Wider Dimensions of the Law and Legal Method

Appendices

TABLE OF CASES

TABLE OF STATUTES

BOOK I

Introduction to Law

Chapter 1

THE NATURE AND FUNCTIONS OF LAW

It is customary to preface a discussion about law with one or two broad generalisations about the nature of human beings. Yet it is sometimes said that one cannot or should not generalise. This is patent nonsense. One can generalise but the generalisation must be supported by evidence, and the danger arises in generalising beyond the particular evidence available. Certain generalisations about human beings are universally valid, such as "all people are mortal" and that "from a global point of view there are limited resources." Some would go further and make other general comments about the human condition, about mankind being basically good or evil. Clearly there are dangers in generalisations of this latter order, and they often hide a particular ideological bias. It is probably better to view human nature as many-sided and sometimes contradictory and leave the subject to theologians to dispute amongst themselves.

"TRUISMS" ABOUT HUMAN NATURE

Professor H.L.A. Hart in his book, *The Concept of Law*,[1] put forward certain generalisations about mankind which he says are truisms, and which, given survival as an aim, afford a reason (or more precisely a set of reasons) why morality and law endure and possess a specific content. The facts are

1. human vulnerability,
2. approximate equality,
3. limited altruism,
4. limited resources, and
5. limited understanding and strength of will.

These are of course vague, and some, such as approximate equality and limited understanding, are perhaps inherently controversial. Also, their status as truisms is ambiguous—since it is not clear whether their self-evidence is to be regarded as apparent on the face of them or only in the light of extraneous considerations which are to be assumed. Hart himself acknowledges that his truisms are based on the philosophical writings of Hobbes and Hume rather than empirical research.[2]

There is some research which has been done by psychologists, indicating a human need for order and predictability in life.[3] Clearly the scientific standing of such research findings may be a matter of controversy—controversy which sometimes challenges the basic claim of social science to be scientific. There are problems of clinical testing, coping with value considerations, and in the scope of the generalisations put forward. It may be that out of considerations such as these Hart relies on truisms and says that the relationship of his truisms to the existence of a common content of morality and law is not a matter of causation (cause and effect) but "natural necessity," by which he seems to mean that they afford practical reasons for such content.[4]

SOCIAL ORDER AND LAW

To a social scientist they afford reasons for social order in the sense of restraint, predictability, consistency, reciprocity and persistence in human behaviour.[5] A solitary individual—a hermit living in complete isolation from other human beings—probably requires nothing more than habits. Habits, according to some scientists, arise because of our limited supplies of mental and physical energy. It is debatable whether the individual family needs anything more than habits, although some families do in fact have rules. When one gets socialisation consisting at least of a number of families the habits, or some of them, seem to begin to crystallise into customs and then into rules.

The existence of such rules used to be explained by reference to a social contract, but the evidence for such a pact in early or present-day primitive communities is not forthcoming. Hume instead explained the existence of social order in terms of habit and self interest[6]; Durkheim in terms of cohesion produced by social solidarity, the principal forms of which were embodied in the law.[7] Others more recently have emphasised particular factors such as a consensus of values, inertia, or conflict and coercion.[8] All of these are themes to which we shall return. Modern industrialised societies are complex systems with many variables operating. The social contract idea, although it has recently been resuscitated is at best a simplistic artificial construction useful perhaps to *justify* the existing order or a better one, but not to explain it.[9] The facts which modern writers identify are useful (perhaps necessary) in an account of social order but they are not individually sufficient to explain it.

In primitive societies when rules are broken and the breach is not the subject-matter of feud, social order is often maintained by a series of unorganised sanctions such as ostracism, ridicule, avoidance and denial of favours. In some societies, such as the Yurok Indians, these were supplemented by go-betweens who acted in a positive but non-judicial way in disputes. Their role is primarily that of diplomats. Amongst the Luhya tribe of western Kenya, the elders intervene and perform a similar role. In such societies the emphasis is on reconciliation of the parties as much as resolution of a particular dispute since there is a need for continuing contact between the parties.[10]

Eventually some of the rules become recognised as laws. In England this was largely a result of adjudication and assimilation by the King's judges. From this you might infer that law in general is a set of particular laws recognised by the judges.

This idea of law is a reasonable one but inadequate. It fails to indicate that people often talk of law not so much in terms of particular laws but in terms of a system. Law is sometimes equated with government and a legal system. In this sense law in our society would include Parliament, the courts, the judiciary, the legal profession and the police and bureaucracy who service the system. Again, some equate law with the legal process, which refers primarily to the legislative and judicial processes—the making of Acts of Parliament and delegated legislation, and the adjudication by judges. This book is principally about law in the sense of a set of laws and the legal process. It refers to the institutions but does not purport to give a detailed treatment of them. The sense in which we refer to law from time to time will, however, be clear from the context.

Law in all three senses of laws, system and process[11] is one of a number of means of social control fostering social order in modern society. The term "social control" was used by an American writer, Ross,[12] as a broad term to cover not only law but also public opinion, religion, education, custom and other less obvious things, such as art. In this broad sense it would cover the unorganised sanctions referred to above. Some recent writers have tended to limit its application to control of deviance.

In what way does law as an instrument of social control help to foster social order? What are its social functions?[13] First, it maintains *public order*. Sometimes this is expressed in the cliché "law and order." This is a woolly term often used for emotive purposes by the less reputable species of politician and is better avoided. Historically, law has evolved as an alternative to private feud and vengeance, and as a supplement to the informal social processes by which men and groups deal with disputes. Law has the advantage over both feud and the more informal alternatives, in that it provides a rationalised and conclusive settlement to disputes which is subject to public scrutiny.

Another aspect of maintenance of public order is the suppression of deviant behaviour. What is regarded as deviant differs as society changes. In an open society this is a matter of public debate and controversy. How far should the area of the law extend and for what reasons? We shall return to this topic later.

Secondly, law fosters social order by *facilitating co-operative action*. Law recognises certain basic underlying interests and provides a framework of rules for giving effect to them. Thus, for instance, it recognises a person's right to freedom from physical injury and protects property. It provides systems for transfer and inheritance of property and formation of groups for peaceful purposes.

Thirdly, it *constitutes and regulates the principal organs of power*. It provides for succession to power and defines who has the right to exercise what kind of power in society. The United Kingdom is peculiar in that it does not have a written constitution. It does, however, have a constitution consisting of a body of particular laws, conventions and traditions which regulate its political life. Finally, law *communicates and reinforces social values*. Law has always enforced some morality. Even the most primitive legal order seeks to regulate matters such as homicide and theft. Bentham[14] and John Stuart Mill[15] discussed the limits within which law should be used to enforce morality. Both favoured a rationalistic approach, and Mill put the emphasis on the value of the maximum freedom for the individual which was compatible with the freedom of others. At the same time they both sought to reform the law so that it reflected their brand of morality, *utility*, the greatest happiness of the greater number. Mill at least perceived a possible contradiction in these attitudes in that utility could lead to the tyranny of the majority and he sought to justify himself by modifying the rigours of utility. More recently the debate has continued between Lord Devlin[16] and Professor Hart[17] and others[18] over the identification of moral standards and the extent of the law's need and right to enforce them. Again, we shall return to this later.

With the growth of collectivism and the welfare state, a wide range of matters formerly left to the individual conscience has been made the subject of state control through law. At other times Parliament has legislated to regulate behaviour in advance of public opinion and has used the law partly as an educative medium on such issues as capital punishment, homosexuality, race relations and sex equality.

The relationship then between law and morality is complex. Analytically the relationship can be crudely represented thus:

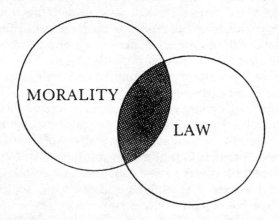

The shaded area represents the area of common ground where law enforces morality. The size of the shaded area is constantly changing. The one great danger with this simplification is that it perhaps suggests a commonly accepted morality in the sense of specific, ascertainable moral rules. In other words, it presupposes the existence of common morality and some consensus on its content. With the growth of relativism in moral beliefs it is becoming more and more difficult to identify a consensus morality. The areas of consensus are yielding ground to opinion and controversy. Any comprehensive view of a legal system must reflect both this tension and the underlying interests represented by existing institutions and pressure groups of varying kinds seeking either the maintenance or reform of the status quo. We shall explore this theme in the third part of this book.

THE NORMATIVE CHARACTER OF LAW AND MORALITY

We have seen the close analytical and causal relationship between law and morality. We are using the word law here in the sense of a set of particular laws. Perhaps it would be better to be even more explicit. The set of laws comprehends *legal rules, principles, standards and concepts*. How can one distinguish between these?[19] An American writer, Dean Roscoe Pound, defines *rule* as a precept attaching a definite detailed consequence to a definite detailed state of facts. He gave as an example a provision in the ancient Code of Hammurabi "If a free man strike a free man, he shall pay ten shekels of silver," and made the point that primitive codes and modern criminal codes are made up of such rules.

His definition of a *principle* is less satisfactory. He adopted the Aristotelian definition of a principle as an authoritative starting point for reasoning. Perhaps a better definition for our purposes would be in terms of a precept of the same basic form as a rule, but expressed at a greater level of generality. An example might be "No man shall profit from his own wrong." Principles often, but do not necessarily have, some ethical content. It is arguable that principles are not made into law in a single judgment and that they evolve rather like custom.[20] They tend to emerge from a number of authorities often as a means of circumscribing a number of particular rules established by those authorities.

A *standard* Pound defined as a measure of conduct prescribed by law from which one departs at one's peril. An example would be the standard of due care to avoid unreasonable risk of injury to others. Standards are perhaps of a greater level of generality than either rules or principles. Standards usually have some element of ad hoc evaluation in terms of fairness or reasonableness. In the case of *Knuller (Publishing, Printing and Promotions) Ltd.* v. *D.P.P.* [1973] A.C. 435, 487A–B (H.L.) Lord Simon of Glaisdale described the operation of standards as follows:

"They depend finally for their juridical classification not upon proof of the existence of some particular fact, but upon proof of the attainment of some degree. The law cannot always say that if fact X and fact Y are proved . . . legal result Z will ensue. Often the law can only say that if conduct of a stipulated standard is attained (or, more often, is not attained) legal result Z will ensue; and whether that standard has been attained cannot be with certainty known in advance by the persons involved, but has to await the evaluation of the tribunal of fact."

A *concept*, broadly speaking, is the general idea of a class of things. Sometimes in legal usage the word category is used instead of concept. Some concepts are ingredients of rules and principles such as the concepts of intention and good faith. Others such as ownership are of wider scope and are used in a broad generic way to embrace a number of rules, principles and standards. To a certain extent conceptual questions are questions about meaning and classification, *e.g.* is a bicycle a vehicle? In law, however, this is frequently complicated by the fact that the law has to make a decision on *borderline* cases for the purposes of social control. We shall examine this problem in more detail later.

Law is not unique in using rules, principles, standards and concepts. Morality also uses them together with attitudes. Morality, however, obviously differs from modern law in that it lacks a legislature and courts to adjudicate on disputes. Nevertheless, in so far as law and morality set out rules, principles and standards they are both said to have a normative character. Normative is derived from the Latin word *"norma"* which literally means a carpenter's measuring instrument, and the term norm[21] is used here to express the notion of a social standard applicable to fact as opposed to the fact to which the standard is applied. The application of a standard involves regulation or evaluation of fact. Law, *in the sense of system and process* can be described in factual statements but the *structure of particular laws* and of morals (other than moral attitudes) is of a different grammatical form from factual statements. It is sometimes said that laws and morals are "ought" rather than "is"; that although their exact wording may differ their structure is ultimately reducible to the form "You ought (or you ought not) to do X." "Ought" is used here in an extended sense, but is perhaps suggestive of something which is or is to be justified in some way. Both law (as a set of laws) and morality can perhaps be justified on rational grounds, but law always falls back on the notion of authority and internal consistency in the use of authority, which is called *legality*. An appeal to authority to clinch an argument in strict terms constitutes a logical fallacy and *proves* nothing, but law as a practical system proceeds on this basis. It is strongly arguable that in its nature as the instrument of organised social control, law has to have recognised authoritative sources and that there has to be a background of coercion and force for it to resort to, to ensure compliance. These are then the most crucial differences between law and morality in our society, that law has clearly recognised authoritative sources and can fall back on institutionalised coercion and force.[22]

THE LEGITIMACY OF LAW

However, even a legal system does not limit itself to force to guarantee its continuance. It seeks in addition to establish and cultivate a belief in its *legitimacy*.[23] Legitimacy according to its Latin origin meant conforming with law or legality. However, it has since acquired a more extended meaning which covers not only conformity with valid reasoning but also the possession of some extra quality of authenticity or genuineness. In the early period of a legal system, legitimacy may be based on *charismatic qualities* of particular rulers or judges. Later it may rest on the sanctity of *immemorial tradition*. Later still this may be in terms of the *impersonal rational authority* of the law—the rule of law not men—accepted both by those who administer the system and by the population at large. The common law shows traces of each of these—particularly tradition—although the emphasis in modern law is now shifting to the third. A general rationality is crucial to the legitimacy of the modern law and it may be, as we shall see in later chapters, that people are now coming to require that every law and legal practice should be justifiable on rational rather than traditional grounds. Rationality, according to the German lawyer and sociologist Max Weber, has two aspects—one a formal logical aspect based on intellectual consistency between the legal rules, principles, standards and concepts, and the other a substantive ideological or value aspect in the sense of conformity with the changing values of society.[24] The first is relatively static and the second dynamic. These represent a conflict or, more precisely, an antimony which is constantly being resolved in the course of legal development.[25] Law must be stable, yet it cannot stand still.[26]

Notes

[1] H. L. A. Hart, *The Concept of Law*, pp. 189 *et seq.*
[2] *Ibid.*, p. 254.
[3] See Edgar Bodenheimer, *Jurisprudence* (rev. ed.), Chap. X.
[4] Hart, *op. cit.*, p. 195.
[5] See Percy Cohen, *Modern Social Theory*, Chap. 2, Hart, *op. cit.*
[6] *Treatise of Human Nature.*
[7] *The Division of Labour in Society.*
[8] See Cohen, *op. cit.*
[9] See the reference to John Rawls' use of the concept in his *Theory of Justice* in Chap. 16, *infra.*
[10] For a fascinating study of such matters see S. Roberts, *Order and Dispute.*
[11] This is based on Roscoe Pound, *Social Control through Law*, p. 40.
[12] E. A. Ross, *Social Control.* For a useful modern discussion, see C. K. Watkins, *Social Control.*
[13] What follows is based on L. Broom and P. Selznick, *Sociology*, Chap. XII. See also M. D. A. Freeman, *The Legal Structure*, Part One.
[14] See Jeremy Bentham, *An Introduction to the Principles of Morals and Legislation*, ed. J. H. Burns and H. L. A. Hart, pp. 281 *et seq.*
[15] *Essays on Liberty and Utilitarianism.*
[16] *The Enforcement of Morals.*
[17] *Law, Liberty and Morality.*
[18] See generally a very useful summary of the debate in Basil Mitchell, *Law, Morality and Religion in a Secular Society.*
[19] What follows is based on Roscoe Pound, *Social Control through Law*, pp. 45 *et seq.*, with obvious modifications. The soundest approach to ascertain the meaning of such terms is to look and see how they are used in legal and moral language. Pound based his view on his familiarity with legal materials although he is a little dogmatic at times. For further discussion of rules and principles, see the materials referred to in the Bibliography.
[20] See Joseph Raz, "Legal Principles and the Limits of Law," 81 Yale L.J. 823, 848 (1972). *Cf.* generally R. Dworkin, *Taking Rights Seriously.*
[21] Sociologists use norm in a different sense. They use it to describe a pattern of regularity in behaviour.
[22] See generally Dennis Lloyd, *The Idea of Law*, Chaps. 2 and 3.
[23] This is based on Max Weber, *Law in Economy and Society*, translated by Max Rheinstein.
[24] *Op. cit.*, p. 6. Weber thought that the Common Law was substantively irrational since it was based too much on reaction to the particular case. See his views criticised by Rheinstein at pp. xlvii *et seq.*
[25] See Benjamin Cardozo, *The Paradoxes of Legal Science*, p. 7.
[26] R. Round, *Interpretations of Legal History*, p. 13.

Chapter 2

METHODS OF SOCIAL CONTROL THROUGH LAW

We saw in Chapter 1 how law is an instrument of social control, helping to maintain social order in a number of ways. Thus it serves to maintain public order, to facilitate co-operation, to regulate the exercise of power and to communicate and reinforce social values.

In this chapter we shall look at the methods of social control through law, at the basic techniques used by the modern law and the areas where they are used. But first, what precisely do we mean when we talk about such methods or techniques? We are thinking here not about sources of law and legal reasoning as such but about various systems that a legislator can adopt to achieve social ends through law. Each general technique really involves a set of particular techniques.

Professor Robert S. Summers, a leading American jurist, has identified these as the five basic techniques used in modern law: penal, grievance-remedial, private arranging, administrative-regulatory and public benefit conferral.[1]

In this chapter we shall adopt his analysis but add two more techniques—the constitutive and fiscal techniques—and rename his last technique the conferral of social benefits. The scheme then is as shown in the diagram on p. 14. It is hoped that by studying that diagram and following this analysis you will appreciate more of the breadth and diversity of the law. At

13

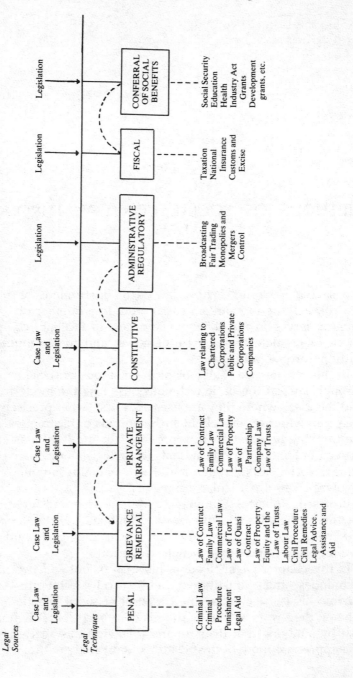

METHODS OF SOCIAL CONTROL THROUGH LAW THE BASIC LEGAL TECHNIQUES

Legal Sources

Legal Techniques

PENAL

Criminal Law
Criminal Procedure
Punishment
Legal Aid

Case Law and Legislation

GRIEVANCE REMEDIAL

Law of Contract
Family Law
Commercial Law
Law of Tort
Law of Quasi Contract
Law of Property
Equity and the Law of Trusts
Labour Law
Civil Procedure
Civil Remedies
Legal Advice, Assistance and Aid

Case Law and Legislation

PRIVATE ARRANGEMENT

Law of Contract
Family Law
Commercial Law
Law of Property
Law of Partnership
Company Law
Law of Trusts

Case Law and Legislation

CONSTITUTIVE

Law relating to Chartered Corporations
Public and Private Corporations
Companies

Case Law and Legislation

ADMINISTRATIVE REGULATORY

Broadcasting
Fair Trading
Monopolies and Mergers Control

Legislation

FISCAL

Taxation
National Insurance
Customs and Excise

Legislation

CONFERRAL OF SOCIAL BENEFITS

Social Security
Education
Health
Industry Act Grants
Development grants, etc.

Legislation

the same time we shall examine in relation to each technique what legal or other social alternatives are open to deal with problems in particular areas.

Let us now examine each of the techniques in the following order:

1. The Penal Technique
2. The Grievance-Remedial Technique
3. The Private Arranging Technique
4. The Constitutive Technique
5. The Administrative-Regulatory Technique
6. The Fiscal Technique
7. The Conferral of Social Benefits Technique

1. *THE PENAL TECHNIQUE*[2]

The first is an obvious one. It involves rules prohibiting certain deviant behaviour, the maintenance of a police force and other enforcement agencies to detect and prosecute violations, together with a system of courts to adjudicate questions of criminal liability. It also involves the maintenance of prisons, custody centres and other such places as a penal system. The criminal justice system is in fact merely the part of the legal system created for the specific purpose of applying the penal technique.

There are some who argue that the very application of the penal technique is made necessary because of the basic injustices inherent in our society which create the tensions leading to anti-social behaviour. If a person is denied reasonable outlets for his or her energies then he or she is likely to react in a manner which society stigmatises as anti-social. Penal techniques are then regarded as involving a labelling process. Those who propound such views often premise their arguments on a conflict model of society, whereas the traditional "establishment" view tends to base itself on a consensus model. The question of what is a just society is obviously an immensely complex value judgment. It is easier to condemn particular practices as unjust than to produce an articulate and convincing conception of the just. This may be because our reaction against injustice is a "gut reaction," a matter of emotion rather than reason. Also, what appears just to one society may seem unjust to another. Unfortunately, criminal laws, once they are part of the legal system, gather a life and momentum of their own and it needs strong public pressure channelled through organised pressure groups and exerted on the legislature to effect change.

Alternatives

What viable alternatives are there to the application of the penal technique in dealing with deviant behaviour? First there is non-intervention. In some areas of behaviour it may be thought that the application of the penal technique is not morally justified or not practicable. An illustration would be private sexual behaviour. Again it might be felt that particular categories of offenders might be better dealt with by a simple warning. This is often done with child offenders. A second alternative which is the symptom of an underdeveloped system is to leave the injured party to obtain his own appropriate redress on the basis of reciprocity—an eye for an eye and a tooth for a tooth. This is a dangerous system and can lead to violence and anarchy. As society develops, matters which relate to public order are taken out of this category. In many societies a third social alternative is censure by public opinion in various ways, which range from the unorganised to organised forms which approximate to modern law. In some societies deviants are treated as mentally ill and dealt with accordingly. Illustrations of this are the treatment of homosexuals in some Indian tribes and, until recently, the treatment of "liberals" in the U.S.S.R. Another social alternative to the application of the penal technique is the use of the fiscal technique. Behaviour which is regarded as anti-social in some way might be taxed heavily. An example of this is the practice of dividend-stripping whereby transactions in shares were carried out by financial manipulators to enable a tax refund to be obtained from the Inland Revenue when no tax had in fact been paid. Parliament introduced sweeping and complex tax legislation to penalise this particular form of deviance.

Effects of the penal technique

What are the particular effects of the application of the penal technique?[3]

First, the existence of the penal system deters some people from committing crimes. Some are deterred by the public enactment of penal prohibitions as such; others by the public announcement by law enforcement agencies that offenders will be brought to trial and punished; others by the physical presence of the police.

Perhaps a larger group accept penal prohibitions as part of the general mores of the society in which they live. Living honestly is a life-style. The existence of penal restrictions as such is almost peripheral to the totality of social factors producing conformity.

Secondly, there is the effect of the penal technique on law-breakers. Clearly the existence of penal prohibitions and the enforcement agencies have been insufficient to inhibit them. Neither have they been inhibited by the general mores of society at large. Their actual motiviation may differ widely; often it will be unknown to the police and the courts even at the end of the day; sometimes it will be unknown to the people themselves. The latter is a characteristic not limited to law-breakers. The devil himself knoweth not the mind of a man.

To the police and other law enforcement agencies the application of penal technique is a job, the efficacy of which is measured in terms of crimes prevented or criminals apprehended.

To the lawyers and the courts the question is first one of proof of fact, the application of legal rules and then one of handling. Has the crime been proved beyond all reasonable doubt? What is the appropriate punishment? How best can the convicted person be dealt with to ensure that he does not break the law again? Or, if that seems a lost hope, how best can society be protected against that person.

To those who work in the penal institutions the job is how to maintain discipline in an institution with these potentially conflicting goals of punishment, rehabilitation of the offender and deterrence from further crimes.

Example. One Saturday afternoon Mr. Brown, an old-age pensioner, is "mugged" outside a Bristol football ground. His wallet containing £20 is stolen and he himself suffers cuts and bruises to his head. Witnesses describe two men who were seen to make the attack and Tom and Dave are subsequently arrested by the police. In an identification parade they are picked out by the witnesses and Mr. Brown as being the men responsible. Tom and Dave are charged with robbery. They are kept in custody overnight and the next morning they appear before magistrates. The case is adjourned for a week but Tom and Dave are refused bail so they are remanded in custody to the local prison.

A week later they appear again before the magistrates and this time the committal proceedings commence. These proceedings are required for all serious charges to determine whether there is sufficient evidence for the case to go to trial at the Crown Court. At this stage, however, Tom and Dave are not on trial. The magistrates, having heard or read the evidence, decide that there is a case for the two men to answer, and they are committed in custody to the Crown Court. Both are granted legal aid.

After several weeks, the case comes up at the Crown Court. By this time, both men have seen their solicitors and barristers and have outlined their defence, which is that, although they had been to the match and were near the scene of the robbery at the time it took place, they were not the people who did it. At the trial Tom and Dave plead not guilty and the jury is sworn in. The prosecution counsel opens the case, stating the main facts on which the prosecution rely and the evidence which they intend to call. This evidence consists of the testimony of the witnesses, including Mr. Brown himself, who identify Tom and Dave as the men who committed the robbery. Each witness is called in turn and takes the oath. He is examined by prosecuting counsel, cross-examined by the respective counsel for Tom and Dave and then re-examined by prosecuting counsel. At the close of prosecution evidence, counsel for Tom and Dave in turn present their case. Tom's counsel makes an opening speech and then calls Tom who gives evidence that he did not commit the robbery. Tom is cross-examined by prosecuting counsel and then re-examined by his own counsel. Tom's counsel then calls his employer, Mr. Jones, who gives evidence that Tom is a man of sound character who has, to his knowledge, never been in any trouble before. There is no cross-examination. Dave's counsel then addresses the court and calls Dave who testifies that he was with Tom at the relevant time and that he too was not involved in the robbery. Dave is cross-examined by prosecuting counsel but there is no re-examination. The prosecution sums up the case against the two men and their counsel reply.

At the conclusion of the evidence and speeches, the judge sums up the case to the jury. He tells them that there is no doubt that Mr. Brown was robbed and that the question is purely one of identity. He warns them of the special need for caution in dealing with identification evidence which he analyses. He then adds that the jury should only return verdicts of guilty against either man if they are satisfied that the prosecution has proved his guilt beyond reasonable doubt. He tells the jury to retire and try to reach a unanimous verdict. After an hour the jury returns and the foreman announces that they have found both men guilty of robbery.

The prosecution then call a police officer who gives evidence that Dave, who is 27, has a number of previous convictions; two for theft, one for burglary and one for causing grievous bodily harm. For this last conviction he has spent a year in prison and was only released six months ago. On the other hand Tom, who is 18, has no previous convictions. The court receives social reports on the two men. These indicate that Dave has experienced a certain amount of difficulty in re-adjusting to normal life since coming out of prison and has also had financial problems. Concerning Tom, the report indicates that he has recently been troubled by the threat of redundancy and that his girl friend has left him. Counsel for Tom and Dave make pleas in mitigation, emphasising many of the points made in the reports. Tom's advocate stresses that the offence is completely out of character; that Tom has recently fallen into bad company, and it appears that his girl friend is ready to come back to him. Dave's counsel points out that Dave has only just come out of prison, has no job and is desperately short of money.

The judge tells the two men that this sort of conduct is far too common and that decent citizens are becoming scared to go out on the streets on Saturday afternoons. He adds that, by any standard, this is a serious offence and one that calls for stern measures. However, having heard the antecedents of both men, he is prepared to be lenient. He sentences Tom to youth custody. Dave is sentenced to two years' imprisonment. Both men are advised that nothing in the judge's summing-up gives any cause to appeal against conviction and that there is no point appealing to the Court of Appeal Criminal Division against the sentences which are certainly on the lenient side for this type of offence.

Thus, you can see the existence of criminal law and criminal procedure. The matter goes before two courts, the magistrates' court for a preliminary hearing and the Crown Court for a full trial. There is also the possibility of further appeal. The case was investigated and brought by the police. Solicitors and barristers are involved in the process of representation. This involves ascertaining the facts, considering the charge, researching the law and then representing the client in court as an advocate in what is an adversarial proceeding. In other words it is a contest rather than an inquisition. In this kind of case, which is pretty serious, the solicitor, having ascertained the facts and considered the charge, instructs (or briefs) a barrister who acts as the advocate in the Crown Court. Barristers have had a monopoly of rights of audience in the higher courts, which include the Crown Court, handling the more serious kind of offence. Whether this division of the English and Scottish legal professions can be maintained much longer is a matter of controversy which you will consider in the legal system part of your studies. Social workers are involved in producing reports on the two men. Then finally there are the youth custody and prison institutions. We have given you a rather detailed example to enable you to get the feel of an actual case. The facts have been built up from practical experience. The procedures and terminology in Scotland are different in a number of respects.

2. *THE GRIEVANCE-REMEDIAL TECHNIQUE*[4]

Professor Summers explains this technique as one which "defines remediable grievances, specifies remedies . . . and provides for enforcement of remedial awards."[5]

This particular general technique involves the statement of substantive legal rules, principles and standards which create rights and duties and remedies to back up those rights. It involves the existence of civil courts to process claims for the establishment of remedies.

This technique is used throughout the civil law. What alternatives to it exist? First, as we have seen, matters which relate to public order are taken out of the category of grievance-remedial and involve the application of the penal technique. Secondly, individuals may seek to provide their own private systems to deal with disputes. They might for example insert a liquidated damages clause in a contract, stipulating precisely how much a defaulting party is to pay to the injured party. Again the parties might decide to deal with the matter solely in terms of insurance cover. An example here would be a crash between two motor vehicles. Many drivers prefer to handle the matter outside court by referring it to their insurance companies who tend to handle the infinite range of motor "accidents" on a "knock-for-knock" basis. Some traders deal on the basis of standard form conditions of Trade Associations, which provide their own mechanisms for dealing with disputes. Often such contracts and indeed commercial contracts generally provide for arbitration which usually but not always avoids adjudication by the courts. An arbitration has the advantage of secrecy, informality and the possible use of a technical expert as arbitrator. It is not necessarily a cheaper procedure. Some contracts are now regulated by the application of the administrative regulatory technique which we shall consider later. Lastly, some disputes are dealt with by collective bargaining by trade unions and other representative bodies, and some by direct political action either in the form of pressure in Parliament or intervention by the Government. Obviously the latter are unusual cases.

Example. The classic case of the application of the grievance-remedial technique is a personal injuries claim in the law of tort.

Let us take an example. Mrs. Smith, a large old lady, is walking down the street in Bath, where she slips on a banana skin which Jim, a student, had just dropped in front of her. She breaks her leg and suffers nervous shock. What can she do? She goes along to Messrs. Whyte & Co., solicitors. Mr. Whyte advises her that she may have a claim in negligence against Jim under the law of tort.[6] The first thing he does is to write a letter to Jim making a claim with the hope of settlement out of court. Jim writes back a letter suggesting that Mrs. Smith should have looked where she was going. He then gets scared and goes along to see a solicitor, Sebastian Black. Messrs. Whyte & Co. consider whether they should try to negotiate further or start suing immediately. They decide to sue for £1,500 damages in the county court and take out a summons on which is endorsed a statement of claim alleging negligence. Sebastian Black enters a defence for Jim denying that Jim owed a duty of care to Mrs. Smith in the circumstances. A duty of care is one of the important ingredients in negligence. Sebastian Black also pleads in the alternative contributory negligence by Mrs. Smith. This means that even if Jim is held to be at fault Mrs. Smith was also careless to some degree in not looking where she was going. Various requests for information are made by both sides and then the parties come before the Registrar of the court for a pre-trial review. The purpose of this is to arrange matters with a view to shortening the hearing before the judge and giving the court officials an idea of how long the case will take.

The case is later heard before Judge Thomas. Mrs. Smith is represented by a barrister, Mr. Briggs. He outlines the facts of the case and calls his client and two witnesses to give evidence. Jim is represented by Sebastian Black since he has a lot of experience of advocacy in the county court. Solicitors have always been allowed to appear in the county court. Mr. Black cross-examines Mrs. Smith and the witnesses. These are re-examined by Mr. Briggs. Mr. Black then presents the case for the defence and calls Jim to give evidence. There is some legal argument on the issue of contributory negligence and whether one can recover damages for nervous shock in such circumstances.

The judge then delivers his judgment holding (1) that Jim was liable in negligence, and (2) that Mrs. Smith was not herself negligent, but that she cannot recover damages for nervous shock. He awards her damages of £850 plus costs.

After the trial, Jim fails to pay and Mrs. Smith consults Mr. Whyte as to enforcement of the judgment. Mr. Whyte advises her that as Jim is a student he is unlikely to have much money or many assets. She could theoretically apply to the court to levy execution on his assets but this is unlikely to be worthwhile. He then manages to negotiate with Mr. Black for Jim to pay by monthly instalments of £25.

You can see from this case that there was a set of substantive laws applicable—the rules, principles and standards of negligence in the law of tort. To enforce her right, Mrs. Smith went to a solicitor who handled the claim first of all informally, later formally by means of court proceedings. The court processed the paperwork, dealt formally with pre-trial matters and provided the forum for rational presentation of the evidence and the law. It then made a decision and provided some machinery for enforcement which in the end the parties did not use. The aggregate of these techniques we call collectively the grievance-remedial technique. It differs at almost every stage from the penal technique. Consider how.

Many writers have suggested that these are the only techniques used by the law. Professor Summers has usefully drawn our attention to the others mentioned above. One which closely relates to the grievance-remedial is the private arranging technique. By providing mechanisms for the private creation of rights which are legally recognised, the law enlarges the scope of matters covered by the grievance-remedial technique. Thus, contracts and property transactions effected by people can be the subject of the grievance-remedial technique.

3. *THE PRIVATE ARRANGING TECHNIQUE*[7]

It is useful to think of the choice of the private arranging technique as one pole and direct governmental action as the other.[8] In between them are many possibilities involving some characteristics of both extremes. Examples of purely private arranging are perhaps marriage, purchase and sale, gifts, making a will, the creation of leases and rights of way and the formation of a club. All of these are left to individual initiative. What the law does here is to provide a framework of rules which primarily determine the validity of the transaction. For example, an Englishman living in Bristol makes a will on the back of a letter from the Inland Revenue and fails to have it witnessed. Is the will valid to transfer his property on death to the people he names, or must the matter be treated as one of intestacy? The law answers such a question by providing detailed legislation and case law which can be consulted. The answer is that the form of will does not matter but it must be in writing and signed in the presence of two witnesses. The will is therefore invalid and the property goes to his next-of-kin under the law of intestacy.

The law also provides a system for the determination of rights and duties and other liabilities. The latter one can subsume under the grievance-remedial technique although there are sometimes situations where people want to have the legal position authoritatively determined without there being a grievance as such. As society becomes more and more collectivist, there is a movement towards direct government intervention in the private arranging area. Dicey's *Law and Opinion in the Nineteenth Century* traced this movement in nineteenth-century England. Thus the law interferes more today in the care and welfare of children, in the regulation of consumer transactions to achieve fair trading, and in order to establish some measure of social control of land. The two principal methods used are state control by direct or indirect ownership, or the application of the administrative-regulatory technique.

Example. Let us take an example of a consumer transaction.[9] Fred buys a tin of baked beans from his local supermarket.

Clearly a private arrangement of purchase and sale of goods governed by the provisions of the Sale of Goods Act 1979 and the general law of contract. This is a transaction to which the law sensibly attaches few formalities. Fred verbally indicates his offer to purchase the beans which the girl on the cash desk accepts on behalf of the supermarket company. He pays for it and the property in it passes to him. He chose it from a stack under a notice which said "2p off our normal price." He was a regular customer at the supermarket and thought that that meant that the cost was 20p since the beans had been 22p for some time, but he is charged 22p. He complains to the shop about misrepresentation but the manager denies his claim. He does not feel that he should go to a solicitor for such a trivial thing but, being a man of principle, investigates his legal position at a Citizens' Advice Bureau. They inform him that he has a possible claim for misrepresentation and that, theoretically, he could use the small claims arbitration procedure in the country court,[10] but that in practice the Registrar will think the matter too trivial to deal with. They also advise him that he should report the matter to his local Inspector, since this probably involves a breach of the Trade Descriptions Act 1968 which imposes a criminal sanction. He does so but the Inspector ascertains that 22p involves a reduction from 24p which is the supermarket company's normal price throughout the rest of the country. Since the company, despite its numerous branches, is regarded in law as one single person it may be that there is no offence committed. Fred is finally advised to write to the Director-General of Fair Trading, a public official whose office was established by the Fair Trading Act 1973, which among other things, safeguards the consumer against unfair consumer practices. He receives a letter from the Director's staff saying that the Director-General is investigating the matter. Fred eats the baked beans muttering something about the law being an ass.

As you can see, the law is developing in this area. Consumer protection is moving into the area of direct governmental intervention in the form of criminal sanctions and a government agency exercising wide powers in relation to such sales. The trouble is it all seems a little remote to people like Fred. There are limits to effective legal action as we shall see in more detail in a later chapter.

4. THE CONSTITUTIVE TECHNIQUE

This technique is one which is closely related to the private arranging technique. Here the law recognises a group of people as *constituting a legal person*, for example a company, separate from the individuals comprised in the group. This is advantageous in a number of ways. Thus the corporation has perpetual succession—it does not die; the members can generally escape personal bankruptcy on its business failure and the corporation enables management to be separated from ownership of capital. The investors in most large companies play a very passive role. Management of the companies' affairs is in the hands of salaried professionals. The earliest forms of incorporation in this country were the chartered corporations which were incorporated by royal grant. Such corporations were responsible for organising a variety of social activities notable amongst which were the development of overseas trade and the colonisation of America. Later, corporations were also created by specific Acts of Parliament but both methods were extremely expensive and by the middle of the nineteenth century Parliament eventually provided for an easier system of incorporation. This was incorporation by registration of certain documents with a public official and the payment of fees and duties. The most common form of corporation today is the limited liability company incorporated in this way. Over the last century a complex system of statute law, case law and informal regulation of corporations has developed.

The institution of a trust whereby one person declares himself a trustee for another, or transfers property to someone else to hold as trustee for the benefit of the transferor or a third person is akin to the constitutive technique, except that no new separate legal person results. Creation of a new legal person is the distinctive characteristic of the constitutive technique. The trust is therefore better regarded as an example of the private arranging technique although in some other countries such like funds are sometimes regarded as legal persons.

5. THE ADMINISTRATIVE-REGULATORY TECHNIQUE[11]

Professor Summers distinguishes this technique from the penal in that it basically exists to regulate wholesome activity rather than prohibiting anti-social forms of behaviour. He distinguishes it from the grievance-remedial mainly on the ground that it is designed to operate preventively before a grievance has arisen. Under this technique, officials adopt regulatory standards, communicate thereon with those subject to them and take steps to ensure compliance. The steps will usually include a system of licensing, inspection and warning letters, often with some further step such as revocation of a licence or the bringing of administrative proceedings, civil litigation or a criminal prosecution as a last resort. This technique has been used much more in the past in the United States than in this country but is increasingly being used here.

Example. A striking example is the setting up of the Office of Fair Trading which we referred to above. Under the Fair Trading Act 1973 and the subsequent competition legislation the Director-General of Fair Trading has duties in respect of protection of consumers, restrictive trade practices and monopolies. The Act also provides for the establishment of a Consumer Protection Advisory Committee and empowers the Secretary of State on the recommendation of the Director-General to make orders prohibiting or regulating practices in connection with consumer transactions which the Advisory Committee have found to have particular adverse effects upon the economic interests of consumers. The Director-General is empowered to institute action against suppliers and traders and other persons in business who persist in a course of conduct which is unfair to consumers and detrimental to their interests. Thus the Act creates a sophisticated set of techniques for regulating trade in the interests of the public.

Another example is the Financial Services Act 1986. The United Kingdom has hitherto resisted the U.S. model of administrative regulation of capital markets through a Securities Commission and has persisted in experiments with self regulation by City of London institutions under the watchful eye of the Bank of England. However, recent scandals, the growing internationalisation of financial services as well as E.E.C. influences have forced something of a change of approach. Now there is a complex pyramid of self regulation under the aegis of a statutory body (the Securities and Investments Board) and ultimately deriving authority from the Secretary of State for Trade under the 1986 Act. This seems the worst of both worlds and is proving costly.

It is very common in this country to have special tribunals of some sort or other as part of an administrative regulatory mechanism. This is much less common in the United States where such matters generally go before the ordinary courts.

6. THE FISCAL TECHNIQUE

The Government raises money to finance its spending by legislation which imposes a variety of levies. Some taxes such as income tax, corporation tax and National Insurance contributions are direct and fall on natural and legal persons. Some are direct and fall on property such as the old death duties and the wealth tax which has been proposed from time to time. Others are indirect and are based on consumption of goods and services. VAT is an example.

Behind the application of the fiscal technique is a complex structure of administration centred on the Commissioners of Inland Revenue and Customs and Excise. National Insurance administration is handled by the Department of Social Security save that the Inland Revenue are now in practice the collectors. Some of the more indirect taxes are collected by the Post Office, *e.g.* TV licences.

7. THE CONFERRAL OF SOCIAL BENEFITS TECHNIQUE[12]

Modern government spends money raised by the application of the fiscal technique on a wide range of benefits and services which in earlier times were left to the individual, to the local community or in some cases to the Church. Examples are education, roads, the National Health Service and Social Security. In the past, such matters were categorised as being outside "lawyers' law." However, this is a somewhat nebulous category which we will consider in more detail later. Increasingly in public law and in so-called poverty law lawyers are rightly turning their attention to them.

Usually these benefits are regulated by statute so there is the basic legal task of construing the statute. Who administers the scheme? How? Is a particular person entitled to benefit? Is the conferral of a particular benefit a matter of right or the administrator's discretion? Is the discretion regulated in any way? Is there a system of appeal? These are all matters which can be regarded as within the legitimate province of law.

The main legal sources of social security law, for example, are a number of consolidating statutes with regulations made thereunder. A number of different government departments are concerned with various aspects—the Department of Employment, the Inland Revenue and the Department of Social Security. The latter are the most important from a claimant's point of view. As far as supplementary benefits, which are aimed at relieving poverty, are concerned there is a separate administrative system with appeals to social security tribunals.

You can see that there are some similarities between this and the administrative-regulatory technique. The main difference lies in the nature of the business dealt with. The member of the public is in the role of a claimant against the state.

Example. Let us take an example of Jill, a deserted wife who has three children. Her husband is out of work and drawing unemployment benefit. She goes along to the local DoS office and obtains supplementary benefit. She may in addition be advised to claim further discretionary benefits and also a rate rebate from her local authority. If she is dissatisfied with the benefits paid to her by the local office she may be advised to appeal in writing to the local Social Security Appeal Tribunal. There is little formality involved and at present legal aid is not available although she may get legal advice and assistance short of representation from a solicitor, under what is popularly known as the Green Form scheme. She would probably be better advised to try to obtain assistance from a voluntary group such as the Child Poverty Action Group who specialise in such matters.

COMBINATIONS OF TECHNIQUES

As we saw in our "baked beans" example, it is possible for the law to use more than one technique to serve in a particular area. Sometimes, as we saw, such an overlap can be unfortunate with none of the techniques adequately dealing with the matter. When new legislation is being considered, the Government must choose which technique or combination of techniques will best achieve its legislative purpose.

THE LEGAL TECHNIQUES AND THE SOURCES OF LAW

In the early history of English law, Parliament was not a very active source of law. Thus, until the nineteenth century, the use of the penal, grievance-remedial and private arranging techniques was largely the result of judge-made law. The development of the great departments of state and the increasing role of government has largely taken place over the last 100 years. The use of the administrative-regulatory, fiscal and social benefit conferral techniques has been through the medium of legislation. The courts still operate to create law in their traditional areas, but more and more innovation, particularly of a general kind, is now the result of legislative intervention.

Notes

[1] "The Technique Element in Law," 59 California L.R. 733 (1971). Also reproduced in *Essays in Honor of Hans Kelsen,* ed. by the *California Law Review* with a Preface by Albert A. Ehrenzweig (hereinafter called "the Essay"). Professor Summers applies his technique analysis to the legal system as a

whole in his anthology *Law, Its Nature, Function and Limits* (2nd ed., 1972) (hereinafter called "Functions").

[2] "The Essay," p. 736.

[3] See "Functions," p. 122.

[4] "The Essay," p. 736; "Functions," Chap. 1.

[5] "The Essay," p. 736.

[6] The law of torts is concerned with civil wrongs which basically do not involve a breach of contract or trust.

[7] "The Essay," p. 741; "Functions," Chap. 5.

[8] Dahl and Lindblom, *Politics, Economics and Welfare,* Chap. 1; "Functions," p. 432.

[9] This is based on an actual case which was the subject-matter of an article in the *New Statesman,* March 8, 1975.

[10] This was introduced to deal with small claims and to avoid the paraphernalia of a full court hearing. See *Practice Direction* [1973] 3 All E.R. 448 for the new procedure.

[11] "The Essay," p. 737; "Functions," Chap. 3.

[12] "The Essay," p. 739; "Functions," Chap. 4.

Chapter 3

CLASSIFICATIONS OF LAW

In the last chapter we considered the various methods through which the law can be used as an instrument of social control. We identified the different techniques and from a social perspective, this is an appropriate classification. However, if you study law as a law student you will soon discover that other forms of classification seem more important to lawyers.

SUBJECT CLASSIFICATIONS

You will probably study law in a series of subject compartments, *e.g.* Tort (civil wrong), Contract, Equity etc., yet if you examine law in the context of a real life problem such as the liability of a solicitor for his careless conduct, you will have to combine your knowledge of the different compartments, Tort, Contract, Equity and others before you will have a full picture of his legal position. If the compartments so overlap in real life, why not study the context and adopt a classification based on the real life problem such as professional liability or housing rights? Indeed there is much to be said for studying law in this contextual way and in recent years a number of stimulating books adopting this approach have been published.[1]

The primary justification for studying law in subject compartments such as Tort rather than in fact based compartments

such as professional liability lies in the way in which the law
has developed and legal reasoning works, *i.e.* by taking principles developed in one particular factual context and treating
them as applicable by analogy within a broader conceptual
context. Thus, within each subject classification you will find a
body of rules and principles which fit together giving a
coherent structure to the law, enabling us to explain its present
state and suggest the ways in which it might develop. In Tort
for example, it is the rules and principles making up the
concept of the duty of care which enable us to do this. In
recent years this concept has been used to develop liability for
economic loss caused by negligence. This development has
greatly increased the potential liability of professional people
such as solicitors and accountants, but many of the cases in
which the development has occurred had nothing to do with
professional people. You could not understand the nature of
the professional person's liability by studying that context
alone. You would have to study the conceptual classification of
Tort.

The importance of understanding law in its subject classification is obvious but it carries with it a danger; the classification
may acquire a momentum of its own and come to dictate the
way in which the law is applied. Thus, lawyers may rigidly
classify their client's claim in terms of Tort and fail to see that
there might have been a successful argument in restitution that
might have been put to the court.[2] At times judges may also
fall prey to the same blinkered thinking. Thus they have
suggested that where there is a contractual relationship
between parties, *e.g.* a customer and a bank, then the courts
must limit themselves to a contractual analysis and not consider any liability in Tort.[3] As we will see in Chapter 8, the
existence of a contract may quite rightly affect the extent of
liability in Tort. But to regard it as excluding any consideration
of Tort is wrong and fortunately not the approach adopted by
most judges.[4]

The warning is clear; conceptual classifications should be the
lawyer's servant not his master. Lawyers should be able to
reason flexibly from the facts to the classifications and then
back to the facts in what Geoffrey Samuel has aptly called a
"snakes and ladders" progression.[5] Perhaps the advent of

computer systems[6] capable of researching all the cases and statutes relating to a particular type of problem will lessen our reliance on conceptual classifications but we should beware of substituting one master for another![7]

In addition to the subject classifications there are three general classifications relating to different legal methods of which you need to be aware in your study of law. We shall discuss them in more detail.

LAW AND EQUITY

The distinction between Law and Equity is not peculiar to our own legal system. It has been said that it appears in the legal development of all progressive societies and certainly it was as significant in the Roman system as in our own.[8] At a philosophical level it may be expressed in this way: Law as a body of rules and principles is by its nature concerned with classes or sets of persons and events rather than individuals and individual instances. The result is, as Aristotle pointed out,[9] that it sometimes fails to achieve adequate justice in the particular case. Equity is a supplementary system which caters more for the exigencies of the particular case. Its principles are more clearly tied to considerations of morality and the conduct of the particular litigants than those of the Law. In the context of our system the distinction is seen in terms of the principles developed by the Common Law Courts on the one hand and the Court of Chancery on the other. To appreciate the distinction we must examine the historical role of those courts.[10]

Prior to the Norman conquest there were different systems of law operating in the different regions of the country. It was the achievement of the Norman Kings to introduce a common system of law applied by Royal Judges through courts in London supplemented by Assize Courts in the regions at which the Royal Judges presided when they undertook a tour or "circuit" of the country. Although older local courts and laws survived, the new courts applying the "common law" came to dominate the legal system. To start an action in these courts a litigant had to purchase a royal writ from the King's

Chancery, *i.e.* his secretariat. Originally the Chancery clerks would simply draft a writ to match the particular type of claim but by the thirteenth century the forms in which they would draft a writ had become fixed and closed, only Parliament being able to authorise a different form to match a new type of claim. Although this rigidity was mitigated to some extent by the use of fictions—allegations of fictitious facts[11]—to give the court jurisdiction, this was not always possible. There was a need for a supplemental agency to avoid injustice.

The practice grew of poor or disgruntled litigants petitioning the King for redress. These petitions were handled by the Chancellor who, in the early period, was a cleric and the Keeper of the King's conscience as well as the head of the Chancery office. At first the Chancellor simply made recommendations to the King's Council but later he made decisions on his own and eventually petitions were addressed to the Court of Chancery. In this early period Lord Chancellors took decisions based on reason and conscience rather than on substantive rules. John Selden, a writer of the seventeenth century contrasted this early approach of Chancery with that of the Common Law in the following rather sarcastic terms[12]:

"Equity is a roguish thing, for law we have a measure, know what to trust to. Equity is according to the conscience of him that is Chancellor, and as it is larger or narrower so is Equity. It is all one as if they should make the standard for the measure we call a foot to be the Chancellor's foot; what an uncertain measure would this be; one Chancellor has a long foot, another a short foot, a third an indifferent foot; it is the same thing in the Chancellor's conscience."

By the time Selden was writing the picture had changed. The Common Law Courts had adopted a more flexible approach by allowing writs to be drafted for the litigant's "special case" and much of our early common law was developed through this "action on the case" as it was called. Conversely, the jurisdiction and rules applied by the Court of Chancery had become more formalised. Equity was becoming a settled system as technical as the common law. Attempts by Thomas More, one of Henry VIII's Chancellors, to produce a reconciliation between the two systems failed and each continued in its separate way until the nineteenth century, developing its own rules often in conflict with those of the other system. Thus one party would be regarded as owning land under the principles of equity and another under the principles of the common law. Again whilst remedies at common law were generally in the form of damages, equity would have a remedy of specific performance, *i.e.* ordering parties to undertake a specific course of action.

Equity's main area of intervention was in property transactions. It created and developed the trust whereby the enjoyment of property could be separated from the ownership of the legal title to the land. The trust was sometimes used as a tax avoidance device but it also enabled property to be left to persons in succession and later facilitated the early growth of the joint stock company. It has proved a singularly useful device for all manner of social purposes ranging from charity to investment and the formation of social clubs. Another area was the field of mortgages where the common law rules were cumbersome and harsh. Equity intervened to protect the borrower and the modern law is based mainly on the equitable rules. Equity intervened in the area of administration of the estates of deceased persons. It also developed an extensive jurisdiction to protect infants where there was property involved. Again it also developed a sophisticated jurisdiction in relation to fraud, a term to which it gave a wide interpretation. Its principal remedy here was rescission of the transaction, cancelling it out and restoring the parties to their original positions if this was possible.

The procedure of the Chancery Court was also different from that of the Common Law Courts; it provided for much greater use of written statements of evidence and for trial by judge alone rather than judge and jury. But its procedure ultimately became its undoing. By the nineteenth century the purpose of the written documentation seemed more to increase the fees of the Chancery clerks than to smooth the way to trial and the limited judicial manpower in the Chancery Court meant years of delay before any trial would be held.[13] The time had come for reform and after legislation in the 1850s which created some procedural uniformity between the two court systems, the Judicature Acts of 1873–1875 merged the courts into a single High Court with a single Court of Appeal. This created the basis of our modern civil court system although one should note that the House of Lords was retained as a final appellate court and at the other end of the spectrum, the County Courts were retained to hear the more minor civil claims.

The single court system introduced in 1875 was charged with applying the rules of both Equity and the Common Law, those of Equity prevailing in the case of conflict. As a result one might have thought that the distinction would be of historical significance only, but this is not the case. In the first place an institutional distinction remains. For reasons of administrative convenience the High Court was separated into three main divisions, Chancery and Queen's Bench and Probate, Divorce and Admiralty.[14] (In more recent times the third Division has become the Family Division and its contested wills and admiralty jurisdictions have been vested in the Chancery and Queen's Bench divisions respectively.) The Chancery Division takes cases which primarily involve equitable principles such as trusts and the granting of equitable remedies such as specific performance and injunctions. The latter are orders by the court to do or refrain from doing some particular act. The Queen's Bench Division takes cases involving the common law principles of contract, tort, etc. The existence of the separate Chancery Division has led to the survival of a separate Chancery Bar, a body of barristers specialising in matters litigated in Chancery. The Chancery Division judges are in turn recruited from that bar. In this way the separate tradition of Equity has been maintained.

Secondly, you will find that in many areas of law the principles of Equity and the common law co-exist somewhat uneasily with neither being subordinated entirely to the other. The question whether a contract is invalidated, *i.e.* rendered of no effect, by a mistake of the parties provides an illustration of this problem. At common law it may only be invalidated if the mistake is fundamental but under the principles of Equity it may be set aside on the basis of a lesser mistake. The courts have not consistently adopted one or other approach with the result that in the words of a leading textbook "no clear answer can be given to the question just when a contract will be rescinded (*i.e.* invalidated), in equity or upheld at common law."[15] Although this kind of uncertainty is both confusing for the student and unsatisfactory for those advising litigants, it does give the courts a chance to develop new legal principles out of the conflict. The continuing tension between Equity and law has then some positive merit but whether this outweighs the disadvantages is a matter of opinion.

Just before we leave the common law/Equity classification, we should note that the term "common law" can be used in two wider senses. First, it is used to describe the whole case law system in its role as a source of law. In this sense it includes both the case law of both the common law and Chancery courts and is used to contrast them with legislation as a source of law. Secondly, it is used to describe the English legal tradition which attaches great importance to the decisions of the judges both in developing case law and interpreting legislation. In this sense it is contrasted with the civil law or civilian tradition of the Continent. This attaches great importance to codes and the commentaries on them written by academic jurists. Under this tradition, decisions of individual judges carry little weight as authorities. Both traditions have been "exported"; that of the common law to the countries formerly subject to British influence which includes the U.S.A. and most of the Commonwealth; that of the civil law to those countries subject particularly to French influence. There are of course other influential and in some cases older legal traditions in other parts of the world and we shall consider them later in Chapter 15.

CIVIL AND CRIMINAL LAW

At first sight the basis of this distinction appears obvious. Civil law in this context refers not to Continental law but to the law which defines the rights and duties of persons to one another and provides a system of remedies, such as damages, specific performance, etc. Amongst the more important examples of civil law are the laws of contract and tort, family law and property law. The smaller civil law cases are usually decided by the County Court, the larger by the High Court. Criminal law on the other hand is, generally speaking, concerned with acts or ommissions which are contrary to public order and society as a whole and which render the guilty person liable to punishment in the form of a fine or imprisonment. Crimes are further subdivided into serious offences such as murder, rape, or burglary, which are normally tried on indictment before a judge and jury in the Crown Court and lesser offences such as traffic infringements or minor assault which are usually tried summarily before lay or professional magistrates in the Magistrates Court.

But the line between civil and criminal law is rather more fluid than this picture shows. In primitive legal systems and in the early development of our own the distinction was hardly drawn at all. Wrongs which we would now regard as crimes against the state were regarded simply as wrongs against the victim entitling him (or his kin were he to be murdered) to be compensated. Only gradually did the idea that such wrongs were the concern of the state take hold. Today the two systems still overlap. A wrong such as assault is classified both as a crime to be punished by the state and a civil offence entitling the victim to compensation. It may give rise to legal action in both the criminal and civil courts. Indeed, a criminal court on finding a person guilty of the crime may both punish him and order him to pay compensation to the victim. Compensation here is a species of criminal sanction.

If we cannot draw such a rigid distinction between the subject-matter of civil and criminal law, we can perhaps draw a clearer distinction between the procedures for trying civil and criminal cases. As we shall see later in Chapter 5 civil trials involve an adversary process in which both sides are treated equally, the alleged facts having to be proved on the balance of probabilities. The criminal trial process differs. To protect an accused person from the danger of wrongful conviction, loss of livlihood and liberty, the rules are weighted in his favour. The prosecution must disclose its evidence to the accused before the trial, it must prove the alleged facts beyond reasonable doubt and in serious cases the accused may only be found guilty by the verdict of a jury whereas in civil cases the issue is normally decided by a judge alone. It is these principles which embody the "presumption of innocence" described memorably by one judge as "the one golden thread . . . always to be seen . . . throughout the web of the English Criminal Law."[16]

The distinction between the methods of trial does pose problems where the same issue can come before both criminal and civil courts. In one notorious case a civil court awarded damages for defamation to a convicted criminal against a newspaper which had stated that he had committed the offences of which he had been found guilty at the criminal trial. He had used the civil process to cast doubt on his conviction by the criminal process. This is no longer possible as legislation now provides that a conviction is admissable as conclusive evidence of guilt in any subsequent civil case.[17]

A potentially more serious problem remains. It is the use of the civil process to pre-judge an issue that is likely to be later tried in a criminal court. Let us take an example. In 1977 the Union of Post Office Workers asked its members to boycott mail bound for South Africa. Had the members carried out the boycott it is possible that they would have been committing a criminal offence and they and the union would have been open to a prosecution in the criminal courts. However, before the date of the proposed boycott, a private citizen, Mr. Gouriet, brought an action in the civil courts asking for a civil court order, an injunction, instructing them not to committ the crime. Ultimately the House of Lords refused his request, partly on the ground that to grant the injunction would be to pre-judge a criminal issue through the civil trial process.[18] In the words of Lord Diplock "an accused has a constitutional right to be tried by a jury and have his guilt established by reference to the criminal standard of proof (beyond reasonable doubt)." To grant the injunction, might in the words of Lord Wilberforce, "in effect convict the subject without the prescribed trial."

The courts have adopted this approach in other similar cases.[19] The civil trial process will not be allowed to undermine that of criminal trial. The criminal and civil courts will not be permitted to compete as did the courts of Chancery and the Common Law. Instead their distinctive roles in the legal system will be respected.

PUBLIC AND PRIVATE LAW

The Roman system of law drew a clear distinction between

Private Law which governed the relationship between citizens and Public Law which governed the relationship between the citizen and the state. This distinction survives in the civil law systems of the Continent which have inherited the Roman Law tradition. In France for example there is a quite separate system of courts for determining matters affecting the state and it applies a body of laws separate from those which govern the relations between private citizens. A contract between a citizen and a French state agency is thus subject to different rules and the jurisdiction of a different court from one made between two citizens.

Our legal system does not draw a distinction between Public and Private law in this sense. We have no separate court system for dealing with matters affecting the state. True, some matters of dispute between citizens and the state such as social security claims are dealt with by specialist tribunals but these are ultimately subject to the control of the ordinary courts through a system of appeal or review. Neither are there Public Law rules entirely separate from the general principles of the Common Law. Contracts between the state and citizens are subject to the same rules as contracts between private citizens. When you study a course called Public Law, you will find that the legal elements of the course such as the rules governing the civil rights of citizens, are simply part of the wider fabric of the common law. The common law is indeed a seamless web spreading over our entire legal system and not allowing for the development of a separate and autonomous body of Public Law principles.[20]

However, in recent years a distinction of a different kind has emerged in our system of law. It is based not on differences between courts or rules of law but rather on the different procedure to be used where the purpose of the case is to enforce the public duties of a state agency rather than to enforce the private rights of a citizen. This distinction between public duties and private rights is not easy to grasp and may seem artificial at times but it has been adopted in recent cases. We shall use one of these cases, *Cocks* v. *Thanet District Council*,[21] to illustrate the distinction and the significance of the procedure.

The case concerned the homeless persons legislation which we shall discuss in more detail in Chapter 10 as an illustration of the problems of statutory interpretation. Put simply, the legislation imposed on Housing Authorities like Thanet D.C. first, a duty to decide whether a person is homeless and if so whether that person is intentionally homeless or not, and secondly, if they have decided that a person is unintentionally homeless, a duty to provide him with permanent housing. In the *Cocks* case the court explained that the exercise of the first duty was a Public Law function. A person could complain about the authority's decision, *e.g.* that they were wrong to find him intentionally homeless, but in so doing he would be exercising a Public Law right. However, the second duty, to house once an uninentionally homeless finding had been made, gave the person a Private Law right to be housed and this imposed a Private Law duty on the authority.

What is the point of this distinction? It is this: there is a special procedure for questioning the exercise of a Public Law function by an administrative authority. It is known as an "application for judicial review." For many years the procedure was only available on a very limited basis. In the 1970s many of these limitations were removed[22] but the procedure still contains a number of safeguards to protect public authorities from unnecessary or undesirable legal harrassment. Thus to protect them from groundless or speculative applications for review, the person questioning their decision must state his case fully when making an application. To protect them and indeed other affected parties from a period of uncertainty as to whether the decision will be questioned, the application must be made as soon as reasonably possible. To prevent the courts usurping the function of the authority, the procedure does not give the court the power to substitute its own decision for that of the authority but confines the court's power to holding the decision invalid and instructing the authority to decide the question afresh in the light of the court's statement of the law. Furthermore, the court cannot find the decision invalid simply on the basis that the court would have taken a different decision, rather the court must find that no authority could have reasonably reached such a decision on the evidence and a proper understanding of the law. However, if a person brings an ordinary civil action against the authority for damages or a declaration, *i.e.* a statement of his rights, none of these safeguards applies. He can bring his action many years after the decision, he need only state his case fully at the trial and the court can in effect substitute its own decision for that of the authority.

All this is fairly clear but for a long time the significance of the distinction was not fully appreciated. The problem lay in the fact that the review procedure was originally limited in availability. In order to escape these limitations and allow aggrieved citizens to challenge authority's decisions the courts permitted them to use the ordinary civil procedure. This practice continued even after the review procedure had been reformed in the 1970s and it was the desirability of this practice which the court had to consider in the *Cocks* case. Cocks had brought an ordinary civil action against Thanet D.C. asking the court to hold that the authority should have decided that he was unintentionally homeless and therefore entitled to housing. The House of Lords refused to allow him to use the ordinary procedure, adopting the view that:

> " . . . it would . . . as a general rule be contrary to public policy . . . to permit a person seeking to establish that a decision of a public authority infringed rights to which he was entitled to protection under Public Law to proceed by way of an ordinary action and by this means to evade the provisions of (the review procedure) for the protection of such authorities."[23]

This then is the main distinction in our system between Public and Private Law. Public Law rights and duties should be enforced by the review procedure not by ordinary civil actions. It is a distinction of method. As Lord Diplock has said, the distinction has been a latecomer to the English legal system and its full implications will have to be worked out over a period of time.[24] One recent suggestion has been for the creation of a Director of Civil Proceedings who would have a discretion to bring public law proceedings himself "whenever he considers this is required in the public interest, rather than requiring citizens to shoulder all the expense that this involves."[25] This would further emphasise the distinction between private law and public law proceedings.

At a substantive level too, there is an increasing realisation that rights and duties concerning public authorities cannot be treated in quite the same way as those between private individuals.[26] In the Spycatcher case for example, the courts took the view that government secrets could not be treated like those of a private citizen and protected from publication simply on the ground that they had been acquired in confidence. It had to be shown in addition that publication would be against the public interest; the reason being that, "in a free society there is a continuing public interest that the workings of government should be open to scrutiny and criticism."[27] In a different context it has been held that the possibility of using the public law remedy of judicial review is one reason for not imposing on the government the same private law liability for tort that might be imposed on a private citizen. However, although these examples suggest that the courts may be beginning to develop a separate approach to public law rights and duties, English law is a long way from the substantive public/private distinction to be found in Roman and modern civilian systems.

CONCLUSION

The three sets of general classifications we have just discussed may not seem of central importance as you study law in its subject classification, but they are in fact of fundamental significance. They reflect differences of method, differences which are to be found in many other legal systems as well as our own. Whilst the subject classifications may change with the demands of society or the perspectives of law teachers, these general classifications are likely to endure in some form or other as expressions of fundamental attributes of legal culture and tradition.[28]

Notes

[1] Two such series of books are the Law in Context books published by Weidenfeld and Nicholson and the Modern Legal Studies books published by Sweet & Maxwell.

[2] See, *e.g. R.C.A. Corpn.* v. *Pollard* [1983] Ch. 135, C.A., and comment thereon by Samuel (1983) 99 L.Q.R. 182.

[3] See *Tai Hing Cotton Mill Ltd.* v. *Liu Chong Hing Bank* [1986] A.C. 80 at 107, P.C. The same approach has also been taken in the Commonwealth. See *Schwebel* v. *Telekes* (1967) 61 D.L.R. 2nd. 470. *Messineo* v. *Beale* (1978) 86 D.L.R. (3rd) 713. *McLaren Maycroft & Co.* v. *Fletcher Developments Co. Ltd.* [1973] 2 N.Z.L.R. 100, C.A.

[4] See, *e.g. Esso Petroleum Co. Ltd.* v. *Mardon* [1976] Q.B. 801, C.A.

[5] Samuel "*Ex Facto Ius Oritur*" (1989) 8 C.J.Q. 53. Samuel makes the point that developments in legal thought often take place at the level of facts; *i.e.* in the way in which they are classified.

[6] Lexis is perhaps the most widely available service in the U.K. It is a "word" based retrieval system so that if you key in a work or phrase, *e.g.* "Professional Negligence" it will give you all the cases in which that phrase has been used. See further Appendix 1 p. 288.

[7] In this context it is interesting to note that the House of Lords has cautioned counsel against the gratuitous citation of unreported cases retrieved from a computer data base. *Roberts Petroleum* v. *Kenney (Bernard) Ltd.* [1983] A.C. 192.

[8] The classic analysis of the role of Equity in the evolution of legal systems is to be found in Sir Henry Maine's *Ancient Law* published in 1861.

[9] Aristotle, *Ethics*, Book V.

[10] See further, J. H. Baker *Introduction to English Legal History*, (2nd ed.), Chap. 6.

[11] *e.g.* the original form of trespass writ contained an allegation that the wrong was committed in breach of the King's peace. Gradually it became accepted that this allegation did not have to be proved, it could be fictitious.

[12] *Table Talk* (ed. by Pollock), p. 43.

[13] The delay and costs of a Chancery action were of course strikingly exposed by Dickens in *Bleak House*. See also Harding, *A Social History of English Law*, Chap. 13.

[14] There were originally other divisions representing the other Common Law Courts but these were abolished after a short time.

[15] Treitel, *Law of Contract* (7th ed.), pp. 244, 245.

[16] Viscount Sankey in *Woolmington* v. *D.P.P.* [1935] A.C. 462 (H.L.).

[17] Civil Evidence Act 1968.

[18] *Gouriet* v. *Union of Post Office Workers* [1978] A.C. 435 (H.L.).

[19] In *Imperial Tobacco Co. Ltd.* v. *Attorney-General* [1981] A.C. 718 (H.L.) the Lords refused to grant the company a civil declaration that its conduct did not amount to a crime. In *Hunter* v. *Chief Constable of West Midlands* [1982] A.C. 529 (H.L.), the same court refused to allow the alleged Birmingham pub bombers to use the civil process to cast doubt on the validity of their criminal conviction.

[20] See generally, Harlow "Public and Private Law; Definition without Distinction" (1980) 43 M.L.R. 241.

[21] [1983] 2 A.C. 286. Another case reported at the same time and taking the same approach is *O'Reilley* v. *Mackman* [1983] 2 A.C. 237.

[22] By an alteration of R.S.C. Ord. 53 subsequently given statutory confirmation in s.31 of the Supreme Court Act 1981.

[23] *Per* Lord Bridge adopting the view of Lord Diplock in *O'Reilley* v. *Mackman, op cit.*

[24] *O'Reilley* v. *Mackman, op. cit.*

[25] Woolf L.J., "Public Law—Private Law: Why the Divide? A Personal View." [1986] P.L. 220.

[26] Geoffrey Samuel in "Govermental liability in tort and the public and private law division" (1988) 8 L.S. 277, presents an interesting discussion of the background to and consequences of the failure of English law to develop a substantive theory of public law rights.

[27] *Att.-Gen.* v. *Guardian Newspapers (No. 2)* [1988] 3 All E.R. 545 at 660 *per* Lord Goff (H.L.).

[28] See further, Stein "Fundamental Legal Institutions" (1982) 2 L.S. 1.

BOOK II

Sources of Law and Methods of Legal Reasoning

Chapter 4

LAW AND FACT

Law is applied to facts. The law is to be found in statutes and court decisions. It can be looked up in text books. The facts are to be found from the evidence, by hearing the witnesses and the experts' opinions. The lawyer then applies the law to the facts and produces the legal decision rather like a computer applying a program to the data. This is often the layman's picture of the relationship of law and fact. It seems simple enough and indeed it does fit the simplest situations. A solicitor advising a client who has purchased defective goods may have little difficulty determining the law and the facts and concluding that his client has been wronged. His difficulty will be the practical one of the deciding upon the best tactics to remedy the wrong without putting his client to the trouble of going to court. Such simple situations are not likely to reach court. Where disputes do reach court, there is likely to be some uncertainty concerning the facts or the law or both. It may be that whilst certain facts are clear others are a matter of inference, that whilst the basic principle of law is clear its scope and application to the facts are not. It is at this point that the simple law/fact distinction breaks down, that the line between questions of law and fact becomes blurred. Perhaps we can best illustrate this problem by examining a particular case.

WHITEHOUSE v. *JORDAN*[1]: *THE BRAIN DAMAGED BABY*

The circumstances which gave rise to this case were tragic. Mr. Jordan was the surgeon who delivered Mrs. Whitehouse's

49

baby. He had initially undertaken what is known in the medical world as a "trial by forceps," *i.e.* he had tried to see whether he could deliver the baby *per vaginam* by using forceps. After deciding that this was not possible he delivered the baby by Caesarean section. After delivery the baby was found to be suffering from irretrievable brain damage. Mrs. Whitehouse claimed that the damage was caused by Mr. Jordan pulling too hard on the baby's head with the forceps and that this conduct constituted the tort, *i.e.* civil wrong, of negligence. She brought a claim on her baby's behalf against Mr. Jordan.

Four main issues had to be decided by the courts: first, did the "trial by forceps" cause the brain damage; secondly, what degree of force was used upon the baby's head by Mr. Jordan; thirdly, what legal duty was owed by Mr. Jordan and fourthly, was his conduct in breach of that duty. The first and third issues were straightforward questions of fact and law respectively. As to the first, the trial judge concluded that the medical evidence showed that the damage was caused by the "trial by forceps." As to the third, the principle of law was clear from previous cases: the surgeon owes a duty to use reasonable care. It was the second and fourth issues that presented the real difficulties.

As to the second issue, the degree of force used, the courts heard the evidence of those present. They told of what they saw and in the case of Mrs. Whitehouse, what she felt. But the question was like so many, one of degree, involving the court in an exercise of judgment, of drawing inferences from the facts presented by the witnesses. Facts inferred in this way are often referred to as secondary facts to distinguish them from the primary facts presented by the witnesses. Thus, Mr. Jordan's uncontradicted evidence that he pulled five or six times with the forceps was a primary fact, whereas the judge's conclusion from the evidence that "it could be that she (Mrs. Whitehouse) was pulled towards the bottom of the delivery bed" was a finding of a secondary fact.

The fourth issue, whether Mr. Jordan's conduct amounted to a breach of duty, involved the court in considering how the standard of reasonable care should apply to a surgeon. Here again the courts had to exercise practical judgment. The principle of reasonable care like many legal principles has a core of certainty and what is often termed[2] a "penumbra" of doubt in its application. Its certain core was that the surgeon should exercise the care that would be expected of a reasonably competent member of his profession. The penumbra of doubt lay in the degree of error of judgment to be tolerated in a reasonably competent surgeon. In resolving this doubt the judges were clearly aware of the broader context of the problem; that the surgeon's professional reputation was under attack; that if they made "findings of negligence on flimsy evidence or regarded failure to produce an expected result as strong evidence of negligence, doctors were likely to protect themselves by . . . defensive medicine . . . adopting procedures which are not for the benefit of the patient but safeguards against the possibility of the patient making a claim for negligence".[3] Some of the judges who considered the case were openly influenced by such factors not only in deciding how the standard of reasonable care should be applied but also in determining how readily secondary facts should be inferred from the primary facts. "The more serious the allegation [of negligence] the higher the degree of probability (or proof) that is required"[4] said one judge. Other judges took the view that surgeons should not be treated any differently from other categories of defendant.[5] Indeed, in one later medical case, a trial judge has commented that if anything "it could be said that the more skilled a person is the more care that is expected of him."[6]

In the event the trial judge concluded that Mr. Jordan had used excessive force and was in breach of his duty whilst the appellate courts, the Court of Appeal and the House of Lords, both held that this was not the case and reversed the decision of the trial judge. Later in this chapter we shall consider why the appellate courts felt free to reverse the trial judge and in the next chapter we shall examine more closely the difficulties faced by the courts in determining what the facts were. For the present the point to be made is that when inferring the secondary facts and applying the legal principles the courts were involved in an exercise of practical judgment. The issues they were considering were neither purely factual nor purely legal in nature. They involved factual, legal and policy considerations which interacted with each other. The law/fact distinction is difficult to apply to this kind of situation.[7]

An alternative way of analysing the issues facing the courts is to distinguish between the different types of question being asked. Three types can be identified.[8] Questions of truth: these turn on the credibility of witnesses. The answers to truth-questions provide the primary facts, *e.g.* the number of times Mr. Jordan pulled. Questions of probability: these involve inference from the surrounding circumstances. The answers depend upon probability rather than the credibility of witnesses. The answers provide secondary facts, *e.g.* that Mrs. Whitehouse was probably pulled down the bed. Questions of description: these turn on an evaluation of the evidence and interpretation of the rules and categories of the law. The answers form an essential part of the judge's decision-making process, *e.g.* that Mrs. Whitehouse was pulled "with such force as to be inconsistent with a trial of forceps properly carried out." Understanding the nature of the question may not help decide whether it should be classed as one of law or fact,[9] but it does serve the factual function of pointing to the factors the court should be considering when giving its answer.

If the law/fact distinction is so difficult to apply, why do lawyers make the effort? Clearly not for any philosophical, or purely theoretical reasons. Rather, it is for practical and functional reasons. We will examine some of these reasons now and we will see that the precise line of the law/fact distinction depends more on the reason for which it is being drawn than upon any abstract definition.

WHO SHOULD DECIDE A QUESTION—LAYMAN OR JUDGE?

In medieval times the English legal system adopted the pattern of having a judge decide questions of law and a jury of laymen decide the questions of fact. Indeed, the issues were often tried separately in both a temporal and geographical sense. The legal questions would be settled first by the judges in London. After hearing the legal arguments of the parties' lawyers (known as the pleadings) the judges would rule on the legal validity of the claim or defence and then set the appropriate factual question to be put to the jury.[10] Frequently the question would be put not by a judge to a jury assembled in London, but rather by a local aristocrat to a jury assembled in the locality where the dispute arose so that the jurymen would be familiar with the circumstances of the dispute. Later the pleadings became a mere formality and both legal and factual issues were decided at the same trial. But the trial judge would still decide the questions of law and ask the jury to answer just the factual questions.

This is still the principle which underlies the trial of criminal charges before a jury. The judge will "direct" the jury as to the law. He will explain the legal definition of the offence charged and the legal rule that the prosecution must prove the accused's guilt beyond "reasonable doubt." The jury is supposed to accept the judge's direction on the law. As far as the facts are concerned the judge may only "sum up" the evidence presented, reminding the jury of the important points and reviewing the performance of the witnesses. He may not direct them to decide the factual questions one way or another, nor may he refuse to let them consider any factual questions merely because the answer seems obvious. As Lord Edmund Davies has recently reaffirmed, the judge can only guard against the possibility of the jury returning a perverse or unreasonable acquittal "commenting on the evidence (maybe even in strong terms provided they fall short of a direction)" and then "he must trust the jury to play its constitutional part in the criminal process."[11] The ultimate decision on factual questions must be left to the jury and their decision will be made by their verdict of "guilty" or "not guilty."

One qualification to this principle is that if the judge considers that the facts alleged by the prosecution could not be sufficient to constitute the offence charged, he will direct the jury to acquit. In this context, the sufficiency of the factual evidence is regarded as a question of law, not because it is so in any real sense but simply because it is the function of the lawyer, here the judge, to decide this question. In other contexts, the judge may direct the terms on which the jury is to consider the facts. Thus, it is for the jury to decide the factual questions whether a person charged with carrying an offensive weapon had a "reasonable excuse" in doing so for self-protection. But the judge may direct them to confine their attention when considering this question to threats which existed at the time when the weapon was being carried.[12] Furthermore, where the jury are free to consider all the facts, they are likely to be greatly influenced by the judge's views as expressed in his summing up of the evidence. Conversely, there are some cases where the jury may appear to have disregarded the judge's direction on the law.[13] In practice then, the law/fact distinction may not be so neat but in theory it is clear and reflects a division between the functions of the professional judge and lay jury.

Until this century civil cases were usually tried by a judge and jury. In theory the same distinction was drawn between questions of law and fact and the functions of the judge and jury. In practice the judges did not trust the lay members of the jury, many of whom in those times might only be semi-literate, to answer the more complex factual questions which might arise in a civil action. Consequently they classified some of these questions such as the construction or meaning of a disputed contract, as being a question of law not fact. As Lord Diplock has remarked, "a lawyer nurtured in a jurisdiction that did not owe its origins to the common law of England would not regard it [such a question] as a question of law at all."[14] But by classifying such matters as questions of law the judges reserved them for their own decision. In this century the judges' belief that the jury's decisions on the facts and particularly on the damages justified by the facts would not produce the desirable uniformity of approach, has led to the gradual abandonment of jury trials. Such trials are now very rare in civil cases save for those concerned with defamation or fraud, where it is still felt that the jury is the most appropriate body to take a factual decision affecting a man's moral reputation. In negligence cases such as *Whitehouse* v. *Jordan* both factual and legal questions are decided by a judge and as we saw the line between the two questions often becomes blurred. However, the technical distinction between the two types of question developed in the days of jury trial still remains and as we will see it may still be relevant and indeed create problems when it comes to deciding what questions are to be the subject of an appeal.

WHO SHOULD DECIDE A QUESTION—TRIAL COURT OR APPEAL COURT?

The adjudicator at the trial, whether a judge or a layman, sees and hears the witnesses. With few exceptions such as Crown Courts hearing criminal appeals from Magistrates Courts, English appeal courts do' not rehear the witnesses. They do not decide the appeal by rehearing the case but rather by reviewing the record of the trial court hearing. The fact that they do not hear the witnesses is a powerful reason for them to respect the findings of the trial court on factual questions, a reason for limiting the grounds of appeal. In some contexts this limitation is partly expressed by drawing a distinction between appeal on the facts and appeal on a question of law. In other contexts this distinction is not expressed but is to some extent observed in practice. The precise form of this limitation on appeals depends on the context and the extent to which it is felt that the appeal court should respect the decisions of the particular type of trial court involved. We shall consider some examples.

Appeals from Jury Convictions

The accused has a right to appeal against his conviction by a jury on any question of law, *e.g.* on the ground that the judge wrongly defined the legal elements of the offence in his direction to the jury. However, where his appeal is based on the application of the law to the facts or on the facts alone, *e.g.* on the ground that the jury should not have convicted at all on the evidence presented, then the accused must obtain the permission (technically called "leave") of the appeal court in order to appeal. If he manages to obtain leave—which is itself statistically unlikely[15]—it is very rare for the appeal court to allow the appeal simply on the basis that the conviction was unreasonable in the light of the factual evidence. To allow such appeals save in the most exceptional cases would undermine the judges' and the public's trust in the jury system and frustrate the desire for speedy and final decisions in criminal cases. Consequently, appeals are normally only allowed where

there has been some technical irregularity in the application of
the law to the facts, *e.g.* where the judge failed in his duty to
warn the jury that a certain type of evidence was unreliable.

Appeals from Tribunal decisions

Tribunals are adjudicating bodies established to decide legal
issues where the ordinary courts are considered to be inappropriate bodies to apply the area of law concerned, perhaps
because their procedure is too formal or because their judges
are insufficiently familiar with the context in which the laws
operate. Thus, social security laws are applied by tribunals
which operate informally so as not to inhibit claimants and
which have adjudicators some of which must have experience
of conditions of poverty. From some tribunals there is indeed
no appeal as such to the ordinary appellate courts although the
ordinary courts may always review[16] and overturn a tribunal
decision on the ground that it rested on an error of law. Where
a straightforward appeal to the ordinary appellate courts is
permitted, it is normally restricted to questions of law and the
courts are likely to be as reluctant to control tribunals by appeal
as they are by review. Thus, speaking of the courts' approach
to reviewing the decisions of social security tribunals, Lord
Denning has commented that Parliament's intention was that
social security legislation

> "should be administered with as little technicality as poss-
> ible. It should not become the happy hunting ground for
> lawyers. . . . The courts should not enter into a meticulous
> discussion of the meaning of this or that word in the Act.
> They should leave the Tribunal to interpret the Act in a
> broad and reasonable way according to the spirit and not the
> letter. . . . The courts should only interfere when the deci-
> sion of the Tribunal is unreasonable in the sense that no
> Tribunal acquainted with the ordinary use of language could
> reasonably reach that decision."[17]

A different approach is taken where there is a right of appeal
within the tribunal system, *e.g.* from the decision of a social
security tribunal to an appellate tribunal known as the Social
Security Commissioner. Here although the right of appeal is

again limited to questions of law, the appellate tribunals have interpreted this broadly and allowed appeals where the original decision did not seem to accord with the facts. Of course in this context there is no fear of the tribunal's function being usurped by an inexpert and legalistic appeal court, rather it is a case of review by a more expert tribunal.

Appeals from civil courts

At first sight appeals from the High Court, *i.e.* the normal trial court for major civil actions, seem the least restrictive of all our examples. A party can appeal to the Court of Appeal on the ground that the High Court judge trying the case was wrong on a question of law or fact and he does not have to obtain permission to make such an appeal. In practice, however, the contrast between the scope of civil appeals and our other examples is not so great. Where the factual findings of the High Court judge are based substantially on his assessment of the credibility of the witnesses, the appellate court "must in order to reverse, not merely entertain doubts whether the decision below is right, but must be convinced that it is wrong."[18] Where the finding of the judge was based not on his assessment of the witnesses but rather on the inferences to be drawn from their evidence, the appellate courts are more willing to intervene. Thus, in *Whitehouse* v. *Jordan* the Court of Appeal and the House of Lords reversed the finding of the trial judge that the surgeon had used excessive force with the forceps. The judge's finding had not been based on the primary facts evidenced by the witnesses; it was based on inferences drawn from their evidence. As Lord Fraser remarked, "in determining what inferences should properly be drawn, an appellate court is just as well placed as the trial judge."[19] In the case, the appellate judges examined the record of the witnesses' evidence given at the trial and concluded that it was not reasonable to infer from these primary facts the secondary fact that the surgeon had used excessive force. From the point of view of the law/fact distinction it is interesting that the appellate judges still regarded this question as one of pure fact. In other contexts where appeals are limited to errors of law this is just the kind of question that appellate judges have been prepared to regard as one of law so as to enable them to review the finding of the trial body.

Appeals and the law/fact distinction

Our examples show that the limitations on a party's ability to appeal against the decision of a trial body depend upon the particular context. They do not depend upon the law/fact distinction although that may be relevant. Thus in the tribunal context it is relevant, for a party can only request permission to appeal to the ordinary courts if there is a question of law. It is not decisive, for the appeal courts may still refuse permission even where there is a question of law. It is relevant in the civil and criminal trial contexts, for the appeal courts are unlikely to allow an appeal unless it raises some question of law or at least mixed law and fact. It is not decisive because it is still open to the appeal courts to allow an appeal on a pure question of fact. It is the appellate court's "feel" for the desirability of review that is decisive. One cannot help the impression that the law/fact distinction, in so far as it is relevant, is often manœuvered to fit with the broader aims of the court.

WHEN DOES A DECISION ON A QUESTION BIND FUTURE COURTS?

In the context of who should decide a question, the law/fact distinction often fails to provide a clear or satisfactory answer. This is not the case where the issue is what part of a decision will bind future courts through the doctrine of precedent. Only the decisions as to purely legal questions will bind. Questions as to how the law applies to the facts or what facts can be reasonably inferred are treated as purely factual questions for this purpose. The point is perhaps best illustrated by the case of *Qualcast (Wolverhampton) Ltd.* v. *Haynes.*[20] The issue there was whether an employer's duty to take reasonable care for the safety of his employees required him to persuade his employees to wear protective footwear. The trial judge felt that he was bound to follow previous decisions in which it had been found that an employer was liable for failing to persuade employees to wear protective footwear. He treated these findings as propositions of law which were binding throughout the doctrine of precedent. The House of Lords allowed the employer's appeal holding that the only purely legal proposition established by the previous decisions was that the employer owed his employees a duty to take reasonable care for their safety. The decision as to how that duty applied in a particular case and whether it required persuasion was one of fact on which the trial judge was not bound. If such decisions were to be treated as establishing propositions of law consequently to be regarded as binding, the precedent system would, in the words of Lord Somervell, "die from a surfeit of authority,"[21] and the judges would in Lord Denning's more colourful phrase "be crushed under the weight of (their) own reports."[22]

Here the consequence of the distinction between propositions of law and fact is clear. But there is a problem. To determine what is the proposition of law applied in a previous case, lawyers need to consider the important or material facts of that case. Sometimes that may lead them to select a proposition of law closely tied to the facts. Sometimes it may be appropriate to select a more general proposition. We explain how this process works in Chapter 7 and in Chapter 8 we provide plenty of illustrations. For the present, the point is that questions of fact cannot be divorced from those of law.

CONCLUSION

Our conclusion must be that the distinction between questions of law and fact is indeed a lawyers' plaything. Their approach to the distinction will depend upon the reason for which it is being drawn. In truth, the distinction is probably most clearly applied to the exercises of law students. In your studies, if your legal education follows the traditional pattern, the facts will be given to you in a tutorial sheet, moot or examination

problem and your job will simply be to apply the legal
principles you have learnt to the given facts. If you go on to
practice law you will not be able to draw the line so neatly. You
will find that the majority of cases concern largely disputes of
fact. You will find that the lawyers' perception of the facts will
influence their interpretation of the law and even, as we noted
in Chapter 3, the category of law to be applied. Nevertheless
our book will follow the traditional distinction. In the next
chapter we shall consider how courts discover the facts and in
the following chapters we will discuss the ways in which they
determine the legal rules and principles to be applied to the
facts.

Notes

[1] [1981] 1 W.L.R. 246 (H.L.).
[2] See H.L.A. Hart, *The Concept of Law*, p. 119 where he introduces this
terminology. He goes on to discuss at pp. 121–132 the reasons why legal
rules inevitably contain an element of uncertainty in their application. He
concludes that such rules like other standards of conduct are "open textured" and that their application to particular facts will always call for an
exercise of judgment.
[3] [1980] 1 All E.R. 650 at p. 659 *per* Lawton L.J. (C.A.).
[4] [1980] 1 All E.R. 650 at p. 659 *per* Lawton L.J. (C.A.).
[5] See the comments of Lords Edmund-Davies and Fraser in the House of
Lords judgment in *Whitehouse* [1981] 1 W.L.R. 246.
[6] Kilner Brown J. in *Ashcroft* v. *Mersey Regional Health Authority* [1983] 2 All
E.R. 245.
[7] It is possible to draw a theoretical distintion between questions of law and
fact. See Murindin, "The Application of Rules: Law or Fact?" (1982) 98
L.Q.R. 587, where the author makes such a distinction and argues that the
application of law to fact is not a question of mixed law and fact but rather a
question of law. However, he notes that in practice lawyers disagree,
regarding the question sometimes as one of fact and sometimes as one of
law.
[8] This classification is taken from W. A. Wilson, "A note on Fact and Law"
(1963) 26 M.L.R. 609.
[9] W. A. Wilson *op. cit.* suggests that while truth-questions are of fact and
probability-questions seem to be of fact, some description-questions are of
law and others are of mixed law and fact.
[10] See Stein, "Fundamental Legal Institutions" 2 Legal Studies 1 at p. 8 where
he points out that in its classical period the Roman Legal System adopted the
same pattern with the lawyer, the *praetor*, settling the legal questions first
and then putting the factual question for decision to the lay *iudex*.
[11] *D.P.P.* v. *Stonehouse* [1978] A.C. 55 at p. 58 (H.L.).

[12] *Evans* v. *Hughes* [1972] 1 W.L.R. 1452. For further examples of this problem see Sneath, *law and fact in Penal Provisions*. He points to the lack of clear distinction between law and fact and comments that what is at stake is not merely an academic or semantic issue, but "who is to decide the guilt or innocence of the accused."

[13] The much-publicised acquittal of Clive Ponting on Official Secrets Act charges may be seen as one such example of a jury asserting its independence. For a report of the case along with a cartoon showing the jury saying "SO THERE" see *The Times*, February 12, 1985.

[14] *Pioneer Shipping* v. *BTP Tioxide* [1982] A.C. 724 at p. 736 (H.L.).

[15] An application for permission must normally be supported by a barrister's opinion. See *Practice Direction* [1980] 1 W.L.R. 270.

[16] There are important technical distinctions between appeals and reviews but they are not relevant to the broad theme of this Chapter.

[17] *R.* v. *Preston Supplementary Benefits Appeal Tribunal Ex p. Moore* [1975] 1 W.L.R. 624 at p. 631 (C.A.).

[18] [1981] 1 W.L.R. 246 at p. 257, *per* Lord Edmund-Davies (H.L.).

[19] [1981] 1 W.L.R. 246 at p. 263 (H.L.).

[20] [1959] A.C. 743 (H.L.).

[21] [1959] A.C. 743 at p. 758 (H.L.).

[22] [1959] A.C. 743 at p. 761 (H.L.).

Chapter 5

FACT FINDING AND DISPUTE RESOLUTION

It might seem obvious that to solve a dispute you must first discover the true facts, but we should remember that this has not always been the case in our legal system and neither is it entirely the case today. For much of the Middle Ages our courts did not find the facts at all, rather they presided over an ordeal. If the disputant survived the ordeal, *e.g.* his hand had not festered after being burnt by a hot iron, then God had intervened in his favour and that proved his allegations. This method of resolving disputes is often referred to as that of "Proof" as opposed to "Trial."[1] It worked because it was acceptable to the parties. Today it would seem irrational and hence unacceptable but we still accept other methods which do not involve finding the facts, *e.g.* mediation of industrial disputes. To understand why this is so we should perhaps remember one further point; there is often no absolute, irrefutable way of determining what facts are true. Truth is as elusive in this as in other contexts. Consequently the question is not how we should find the truth but rather what are the acceptable means of dealing with a dispute as to the facts.[2] In this chapter we shall examine the two main approaches taken by adjudicators, the adversarial and inquisitorial methods, and then after comparing the merits of these methods, examine briefly the other approaches adopted in our society.

THE ADVERSARIAL METHOD

The adversarial method is one which gives the parties and their lawyers a great deal of control over the way in which facts are collected and presented. Each party to the dispute will collect its own evidence in the form of witnesses, expert opinions, etc., and will present that evidence to the court in the way most favourable to its own version of the facts and adverse to that of the other party. The role of the judge is limited to that of an umpire, ensuring that the evidence is presented in accordance with certain ground rules such as the rule that a lawyer must not ask his own party's witnesses questions which "lead" them to a particular answer, *e.g.* "You did see X, didn't you?" The judge must not intervene to question a witness himself save to clarify an ambiguity in the witness's answers.[3] When all the evidence has been presented he must decide which version of the facts he prefers. He may very well feel that some important evidence is missing, that the lawyers have failed to ask the right questions or call all the relevant witnesses but there is nothing he can do about that. He must make up his mind on the basis of the evidence presented by the two adversaries.

It is perhaps easier to understand the adversarial method by looking at a particular case, and we will take as our example *Whitehouse* v. *Jordan*[4] which we have already discussed in the last chapter. Mrs. Whitehouse, you may remember, had alleged that Mr. Jordan, the obstetrician, had negligently pulled too hard with the forceps when attempting to deliver her baby. Her evidence consisted of her own story that she had been lifted *up off* the delivery bed by the pulling and the evidence of two expert witnesses, retired obstetricians, who having read the hospital notes and heard her story concluded that she had been pulled *down off* the bed and that Mr. Jordan must therefore have been acting negligently. For Mr. Jordan there was his own evidence. He could not remember the facts in any detail but on the basis of his notes concerning the delivery and his usual practice he was certain that he could not have pulled so hard. In his support was the evidence of his junior colleague present at the delivery, that of his superior to whom he reported the events and that of four consultant obstetricians who concluded from the hospital notes that he had not acted negligently. The evidence of the two midwives present at the delivery was not presented by either side seemingly because they could not be traced, a pity as they

might have appeared to have been more neutral observers of
the facts than either of the parties.

At the trial Mrs. Whitehouse's barrister questioned her and
her witnesses so as to bring out their story and opinions. This
process is known as the *examination in chief*. After he had
questioned each witness, Mr. Jordan's barrister cross questioned them, trying to shake their evidence, probing the
conflicts as between being pulled *up* or *down* off the bed. This
process is called the *cross-examination*. The same method was
then applied to Mr. Jordan's witnesses. Perhaps a flavour of
this process can be gained from a short extract from the
questioning of Mr. Jordan's junior colleague. First the examination in chief:

> "Q.   It was suggested somewhere that the forceps were
>   used in such a way that the patient was lifted from
>   the bed. Did you see anything like that?
> A.   No. Physically lifted off the bed?
> Q.   Yes.
> A.   Definitely not.
> Q.   If you had seen something of that nature, do you
>   think you would have remembered it?
> A.   I am sure I would have remembered it from the
>   fantasticness of it."

Now the cross-examination:

> "Q.   You have no recollection of her having to be moved
>   back into a better position on the table?
> A.   Continually moved back following the forceps?
> Q.   Following the tractions.
> A.   No, oh no."

On the basis of all this conflicting and in some respects
incomplete evidence the judge had to make up his mind and
he concluded that on the balance of probabilities Mr. Jordan
had pulled too hard and was liable. As you know from the last
chapter, the Court of Appeal and the House of Lords held that
the evidence did not justify this conclusion. The conflict of
judicial opinion illustrates more clearly than the conflicts of the
witnesses, the difficulties of finding the facts.[5]

Civil litigation like that in *Whitehouse* is the classic illustration of the adversarial method. The process involves neutrality between the parties. Neither side is forced to disclose more of its evidence before the trial than the other. At the trial although the plaintiff bears the burden of proof, *i.e.* in the absence of any evidence he loses, the standard or extent to which he must prove his case is simply "on the balance of probabilities" a standard which favours neither party. However, in some adversarial contexts this neutrality may be modified for policy reasons. It may be modified by evidential presumptions or rules altering the burden of proof.[6] An example in the civil context is the maxim *Res Ipsa Loquitur* which literally means the matter speaks for itself. Thus, if the steering wheel of your new car falls off in your hands it seems to suggest in itself that the manufacturer was negligent and following the maxim it would then be for the manufacturer to show that there was some other explanation. Underlying this use of the maxim is clearly the policy consideration that it would be difficult for the car owner, knowing nothing of the manufacturing process, to present evidence identifying the precise element of negligence. The most significant policy modifications are made in the context of criminal procedure. Here, for example, the prosecution has to reveal its evidence to the accused before trial thus enabling the accused to prepare an answer, but there is only a very limited duty on the accused to disclose his evidence to the prosecution. Again, at the trial the prosecution must prove its case not on the balance of probabilities but to a much higher standard, "beyond reasonable doubt." Underlying this and other rules of criminal procedure is a social policy of favouring the accused at the expense of the prosecution. The presumption of innocence is not simply a legal rule: it is a declaration of social policy.

THE INQUISITORIAL METHOD

The characteristic of this method lies in the fact that the adjudicating body has considerable control over the way in which the evidence is collected and presented. Just as there are varieties of adversarial method, there are also varieties of inquisitorial method. We can illustrate two such by reference to the system for determining disputes about Industrial Injury Benefit. A person is entitled to benefit if he satisfies a number of conditions including (1) that he is an employee rather than being self-employed and (2) that his injury was caused by an accident at work. Disputes as to the first issue are determined by a government minister, the Secretary of State. In practice this usually means that a civil service lawyer will conduct an inquiry and report to the minister who will then make his decision. If the decision goes against the claimant he can appeal to the ordinary courts and have the decision overturned if it was supported by no evidence. Subject to this check, the process is a good illustration of purely inquisitorial method, with the decision maker or his investigator in absolute control of the collection of evidence. Disputes as to the second issue are resolved by a tribunal. At first sight the proceedings before the tribunal may appear adversarial in nature; the claimant will present his case and then the social security officer will present the administration's view of the facts. But appearance deceives; the officer is regarded more as an investigator providing information for the tribunal than as an adversary of the claimant; similarly the claimant's role is to provide information and answer questions. The tribunal controls the proceedings: indeed, it may appoint its own expert assessor. The method is modified inquisitorial: the tribunal does not investigate itself but adopts an inquisitorial attitude whilst relying on the information and investigation of others.

As with the adversarial method, it is easier to appreciate the nature of the inquisitorial method by taking an example, and ours is *Ex p. Moore*,[7] a case concerning the second issue discussed above—causation of injury. Ms. Moore had suffered from a form of slipped disc which she claimed was due to her bending at work in her job as a crane driver. The tribunal held against her and she took her case to an appeal tribunal. Before this tribunal a consultant surgeon gave evidence on her behalf. Government medical officers gave evidence suggesting that the disc problem was caused by a pre-existing condition and not the bending. The tribunal also heard reports of the opinions of two other doctors given in previous cases as to the likely causes of disc problems. These doctors did not appear before the tribunal and could not therefore be questioned in an adversarial way by Ms. Moore. Nevertheless, the tribunal relied on their opinions and those of the government doctors in concluding that the weight of evidence was against Ms. Moore. Ms. Moore then asked the ordinary courts to overturn the decision on grounds that by taking account of the reports of the doctors who had not been questioned, the tribunal acted against the principles of natural justice which required a fair hearing. The Court of Appeal dismissed her claim. Lord Justice Diplock drew attention to the essentially inquisitorial nature of the tribunal in the following terms:

" . . . there is an important distinction between the functions of an insurance tribunal and those of an ordinary court of law, or even those of an arbitrator . . . a claim by an insured person to benefit is not strictly analogous to a *Lis Inter Partes* [adversarial litigation]. Insurance tribunals form part of the statutory machinery for investigating claims, that is, for ascertaining whether the claimant has satisfied the statutory requirements which entitle him to be paid benefit out of the fund. In such an investigation, neither the insurance officer nor the Minister (both of whom are entitled to be represented before the insurance tribunal) is a party adverse to the claimant. If an analogy be sought in ordinary litigious procedure, their functions most closely resemble those of *amici curiae* [literally friends of the court]. The insurance tribunal is not restricted to accepting or rejecting the respective contentions of the claimant on the one hand and of the insurance officer or Minister on the other. It is at liberty to form its own view, even though this may not coincide with the contentions of either . . . "

In subsequent cases concerning similar tribunals[8] and also planning enquiries,[9] the ordinary courts have re-emphasised that the principles of natural justice cannot apply in the same way to inquisitorial proceedings as they do to the adversarial proceedings of civil litigation.

MERITS OF THE METHODS

For the most part English lawyers practise before the ordinary criminal and civil law courts under the adversarial method.

Despite the social and numerical importance of tribunal cases,[10] lawyers rarely appear before tribunals and perhaps for that reason they tend to be suspicious of the inquisitorial method. The familiar is to be preferred to the unfamiliar. As a warning against such a bias we can do no better than to quote from the judgment of Lord Diplock in a case where the inquisitorial method of a planning enquiry was challenged on the grounds of natural justice:[11]

> "It would, in my view, be quite fallacious to suppose that at an inquiry of this kind the only fair way of ascertaining matters of fact is by the oral testimony of witnesses who are subjected to cross-examination on behalf of parties who disagree with what they have said. Such procedure is peculiar to litigation conducted in courts that follow the common law system of procedure; it plays no part in the procedure of courts of justice under legal systems based on the civil law, including the majority of our fellow member states of the European Communities."

What then are the real merits of the adversarial method? American research[12] based on psychological analysis suggests that it may have two direct advantages; first, it may reduce the element of bias in the decision maker. In an adversarial process such a person may make up his mind later and on fuller evidence than he would in an inquisitorial process. Secondly, it may lead the lawyer for a party with a weaker factual case to put forward a fuller version of the facts than he would in an inquisitorial context. However, perhaps the most significant finding of the research is that the adversarial process was more acceptable to the parties than the inquisitorial process and this was true both for "parties" in the experimental research who were brought up in the American tradition of adversarial process and for parties brought up in the French tradition of inquisitorial process.

Are there any disadvantages? Clearly there are. First, the adversarial method promotes the "sporting" theory of justice. Those with the best (and often these are the most highly paid) lawyers are the most likely to win the game. It may lead to other problems. In *Whitehouse* for example, the judges were strongly and rightly critical of her lawyers for "doctoring" the expert evidence, persuading their own experts to take a particular line. But this is an almost inevitable side-effect of the adversarial method. Ironically it may still be the "sporting" nature of the process which makes it so acceptable—every party has his day in court, his chance to win. Secondly, giving control to the parties is both expensive and fraught with the possibility of endless delay. Sometimes parties may do this simply as a tactic to force the other side into a settlement but where a trial finally takes place it may be many years after the incident, nine years in the *Whitehouse* case. This points to the third problem, the fact finding efficiency of the system may be impaired. The delay may mean that winesses are unable to remember the facts, as was the case with Mr. Jordan, or they may have simply disappeared, as was the case with the midwives. In 1989 the Lord Chancellor's Department introduced reforms aimed at overcoming some of these problems.[13] Parties will have to disclose more of their own evidence to each other prior to trial and this "cards on the table approach" should make for fairer trials and pre-trial settlements. Court officials will have powers to stop delaying tactics by the parties. Judges will read much of the evidence and arguments before trial and this will give them more opportunity to control the trial itself. Whether these and other reforms will succeed in their aim depends upon whether they produce a change in lawyers' traditional attitudes towards the adversarial process so that it is seen more as a way of resolving a dispute and less of a way of continuing a fight.

The advantage of the inquisitorial method lies in the fact that court control will limit the costs and the delay. This is particularly important where a high volume of disputes about relatively small sums has to be decided. This is the case in the social security context, *e.g.* claims for industrial injury benefits and other benefits. It is not surprising that it is in this context that we have made the greatest use of the inquisitorial method in the United Kingdom. The method has a further important advantage in this context; its success does not depend so much on the disputants being legally repesented but rather on the efficiency of its investigatory process. This is just as well as the majority of social security claimants cannot afford to pay for a lawyer and the state does not provide legal aid for them to be represented. Recognising these advantages, the Lord Chancellor's Department has recently proposed that courts hearing both small consumer claims and housing disputes should act in a much more investigatory manner. The trend towards adopting inquisitorial methods is bound to continue as government and litigants seek more efficient means of resolving disputes; it would be a pity if lawyers were not able to change their adversarial attitudes and make a positive contribution to these new developments.

NON-ADJUDICATORY METHODS

We began this chapter by noting the significance of non-adjudicatory methods of dispute resolution, and this is a theme to which we must briefly return. It is obvious that some types of disputes are rarely subject to adjudication by either adversarial or inquisitorial methods. Most industrial relations disputes are resolved by bargaining between the parties or possibly by mediation, *i.e.* a process under which a third party suggest a possible settlement but the two parties are left to decide whether to accept it. Adjudicatory methods, whether by inquiry, arbitration or still less court trial, are rarely acceptable to the parties in industrial relations. Such parties must carry their constituents, the employees and the company men, with them in the resolution of a dispute and they are less likely to do so if they are seen to have relinquished their power to a third party adjudicator.

What is less obvious is that these methods of dispute resolution are equally significant in the context of disputes which are normally regarded as appropriate for adjudication.

Mediation is being used in the United States, Australia and New Zealand[14] to deal with a range of criminal as well as civil cases involving parties who have some form of continuing relationship with each other, whether as neighbours, fellow workers or members of the same household or organisation. In many such cases, as in labour disputes, the "win-lose" outcomes of adjudication may work against future harmony between the parties. Moreover, the incident which triggers legal system intervention, for example an assault, seems often to be only a symptom of underlying tensions. Unlike a court which gives judgment with respect to the particular claim or charge before it, mediators assist the disputants to explore their differences and to develop a mutually acceptable formula for future co-existence.

It should also be realised that most civil disputes are settled before trial. In the commercial context the parties will often bargain rather than even start the pre-trial process. In the personal injury context, they will often start the pre-trial process of collecting evidence, but they frequently do this and devise their pre-trial tactics with the aim of forcing a good settlement rather than having the case adjudicated.[15] In recent years American Courts have encouraged parties to use various forms of Alternative Dispute Resolution (A.D.R.) systems in an effort to produce cheaper, faster settlements.[16] The Lord Chancellor's Department has suggested that A.D.R. systems might also have a role to play in the English system. In the context of criminal cases, bargaining is again important. There is considerable evidence to suggest that the practice of plea bargaining, under which the accused pleads guilty in return for a lighter sentence, is rife.[17] Many would see this as undermining criminal justice and the presumption of innocence, trial by jury, etc. But it appears to be acceptable to the participants. It avoids the time, expense and uncertainty of a trial. It enables the parties to control their own fates rather than relinquishing the power to an adjudicator. What it ignores is the wider interest of society in seeing the innocent acquitted and the guilty properly sentenced.

One final comment: there are perhaps some disputes which can be avoided entirely. Lord Justice Lawton suggested in the *Whitehouse* case that the victims of medical mishaps such as the Whitehouse baby "should be cared for by the community rather than by the hazards of litigation."[18] This could be achieved by a system of state compensation paid not on proof of negligence but simply on proof of injury. Such a scheme has been introduced in New Zealand. Similarly, it has been suggested that some criminal offences should be de-criminalised, *i.e.* either disregarded or treated as contraventions subject to an on-the-spot fine.[19] Clearly this approach would reduce the number of disputes requiring resolution. These questions obviously raise issues of social policy, but this is true of all legal methods.

Notes

1 For a legal historian's account of methods of "proof" and the gradual move to methods of trial, see Baker, *Introduction to English Legal History* (2nd ed.), especially pp. 63–65. For a more general over-view of the social policies inherent in these methods see Shapiro, *Courts: A Comparative and Political Analysis*, especially pp. 37–49.

2 It is important to remember this point; the jury has been much criticised as an inefficient, irrational and unpredictable fact finder but, as one commentator has put it, "We must ask not . . . does it tell us the truth? But rather something like: do we want convictions and possible loss of liberty to depend on a system which is ultimately based on decisions of a 'little parliament?' " See Bankowski, "The Value of Truth: Fact Scepticism Revisited" (1981) 1 L.S. 257.

3 *Jones* v. *N.C.B.* [1957] 2 Q.B. 55. The complex appeal problems and enormous costs that may result if the judge does intervene in the questioning, taking upon himself the role of the barrister, are well illustrated by *Prudential Assurance Co.* v. *Newman (No. 2)* [1981] Ch. 257.

4 [1981] 1 W.L.R. 246, (1980) 125 S.J. 167, [1981] 1 All E.R. 267 (H.L.).

5 Appeal courts may be no better at finding the facts than the trial court but the procedure must stop somewhere. As Lord Simon put it in the *Ampthill Peerage* case [1976] 2 W.L.R. 777, [1977] A.C. 574. "Since judges and juries are fallible human beings we have provided appellate courts which do their fallible best to correct error. But in the end you must accept what has been decided. Enough is enough!"

6 See Eggleston, *Evidence, Proof and Probability*, Chap. 8.

7 *R.* v. *Deputy Industrial Injury Commissioner Ex parte Moore* [1965] 1 Q.B. 456.

8 *R.* v. *National Insurance Commissioner Ex p. Viscusi* [1974] 1 W.L.R. 646 (C.A.).

9 *Bushell* v. *Secretary of State for Environment* [1981] A.C. 75.

10 Social Security tribunals of one kind or another hear around 100,000 cases a year, many times more than the number of cases heard by the classic adversarial procedure in the High Court.

11 *Bushell* v. *Secretary of State for Environment* [1981] A.C. 75.

12 Thibaut & Walker, *Procedural Justice: a Psychological Analysis*; Lind & Tyler, *The Social Psychology of Procedural Justice*. See also, Danet and Bogoch "Fixed Fight or Free for All" (1980) 7 B.J.L.S. 36.

13 These reforms resulted from the Lord Chancellor's Department's *Civil Justice Review*, published in 1988.

14 See Jane Chart, "Experiments in Community Mediation" (1981) 1 Canta L.R. 271, and Jan Cameron, "Community Mediation in New Zealand" (1988) J.S.W.L. 284.

15 For some discussions of the implications of civil procedure in the settlement context see *Atiyah's Accidents, Compensation & The Law* (4th ed.), Chap. 22.

16 See Williams, "Should the State provide ADR Services?" (1987) C.J.Q. 142.

17 See Baldwin & McConville, *Negotiated Justice*.

[18] See also the suggestion of the same judge in *Dennis* v. *Charnwood B.C.* [1982] 3 All E.R. 486 that "a compensation insurance scheme for builders of houses might provide better justice than the uncertainties of litigation." The litigation in that case involved action against a local authority who were allegedly negligent in approving of the foundations of a house 27 years before the eventual trial of the issue.

[19] (1981) 131 N.L.J. 766.

Chapter 6

DETERMINING THE LAW

Having found the facts, how do we determine the law which applies to them? In this chapter we shall consider some general aspects of this question, examining the sources of the law, the language in which they are expressed and the nature of the reasoning process by which they are applied to the facts.

SOURCES OF LAW

Any Law Library contains volumes of reports of case decisions and statutes. These are the two main sources of our law. Judgments in cases are sources of law, for what a court declares the law to be in one case has "authority" in the sense that it must be taken into account by other judges (and consequently legal advisers) when they are determining what law should apply to other similar fact situations. If, say, you want to know whether a professional man such as an accountant owes a duty of care to someone who has suffered a loss as a result of his actions, you will be able to find the likely answer by consulting previous case decisions in which a court has declared the extent of a professional man's duty. These "authorities" provide the guidelines for both future cases and legal advice generally. In chapter 7 we explain the rules of precedent which establish how previous decisions must be taken into account in subsequent cases and in chapter 8 we examine one particular legal topic to show how case law authorities gradually develop the law over the years.

Until the nineteenth century, case law was the main source of law, statutes being of relatively minor importance. But today their roles are reversed, indeed some would say that statutes are too dominant, that our system is "choking on statutes" many of which are in need of repeal or amendment if only the legislature had time.[1] The reasons for the growth of statutes as a source are several. Partly, it is because the social and economic problems of the twentieth century have demanded more sophisticated legal techniques than can be provided by case law alone. The regulatory or benefit conferral techniques discussed in chapter 2 require laws establishing complex pro-cedures, requirements, rights and duties which can only be expressed with sufficient precision in a statute. Again the speed of change has far out-stripped the capacity of case law alone to create new rules. Thus the regulation of credit cards or data banks cannot be left to await the development of suitable case law principles. It requires an immediate response which can only be provided by the legislature. Legislation has another important advantage as a source; it attracts widespread publicity. If the aim is to influence behaviour, *e.g.* persuading car occupants to wear seat belts, it is best achieved by a well publicised statute rather than by a little heard-of case law decision.[2]

Although the legislature passes statutes, it does not apply them. The task of applying the provisions of a statute to a particular fact situation is ultimately one for the courts and in exercising this function judges are called upon to interpret the meaning of the statute. To appreciate the role of statutes as a source of law, it is then necessary to understand the approaches to interpretation which the courts adopt. Indeed the appellate courts probably spend more of their time on cases involving statutory interpretation than on those involving case law.[3] In chapter 9 we will consider in detail the judicial approaches to interpretation and in chapter 10 we will examine some of the problems that may arise by reference to one particular statutory provision.

Our membership of the European Community has added a third and increasingly important source of law. The rulings of the E.C. institutions now create law that is applicable within the United Kingdom. In chapter 13 we consider the nature and operation of this source of law.

One comment should be made about the sources as a whole. They do not provide a neatly ordered legal framework under which one particular fact situation is covered by one particular source of law. Rather the sources frequently overlap and on occasions conflict. Different case law sources may be potentially applicable to the same fact situation. The conflict between the case law authorities of Equity and the Common Law, discussed in chapter 3, are but an extreme example of this problem. Statutes may also overlap in a particular context. There may occasionally be a conflict between their provisions or the way in which they have been interpreted. Both statutory and case law sources may overlap, it being left to the courts to resolve their competing claims to be applied to the situation in question. By contrast, it might seem that the sources of the civil law systems, namely codes supplemented by doctrine, *i.e.* learned writings, present a clearer picture. It has been said that whilst the framework of sources of the civil law systems possesses the order of a Louis XIV formal garden, that of our system is more akin to Hampton Court Maze.[4] However, whether formal garden or maze, it is perhaps the language in which the sources are expressed that presents the main and inevitable obstacle to their straightforward application to facts.

LEGAL LANGUAGE

Laws can be expressed in highly specific language. Consider the statutory provisions concerning social security. They specify in great detail the requirements for claiming a particular benefit. There will usually be little doubt how they should apply to the facts of a particular case. This is just as well. The social security system could ill afford the time or money necessary for resolving legal doubts on a large scale. Its tribunals are more concerned with establishing the facts of a case. But it would be difficult to express all our statutory rules in this detailed way. The sheer volume of the resulting law would be unwieldy and somewhat lacking in coherence. In any case, it is often not possible to anticipate all possible eventualities and draft laws specifically to meet them. Consequently, statutory provisions are often pitched at a higher level of generality. Thus, the housing legislation, which we examine further in chapter 10, provides that a homeless person must be permanently housed unless he is "intentionally homeless." The statute provides little further guidance as to the meaning of this phrase. It is left to those applying the statute to determine how the general phrase applies to particular facts.

The same characteristics of legal language can be seen in relation to case law sources. It is possible to regard the proposition of law for which a case is authority in narrow, specific terms. Thus, the famous case of *Donoghue* v. *Stevenson*[5] could be regarded as establishing that a manufacturer of ginger beer owes a duty not to allow snails to get into the product, that being the specific fact situation before the court. But to express authority in this highly specific way would not be very helpful. It would make it difficult to produce future case law decisions. It would hinder the development of broader case law principles. Consequently, its authority has been viewed at a higher level of generality. It has been taken as establishing that a manufacturer of consumer goods owes a duty of care. Obviously it may be difficult to determine the correct level of generality and this is a problem we consider further in chapter 7, but what is clear is that case law authorities should be viewed at some level of generality.

Generality or the potential for generality is, then, one important characteristic of much legal language. It means that there is necessarily an element of practical judgment as to whether the law should apply to particular facts. Every fact situation is unique and inevitably there will be tension between the generality of laws and the exigencies of a particular fact situation.

A second and related characteristic of legal language is its use of abstract concepts, concepts which do not take their meaning from sensed experience, but are normative in character. This adds to the element of doubt and resulting tension. We can illustrate the significance of abstract concepts by reference to the law of contract.[6] Early legal systems such as the Babylonian, Hebrew or our own Anglo-Saxon did not possess a concept of a contract under which both parties were legally obliged to perform promises. Instead they recognised simply that a physical exchange of goods for money would transfer possession of the goods from one person to the other. Their ideas were based on what they could see and sense. Abstract concepts were introduced by the Greeks in the fields of mathematics and philosophy. They saw that a form of reality could exist in the world of ideas. This form of conceptual thinking was absorbed into Roman philosophy and law and then much later, through the early universities, into medieval English law. It eventually enabled lawyers to regard particular types of relationship between parties as amounting to the abstract concept of a "contract" under which the promises of both would be legally binding. Indeed conceptual thinking came to dominate English common law. It has been said that English property law was gradually transformed into a science which was so mathematical in its precision that it can be compared with calculus. This analogy is misleading in one sense for it suggests that the use of concepts will produce a correct answer. Concepts are more like chess pieces. They can be manœuvred to produce certain results but the players have a choice as to the move. Similarly, lawyers and judges often have a choice as to how they will move the concepts.[7] The way in which they are moved and are applied to facts involves a process of reasoning and it is to this that we now turn.

LEGAL REASONING AND LOGIC

Lawyers are often thought of as having logical minds. This gives the impression that legal reasoning itself is or should be governed by logic. Certainly logic plays an important role in legal reasoning but as we will see it is only part of the story.

When we refer to logic we are often thinking of the deductive form of argument knows as *the syllogism*. It goes like this:

All men are mortal—Major Premise
Socrates is a man—Minor Premise
Therefore Socrates is mortal—Conclusion.

A lawyer advising his client as to the application of a detailed statutory provision will employ this type of reasoning. The statute is the major premise, the lawyer identifies his case as falling within the statute and then deduces as the conclusion the way in which it applies to his client. Deductive logic is only applicable once a clear major premise has been established. If the source is not a statute but case law, no major premise is likely to be clear from just one case decision. Instead, the lawyer will have to examine several cases to find a major premise which underlies them all. He will have to reason from particular case decisions to a general proposition. This form of reasoning is often referred to as inductive logic as opposed to deductive logic where the reasoning is from the general proposition to the particular conclusion in the case itself. Thus, a lawyer advising on the application of case law to a particular situation will employ, first, inductive reasoning to find a general proposition of law, and then deductive reasoning to determine how it applies to the facts.

Judges too make use of inductive and deductive logic when deciding cases. Lord Diplock explained very fully how a court uses this form of reasoning in the case of *Dorset Yacht* v. *The Home Office*[8] which concerned the question whether Borstal Officers owed a duty of care to the public to prevent escapes by those in their custody. He said that the court should proceed:

" . . . by seeking first to identify the relevant characteristics that are common to the kinds of conduct and relationship between the parties which are involved in this case for decision and the kinds of conduct and relationships which have been held in previous decisions of the courts to give rise to a duty of care.

The method adopted at this stage of the process is analytical and inductive. It starts with an analysis of the characteristics of the conduct and relationship involved in each of the decided cases. But the analyst must know what he is looking for, and this involves his approaching his analysis with some general conception of conduct and relationships which ought to give rise to duty of care. This analysis leads to a proposition which can be stated in the form;

'In all the decisions that have been analysed a duty of care has been held to exist wherever the conduct and the

relationship possessed each of the characteristics A, B, C, D,
etc., and has not so far been found to exist when any of
these characteristics were absent.'
   For the second stage, which is deductive and analytical,
that proposition is converted to:
'In all cases where the conduct and relationship possess
each of the characteristics, A, B, C, D, etc., a duty of care
arises.' The conduct and relationship involved in the case for
decision is then analysed to ascertain whether they possess
each of these characteristics. If they do the conclusion
follows that a duty of care does arise in the case for
decision.''

In this extract Lord Diplock adds one further element to the
model of inductive and deductive reasoning, namely that at the
inductive stage the analyst must have some idea of what he is
looking for. In other words he must categorise the issue and
decide which previous decisions are so closely analogous to the
issue in question that they can be used as a basis for inducing
the relevant proposition of law. Judges and legal advisers
frequently use this form of reasoning, arguing that previous
decisions are or are not sufficiently similar to be relevant to the
issue in question. Analogical reasoning of this kind is not
strictly logical. It is a looser form of reasoning which raises
broader issues.

Lord Diplock went on to stress one further limitation upon
logical reasoning in the following terms:

"But since *ex hypothesi* the kind of case which we are now
considering offers a choice whether or not to extend the
kinds of conduct or relationships which give rise to a duty of
care, the conduct or relationship which is involved in it will
lack at least one of the characteristics A, B, C or D, etc. And
the choice is exercised by making a policy decision as to
whether or not a duty of care ought to exist if the characteristic which is lacking were absent or redefined in terms
broad enough to include the case under consideration."

Cases which involve a question of what law should be applied
come before the courts precisely because there is no purely
logical answer to the question. Instead there is a choice which,
according to Lord Diplock, is exercised by making a policy
decision. But how does the judge make this decision?

Obviously he will be influenced by the rhetoric of the parties' counsel, by the way in which they have framed the issue and the analogies they have suggested.[9] He may have his own personal views, although on legal matters these are likely to have become "institutionalised" over the years of practice before the courts.[10] Perhaps the most important influence on his choice is the knowledge that he will have to justify his decision in a reasoned judgment. It is to this "justificatory" nature of legal reasoning that we now turn.

LEGAL REASONING AND JUSTIFICATION

How will a judge justify his decision? Obviously he will appeal to authority, to the sources of law, the past precedents and the statutory wording. Until the last 20 years or so, this might have been the limit of his expressed justification. Judgments were often written in such a way as to suggest that the authorities provided an obvious answer.[11] Nowadays the judges are more willing to recognise that the authorities present a choice and that their decision can be properly justified in other terms.

Professor Neil MacCormick, in his book *Legal Reasoning and Legal Theory*, suggests that two factors in particular may be considered by a judge when justifying his decision. The first is the extent to which a proposed decision will cohere with existing principles and authorities: the greater the inconsistency with the existing legal framework that will result from a proposed decision, the less likely it is to be adopted. The second concerns the broader consequences of the decision for potential litigants, the legal system and indeed the role of law in society. Will these consequences be acceptable in terms of justice or common sense? Other writers have made similar suggestions and if you examine the judgment of Lord Oliver in the *D & F Estates* case, which we have set out as an appendix to chapter 8, you will see an example of a judge employing justificatory arguments of this kind. When you have read that chapter you will understand more of the background to the case and the basis of the principle. Of course, the fact that Lord Oliver justified his decision in terms of coherence and conse-

quence does not prove that he is right. In previous cases the
Law Lords had employed just the same kind of arguments to
the opposite effect. What it illustrates is simply the process of
reasoned justification.

Other types of argument may be used as justification. Judges
may refer to common sense, the supposed view of a reasonable
man[12] or they may refer to notions of justice and fairness.[13] In
chapter 10 we describe the way in which the courts have
interpreted the statutory phrase "intentionally homeless" and
there you will see examples of the appeal to common sense
and other factors to justify a particular decision. Some critics
see such arguments as merely playing with language. They
argue that if judgments are "deconstructed" by unravelling the
linguistic devices, the emptiness of legal reasoning will be
revealed. This view, often associated with the movement
known as "Critical Legal Studies," challenges conventional
thinking but to some extent depends upon setting up an easy
target: if legal reasoning purported to provide a scientific route
to the truth one would have more sympathy with the critics,
but that is not its nature. Rather, as Professor John Wisdom
has put it, legal reasoning is "not a chain of demonstrative
reasoning. It is a presenting and re-presenting of those features
of the cases which severally co-operate in favour of the
conclusion. . . . The reasons are like the legs of a chair not the
links of a chain."[14] In this respect legal reasoning employs the
process of practical reasoning we all use in everyday life. We
tend to weigh a collection of reasons for or against a particular
decision rather than think in terms of deductive logic.

However, whilst in our own practical reasoning we can take
into account anything within our own knowledge, it is important to realise that a judge can only properly take into account
those considerations which can be adequately argued before a
court of law. We must now consider this institutional limitation
on the nature of legal reasoning.

THE LIMITS OF LEGAL REASONING

The limitations of the judicial process were described by Lord
Simon in *Miliangos* v. *Frank George*,[15] a case which raised broad

issues of monetary theory and international commerce. Lord Simon refused to consider these issues. To do so would require "the contribution of expertise from far outside the law . . . for which judges have no training and no special qualification merely by their aptitude for judicial office." He continued, "All such experience as I have had of decision making within and without the law convinces me that the resolution of (these issues) demands a far greater range of advice and a far more generally based knowledge than is available to a court of law— even one assisted by the most meticulous, cogent and profound argument of counsel." Finally, he emphasised the limited role of a judge:

> "the training and qualification of a judge is to elucidate the problem immediately before him, so that its features stand out in stereoscopic clarity. But the beam of light which so illustrates the immediate scene seems to throw surrounding areas into greater obscurity; the whole landscape is distorted to the view. . . . The very qualifications for the judicial process thus impose limitations on its use."

This point is fundamental. At a more philosophical level it is reflected in the writings of Professor Ronald Dworkin, Professor of Jurisprudence at Oxford University.[16] Dworkin argues that judges do not decide cases on the basis of policy in the sense of giving effect to particular social or economic goals. Policy in this sense must be left to the legislature. Instead judges decide cases on the basis of principle in that they seek to give effect to rights that individuals should be regarded as possessing. His views have been controversial not least because some judges do profess to decide cases on the basis of policy[17] (although Dworkin would argue that they are using policy to support a principle rather than to undermine it). Seen in the light of Lord Simon's comments there would seem to be a lot in what Dworkin argues and certainly leading judges both on[18] and off[19] duty have supported his view that a principle which entitles a litigant to judgment should not be overridden on the grounds of a utilitarian policy calculation. We return to this topic in chapter 16.

CONCLUSION

Determining what law applies to a particular fact situation can be as difficult as discovering the facts themselves. The sources of law do not always present a clear, logical pattern suggesting the right answer. The generality and abstract nature of many legal rules may mean that it is not self-evident how the rules should apply to the facts. The nature of legal reasoning makes it difficult to predict how the courts will resolve hard cases where there is a choice as to how the law should apply to the facts. These then are the general problems that arise in determining the law. In subsequent chapters we shall examine in detail the nature of the three main sources in our system, case law, statutes and E.C. regulations, directives and decisions. Finally in this section of the book, we shall consider the relevance of our common law system of codes and doctrine, sources which are fundamental to civil law systems.

Notes

[1] See Calabresi, *A Common Law for the Age of Statutes.* Calabresi suggests that courts should take upon themselves the power to discard obsolescent statutes.

[2] Case law in the 1970s did establish that a person not wearing a seatbelt would not be able to recover as much compensation for a road accident injury as one who was wearing a belt. It is unlikely that the case law influenced behaviour. That was left to the "clunk click" campaign and the Motor Vehicles (Wearing of Seat Belts) Regulations 1982, which made failure to wear a belt a criminal offence.

[3] This is evident from the survey of House of Lords decisions in 1979/80 by Rawlings and Murphy, "The writing of judgments in the House of Lords" (1979) 44 M.L.R. 617, 45 M.L.R. 34.

[4] See the observations of Weir in his *Casebook on Tort* (5th ed.), p. 2, on the relative merits of the common law of tort as against the French and German systems.

[5] [1932] A.C. 562.

[6] The following account is based on the article by Smith, "The Unique Nature of the Concepts of Western Law," (1968) 46 C.B.R. 191.

[7] See the classic article on the role of concepts by Hart, "Definition and Theory in Jurisprudence," (1954) 70 L.Q.R. 37.

[8] [1970] A.C. 1004.

[9] See the interesting description of the influence of counsel's arguments in Patterson, *The Law Lords* pp. 49–65.

[10] The institutionalised views of a judge may still influence his decision. Whether the influence is desirable is debatable. See Griffiths, *The Politics of the Judiciary* and Devlin, "Judges, Government and Politics," (1978) 41 M.L.R. 501.

[11] The reasons for this "formalist" approach of the judges prior to 1960 and for the subsequent change to a more open approach are explained in Stevens, *Law and Politics*, especially Chaps. 10 and 12.

[12] See, *e.g.*, the judgment of Megarry V.C. in *Ross* v. *Caunters* [1980] Ch. 297.

[13] This was commonly the case in the judgments of the former Master of the Rolls, Lord Denning. He gives his own views on decision making in his book *The Family Story*, s.7.

[14] *Philosophy and Psycho-Analysis*, p. 157.

[15] *Miliangos* v. *Frank George (Textiles) Ltd.* [1976] A.C. 443.

[16] See Dworkin, *Taking Rights Seriously*, Chap. 4.

[17] See, *e.g.*, the judgment of Lord Denning in *Spartan Steel & Alloys Ltd.* v. *Martin & Co. (Contractors)* [1973] 1 Q.B. 27.

[18] See, *e.g.*, the judgment of Lord Scarman in *McLoughlin* v. *O'Brian* [1982] 2 W.L.R. 982. See further Chap. 16.

[19] See, *e.g.*, the biting defence of Dworkin's views by Mr. Justice Hoffmann in his review of *Judging Judges* by Simon Lee, (1989) 105 L.Q.R. 140. Hoffmann J. comments that "Dworkin is one of the few writers on general jurisprudence who accepts and engages with the reality of what judges have to do."

Chapter 7

CASE LAW

Case law is the product of judicial reasoning in deciding cases in particular fact situations. As a source of law it is like a mosaic where the pattern emerges as the work develops. To those whose conceptions of rationality are rooted in logic this may seem intellectually imperfect. But, as the great American judge Oliver Wendell Holmes, Jr. wrote[1]: "The life of the Law has not been logic; it has been experience." Indeed, if one examines the oath taken by English judges one can see that the function of a judge is not to produce a system of rules or an institutional work possessing logical symmetry but "to do right to all manner of people after the laws and usages of this Realm without fear or favour, affection or ill-will."[2] The function of the judge is to apply the general legal rule or principle to the particular fact situation, which may at first sight appear to be a deductive process, but it is also to "do right" in that situation. This seems to imply an evaluation which goes beyond the law itself and which must be made in accordance with the "law behind law," *i.e.* the basic underlying values of the legal and ultimately the social system.[3] Obviously there are difficulties in the execution of this role—there is what a sociologist would call a role conflict.[4] Judges differ in their personalities and attitudes and this difference reflects itself in their interpretation of their role and the resolution of role conflict which comes to the fore in deciding borderline or difficult cases.

In the early period, in the absence of a body of law, the judges had regard to customs and usages and assimilated them into a single set of rules, principles and standards. In this process notions of what was right played a crucial part. In the determination of what was right in this period men stressed the desirability of producing public order. It is only when this state of affairs is established that values can be given recognition.[5]

ANALOGY, RULES AND PRECEDENT

Once the decisions of the judges are remembered and recorded the system develops the eminently reasonable practice of treating like cases as like.[6] This produces convenience and consistency. The basic method of reasoning at this stage is by analogy. Analogy proceeds on the basis of a number of *points of resemblance of attributes or relations between cases.* It rests not just on the number of attributes or relations which are found to exist in common, but also and more particularly on the relevance and importance of such attributes or relations. These are matters ultimately of practical judgment.[7] Further, unlike the use of analogy in the physical sciences, which tends to proceed on the basis that because I know X and Y resemble each other in so many ways I believe that in fact they probably resemble each other in every way, law being normative proceeds on the basis that because X and Y resemble each other in these ways they ought to resemble each other in every way and thus be governed by the same legal rule or principle. John Stuart Mill pointed out that the use of analogies in the sciences served as "mere guideposts, pointing out the direction in which more rigorous investigations should be prosecuted."[8] In law on the other hand the process concludes not with an inference based on probabilities and further investigation but with the use of the resemblance as the basis of a normative step—the application of the old rule to the new case.

The main debate thus takes place about the material similarities and dissimilarities in the facts but this is really only the tip of the iceberg. Underneath is the complex question of the desirability and expediency in extending the rule to the new fact situation. This is a question of policy and the values accepted by the legal system both in relation to the instant case and in relation to society at large.[9] Formerly judges were reluctant to articulate such factors in their decision-making. Nowadays there is an increasing tendency for them to articulate them and to engage in a broader ranging justification of their decisions.

Legal reasoning by analogy thus involves two processes— analysis and justification. It involves comparing concepts or preconceptual clusters of cases. This involves analysis but the analysis is taking place in the context of decision-making. We are concerned not only with resemblances but also with what resemblances are material or significant for the purpose of the development or restriction of a legal concept. This latter aspect involves justification and justification involves evaluation of consequences.[10]

Case law also involves reasoning by rules.[11] In the formulation of rules the judges use normal classification techniques. They identify categories or concepts and species within them. Species are members rather than parts. Historically, however, the development tends to be an evolutionary movement from the particular to the general in the sense that the courts from case to case identify a number of particular species and later formulate a general concept or rule to embrace them all. The categorisation and rule formulation aspects of case law thus have a distinctly inductive character.

Again, as the law develops, broad statements of principle are made which are pitched at a higher level of generality and these often epitomise basic values or traditions of the legal system. Examples of this are the principle "No man shall profit from his own wrong," or some of the so-called maxims of Equity such as "He who comes to Equity must come with clean hands." As we have seen, usually but not necessarily they express some ethical value recognised by the law.

It is useful to contrast English and Scots law at this stage.[12] Scots law developed out of an indigenous common law which was later influenced by Roman law and synthesised in institutional writings. After the Act of Union it naturally came under the influence of English law and superimposed a system of case law on a civilian and institutional foundation. In consequence of this tradition and certain specific legal procedures[13] in Scots law, the courts seem less concerned than English courts with the mere facts of a precedent. The emphasis is placed instead on legal principles, and the debate is often based on a choice between conflicting pronouncements of principle. Another way of putting this is that the Scots courts stress the rule aspect rather than the reasoning by analogy aspect of case law. This is less so, however, where a precedent of the House of Lords is concerned. Here the Scots courts seem to adhere more to the English pattern. Paradoxically, one can nevertheless discern the former attitude reflected in the speeches of Scottish Law Lords in English appeals.

Sometimes, once a rule or principle has been established, it is used in a manner that suggests deduction and the process of reasoning assumes a deductive form. A classic example of this is Lord Atkin's famous neighbour principle in *Donoghue* v. *Stevenson*[14] in 1932 which attempted to lay down a basic general test of a duty of care in negligence. In this he formulated a principle wide enough to cover the earlier cases. An extract from his speech is set out in chapter 8. The principle which he laid down has often been used as a starting point in subsequent cases.[15] The residual elements involved in the process, however, prevent the process from being a strictly logical one. There are elements of discretion, as we have seen, first in the selection of the major premise and in its precise formulation. No case law rule or principle is ever settled for all time. Secondly, there is often some degree of selection involved in the formulation of the minor premise. This is at the level of fact.

Also, as we have seen in chapter 6, conclusions do not follow as a matter of logical necessity in legal cases but as a matter of choice. The process of choice is not thereby necessarily irrational. The judge has heard the arguments on both sides and weighed them up. Policy and value considerations enter into it to some extent. (We explore these factors later in chapter 16.) The judgment records the inferences drawn, but this may be a rationalisation of the mental process involved. It will also be concerned not only with rationalising the inference drawn, but also justifying it. The two are inextricably joined in case law reasoning.

English case law thus is the product of practical reasoning emerging from decision-making, and combining the attributes of reasoning by analogy with those of reasoning by rules. With regard to the ingredients of rules it adopts what might be described as a shifting classification system which is anathema to traditional logicians who see the world in a static, finite form. A rule or principle may be extended or contracted as the need arises. To a certain extent and within certain conventional limits, the judge is free to choose the precise rules by which they are to be bound. The limits are prescribed by the vague criteria of analogical reasoning and the more precise criteria of *stare decisis* or the doctrine of precedent. In any event, rules in any sphere of life never bind in an inexorable sense. There is flexibility inherent in their structure and often in their content. Language cannot attain the precision of the more abstract symbols used in mathematics and the use of standards such as reasonableness ensures a residual discretion in many cases. This is not to say that the process is entirely discretionary. Rather there are pockets of discretion within a framework of rules.[16] Principles and standards, being pitched at a greater level of generality than rules, afford more scope for judicial discretion.

THE FORMULATION AND APPLICATION OF CASE LAW RULES[17]

Let us now consider the doctrine of precedent in more detail. What is it that is the binding element in a case? To what extent is a later court bound? Assuming that the later court can be bound, which courts bind which courts in the legal system? What we are mainly concerned with here is the aspect of case law which involves reasoning with rules, although it is impossible to separate this completely from the analogical aspect. You may find it useful at this stage to refer to Appendix 2 which sets out a specimen law report.

THE RATIO DECIDENDI

The actual decision on the facts of a case, which is often described by the Latin phrase *res judicata*, is binding only on the parties to the action. A distinction is made between this and the *ratio decidendi* which is something more abstract and which is absorbed in to the general body of law. It is clearly an abstraction. Can one define it any more precisely? *Ratio decidendi* does not seem to have been widely used in English law until the nineteenth century. It is not mentioned at all in an early work on precedent, *The Science of Legal Judgment* written by a barrister, James Ram, in 1834. Rule or principle of a case are used but not *ratio decidendi*. On the other hand the term is used in John Austin's *Lectures on Jurisprudence*,[18] which were the first detailed academic treatment of precedent. Austin was much influenced by the German jurist, Thibaut, and the term is used by Thibaut in contrast to *ratio legis*. It was also used by the eminent Scottish judge and legal writer, Lord Kames, in the eighteenth century. Now where does all this leave us? It is suggested that the Latin term which was not a Classical Roman law concept, probably came into use through canon law and continental law usage. It probably acquired acceptance amongst English lawyers through its adoption by Austin as a convenient term. We should not, however, make too much out of the Latin. Its value is simple as a convenient term to sum up the flexible method of case law reasoning. The courts have not tied themselves down to any one definition of *ratio decidenti*, but have simply used it as a means of bridging the gap between reasoning by analogy and reasoning with rules.

Some jurists have thought that in the absence of an *authoritative* definition perhaps the solution is to establish a technique of identifying a *ratio* in a particular case rather on the basis of ''I may not be able to define an elephant but I know one when I see one.''

Goodhart's Test

The most influential test is that of Professor Goodhart who, though American, spent most of his professional life in England and was Professor of Jurisprudence at Oxford. His approach is centred on the facts treated as material by the trial judge. He summarised his rules for finding the *ratio decidendi* of a case as follows[19]:

"(1) The principle of a case is not found in the reasons given in the opinion.

(2) The principle is not found in the rule of law set forth in the opinion.

(3) The principle is not necessarily found by a consideration of all the ascertainable facts of the case, and the judge's decision.

(4) *The principle of the case is found by taking account of (a) the facts treated by the judge as material, and (b) his decision as based on them.*

(5) In finding the principle it is also necessary to establish what facts were held to be immaterial by the judge, for the principle may depend as much on exclusion as it does on inclusion."

A conclusion based on a hypothetical fact is a *dictum*. By hypothetical fact is meant any fact the existence of which has not been determined or accepted by the judge.

The main reasons for these general rules are that as regards (1), the courts often state their reasons too widely and sometimes incorrectly—but the cases are nevertheless authoritative; as regards (2), sometimes there is no rule stated; as regards (3), (4) and (5), it is the facts which the trial judge regards as material which are important. In Goodhart's words "It is by his choice of material facts that the judge creates law."

Professor Goodhart has subsequently explained that he was trying to provide a guide to the method which he believed most English courts followed when attempting to determine the *ratio decidendi* of a doubtful case.[20] His test seems useful[21] and yet it must be admitted that the courts do not always work in this way. As Sir Rupert Cross put it neatly " . . . although it is always essential and sometimes sufficient in order to arrive at the *ratio decidendi* of a case to consider the facts treated as material by the court and the decision based on those facts, it is sometimes necessary to do a great deal more."[22] It is then, as he says, necessary to examine the way in which the case was argued and pleaded, the process of reasoning adopted by the judge and the relationship of the case to other decisions. It is also necessary to consider the status of the court itself since there is an increasing tendency by lower courts to adopt a more elastic view of what binds them when a matter has been fully argued before a higher court.

Stone's Critique

In an article in the *Modern Law Review* in 1959[23] Professor Julius Stone made some very convincing criticisms of Professor Goodhart's theory. He started from the premise that Goodhart is attempting to produce a prescriptive rather than a descriptive theory. This, Stone thinks, is his big mistake. *The process is basically one of choosing an appropriate level of generality. There is thus implicit in a decided case a number of potential rationes decidendi.* Stone analyses *Donoghue* v. *Stevenson* (the famous case of the alleged snail in the ginger beer bottle) and shows how the range of facts could be stated at alternative levels. He lists them as follows:

(a) *Facts as to the agent of harm.* Dead snails, *or* any snails, *or* any noxious physical foreign body, *or* any noxious foreign element, physical or not, *or* any noxious element.

(b) *Fact as to vehicle of harm.* An opaque bottle of ginger beer, *or* an opaque bottle of beverage, *or* any bottle of beverage, *or* any container of commodities for human consumption, *or* any containers of any chattels for human use, *or* any chattel whatsoever, *or* any thing (including land or buildings).

(c) *Fact as to defendant's identity.* A manufacturer of goods nationally distributed through dispersed retailers, *or* any manufacturer, *or* any person working on the object for reward, *or* any person working on the object, *or* anyone dealing with the object.

(d) *Fact as to potential danger from vehicle of harm.* Object likely to become dangerous by negligence, *or* whether or not so.

(e) *Fact as to injury to plaintiff.* Physical personal injury, *or* nervous or physical personal injury, *or* any injury.

(f) *Fact as to plaintiff's identity.* A Scots widow, *or* a Scotswoman, *or* a woman, *or* any adult, *or* any human being, *or* any legal person.

(g) *Fact as to plaintiff's relation to vehicle of harm.* Donee of purchaser, from a retailer who bought directly from the defendant, *or* the purchaser from such retailer, *or* the purchaser from anyone, *or* any person related to such purchaser, *or* other person, *or* any person into whose hands the object rightfully comes, *or* any person into whose hands it comes at all.

(h) *Fact as to discoverability of agent of harm.* The noxious element being not discoverable by inspection of any intermediate party, *or* not so discoverable without destroying the saleability of the commodity, *or* not so discoverable by any such party who had a duty to inspect, *or* not so discoverable by any such party who could reasonably be expected *by the defendant* to inspect, *or* not discoverable by any such party who could reasonably be expected *by the court or a jury* to inspect.

(i) *Fact as to time of litigation.* The facts complained of were litigated in 1932, *or* any time before 1932, *or* after 1932, *or* at any time.

Stone is convinced that Goodhart's neglect of this and his concentration on "material" facts has led him into error. Apart from some indication from the earlier cases one starts off from the position that a *ratio* is only prescriptive for a later case whose facts are "on all fours" in every respect. Outside this range the question is always whether in the later court's view the presence in the instant case of *some* of the facts at *some* of their levels of generality is more relevant to its present decision than is the *absence* of the rest of them. To Stone this is not a question of the "materiality" of facts to the decision in the earlier case imposing itself on the later court. "It is rather a question of *the analogical relevance* of the prior holding to the later case, requiring the later court to choose between possibilities presented by the earlier case."

It would seem that Professor Stone has made some convincing points and that it is a mistake to seek either for a prescriptive definition of the concept of *ratio decidendi* or to expect a case to yield up a single *ratio* in any event. It is more easily intelligible in terms of a *technique or process of abstraction and generalisation* which assumes its importance in later cases. The general point needs to be reiterated that ultimately it is the later court, considering the case in the light of the exigencies of the case before it, which is in *practical terms* the arbiter of the appropriate level of generality, at least until the later case itself is reviewed in a subsequent case. Obviously in the meantime textbook writers can hazard *an opinion* as to the scope of the *ratio*. Perhaps this means at the end of the day that *ratio decidendi* is a flexible notion which is "fuzzy at the edges" and purposely left so by the courts for policy reasons because it itself is not so much a rule as *an analogical technique used to create a rule*. *Ratio decidendi* thus in ordinary, loose usage can refer to the technique and to a particular rule actually produced or likely to be produced by the technique.

OBITER DICTUM

Orthodox legal thinking juxtaposes to *ratio decidendi* the concept of *obiter dictum* or *dicta*. The two are regarded as opposites although this overstates the case. Can one be more explicit than this?

One approach is to define *obiter dictum* as a "statement of law" in the judgment "which could not logically be a major premise of the selected facts of the decision."[24] This approach rests on two erroneous assumptions. First, it assumes that the process is a logical one and secondly in any event it tries to turn logical deduction upside down. It is not possible from a conclusion and a middle premise to arrive at one single major premise or to put it in simpler terms one cannot logically start at the end and work back to the beginning. If one cannot identify what is logically *the* major premise by this process *a fortiori* one cannot identify what is *not* the major premise. All that one can do is to state *a range* of possible major premises or things incapable of being the major premise.

Professor Goodhart on the other hand, as we saw, approached the matter from the point of view of the facts and said that an *obiter dictum* is "a conclusion based on a fact the existence of which has not been determined by the court."[25] Now, as Sir Rupert Cross pointed out, there is a distinction which can be drawn between statements based on facts, the existence of which has been denied by the court and statements based on a fact the existence of which has not been determined by the court.[26] The latter may arise where the court gives a preliminary ruling on a point of law on assumed facts. Indeed, such an event is common in Scots law, and the leading case in the law of torts, *Donoghue* v. *Stevenson* arose in this way.[27] In such cases the ruling can be regarded as *ratio decidendi*, whereas in cases where the facts are denied by the court the statements are purely *obiter*.

Clearly the whole conception of *obiter dictum*, involving the negation of *ratio decidendi*, is affected by the fuzziness of *ratio*. Both *ratio* and *obiter* are analogical techniques. *Ratio* gives rise to a rule to follow; *obiter* to something of less force than a rule but which might be worth following. It has less force because the matter might not have been adequately thrashed out.

Within the category of *obiter dictum* there nevertheless seems to be a number of species with varying degrees of authority. Where the *dicta* are clearly irrelevant to the case in which they occur they are sometimes called mere *gratis dicta*.[28] Where they relate to a collateral issue in the case they are sometimes said to be *judicial dicta*.[29] Where the matter is heard on appeal, particularly in the House of Lords, the court sometimes in order to settle the state of the law in a particular field asks counsel to address them on the law and then makes general statements about the law. These are regarded as a superior species of *obiter dicta* and are likely to be followed in the High Court.[30]

Sometimes, a later court faced with an inconvenient decision interprets the ruling as *obiter* in order to resist being bound by it. Mr. Dias has argued that "The distinction in such cases between *ratio* and *dicta* is but a device employed by subsequent courts for the adoption or rejection of doctrine expressed in previous cases according to the inclination of the judges."[31] This would amount to an overstatement of the case if we interpreted Mr. Dias's inclination as whim and regarded this as true of all *obiter dicta*. The process is a little more sophisticated than that, as we have seen.

FINDING THE RATIO OF DECISIONS IN APPELLATE COURTS[32]

So far what we have said about *ratio decidendi* and *obiter dicta* has been built on the model of a decision by a single judge. Obviously it applies to first instance decisions in the High Court and county court. The Court of Appeal and House of Lords, however, sit with more than one judge. How does one extract a *ratio* if all the judges give separate judgments? One starts with a simple proposition—follow the majority. This proposition, however, begs a number of questions. First, while one can always discern their decision, their individual reasons may differ. There is authority for the view that if there are two grounds given for a decision by different judges or groups of judges the narrower ground should prevail as the *ratio*. It cannot be said, however, that this is firmly established practice. Secondly, the case may be fragmented into a number of different issues and there may be different majorities on different issues. It has been held by the Court of Appeal in an interlocutory appeal[33] that where there is no discernible *ratio decidendi* common to the majority in the House of Lords, the Court of Appeal is not bound by the reasoning in those speeches and is free to adopt any reasoning which appears to be correct provided it supports the actual decision of the House. It is likely that a similar practice would be adopted in relation to decisions of the Court of Appeal, although there is no authority on the point. Last, the above proposition assumes that the matter is one which is governed by strict rules, whereas the judges seem sometimes to treat it as practice which can be discarded if it stands in the way of justice in the particular case.

Where the court is equally divided there is a clear practice in the House of Lords to dismiss the appeal on the principle *semper praesumitur pro negante* ("The presumption is always in favour of the negative").[34] In other words, the *ratio* of the court from which the appeal came becomes the *ratio* of the House of Lords when the House of Lords is evenly divided.

The position in the Court of Appeal is not so clear. In *The Vera Cruz*[35] in 1880 it was said that a subsequent Court of

Appeal was not bound by a previous decision of that court when the earlier court was evenly divided. Brett M.R. said that the practice of following other courts of equal status was based on judicial comity and this did not exist where an earlier court was equally divided. This practice did not apply to the House of Lords. The reasoning is not very convincing and the practice laid down by him was not followed in *Hart* v. *The Riversdale Mill Co. Ltd.*[36] in 1928, where the Court of Appeal regarded itself as bound by the decision of an equally divided Court of Exchequer Chamber, the forerunner of the present Court of Appeal. *The Vera Cruz* approach was, however, followed in *Galloway* v. *Galloway*[37] in 1954 although neither *The Vera Cruz* nor *Hart's* case seems to have been considered.

The practice, therefore, is not well settled. The present state of the authorities is muddled, and a clear, rationally justified rule has still to be laid down. In practice, however, the problem is not likely to be acute since the Court of Appeal normally sits with three judges, except on interlocutory matters when there are two. The latter are pre-trial matters, which are usually of less importance, and the decisions are not often reported.

Exceptional Cases

You may from time to time come across two rather anomalous types of case. The first is a case which was the subject of a resolution of the judges meeting informally in the Exchequer Chamber to hear legal arguments. These often arose out of actual cases but were dealt with not as a species of appeal, rather as a moot. Once a point had been resolved in this way it was authoritative and could not be reopened before the courts. The Court of Exchequer Chamber has long since disappeared but there is a similar kind of procedure under section 36 of the Criminal Justice Act 1972 known as an Attorney-General's reference. The matter arises out of the actual case where an accused has been acquitted but the Crown wish a point of law to be resolved. The matter is referred by the Attorney-General to the Court of Appeal (Criminal Division) for a determination. The opinion is treated in practice as equivalent to a *ratio decidendi*.

DISTINGUISHING CASES

Instead of following or refusing to follow an earlier case the court may distinguish it. This differs from a refusal to follow or overruling of the previous case which are courses only open to a c rt which is not bound to follow a decision of the earlier court. In distinguishing, certain factual differences are found which justify the court not following the earlier case while still accepting that the earlier case is good law.

The recognition of similarity and difference between cases lies at the root of English legal reasoning, as we saw earlier in this chapter. Because of the vagueness surrounding the concept of *ratio* and the possibility of distinguishing cases, some argue that the courts are never really bound. To a certain extent this seems to arise out of a failure to appreciate what is meant by being bound in this context. The expression conjures up to some the idea of a person wrapped in chains and physically compelled to do a particular thing. Judges are clearly not bound (even metaphorically) in this way. Further, there is always in the nature of things going to be some factual difference between cases. What is it that stops the judge from always using the difference to formulate a new rule? As we have seen, convenience and consistency play a large part. Distinguishing cases in fact involves more than just identifying a factual difference. It involves using it as a justification for departing from the ruling in the earlier case. The court's acceptance of the distinction as a basis for departing from the earlier ruling usually rests on some notion such as morality, social policy or common sense.[38] Often one hears these summed up in a general reference to justice or to public policy or just plain policy. We return to the questions of policy and values in chapter 16.

Professor Glanville Williams in *Learning the Law* divides distinguishing into two types—restrictive and non-restrictive.[39] The latter, he says, occurs where the court accepts the expressed *ratio decidendi* of the earlier case and does not seek to curtail it, but finds that the case before it does not fall within it because of some material difference of fact. Restrictive distinguishing cuts down the *ratio decidendi* of the earlier case by treating as material to the earlier decision some fact which the earlier court regarded or appeared to regard as immaterial. It can be seen that this view is inconsistent with Professor Goodhart's view that the judge in a case is the arbiter of what are material facts. Professor Williams in fact rejects that view and also argues that the judge does not have an unlimited discretion to jettison facts as immaterial.[40]

Since two of the leading jurists differ on such a fundamental point it might be asked how can we ascertain the true position? The answer would seem to be that distinguishing cases is a complex process which cannot easily be reduced to one fixed formula. The best way to understand it is to examine the ways in which different judges approach their task. This involves reading the cases. It would seem that there is scope here for socio-legal research identifying the types of situations in which judges distinguished cases and the justification they used. The problems, of course, are the building of a comprehensive research framework and the fact that one would be largely limited to reported cases, which in some respects represent the pathology of the legal system (the abnormal cases) and are thus not a true random sample of all cases before the courts.

Persuasive Precedents

A distinction is drawn between binding precedents and persuasive precedents. We examine the detailed ground rules of *stare decisis* shortly. The basic rules are that courts are bound by higher courts in the same hierarchy. In the United Kingdom, Scotland and Northern Ireland are separate jurisdictions although they have a common system of appeal to the House of Lords. The decisions of Scottish and Northern Irish courts are not binding on English courts but are of persuasive authority. The same is technically true of decisions of the House of Lords sitting on Scottish and Irish appeals although where the law is the same in practice they are treated as binding. Other persuasive authorities are decisions of Commonwealth countries and the Irish Republic. American court decisions, particularly of the superior courts, are persuasive, although less so today than formerly. Technically the recommendations of the Judicial Committee of the Privy Council sitting as an appeal court from the Commonwealth are persuasive, but they are usually accorded considerable weight and followed. *Obiter dicta* of any court even a higher court are merely persuasive, although in practice they are often followed especially when they are the considered dicta of a higher court.

Practical Factors affecting the Weight of a Precedent

Too much can be made of the binding/persuasive distinction given the flexibility within the system. Certain practical factors seem to affect the attitude of the courts towards particular precedents. Generally the greater the age of a precedent the greater will be the reluctance of the courts to disregard it even if they think that the reasoning in it is not convincing. This is particularly so in property cases where whole conveyancing systems may have been built up on it. On the other hand where circumstances have changed rendering the precedent inappropriate to modern conditions the courts may disregard it.

The status of the court and its composition are relevant factors. If the precedent is of an inferior court or if the judges were less than distinguished this will affect the value of the case as a precedent. Certain judges such as "Lord" Coke, Lord Mansfield, Lord Blackburn, Bowen L.J., Lord Atkin and Lord Reid are very much judges' judges and their views carry great weight. This is interesting as an example of authority within a system of authority. It is important to determine whether the court was unanimous or whether there were strong dissenting judgments. Also a reserved decision which will often be indicated by the Latin *'curia advisari vult'* is of greater authority than an unreserved decision. The adequacy of the report is another important factor. Early cases were often inadequately reported by modern standards and some law reporters had a reputation for ignorance and neglect. Recently the House of Lords have criticised the gratuitous citation of unedited transcripts of unreported cases. The subsequent history of a precedent is also very significant. Has it been followed in later cases and approved by learned writers? A further factor is whether the case was fully argued or the particular point taken, or a relevant authority cited. Also, subsequent courts are responsive to arguments based on the unjust or absurd consequences which ensue from a previous case. This factor will often be linked with a change in social conditions which renders the earlier decision socially obsolete.

These factors then will influence the later court in determining whether or not it regards itself as bound by the earlier decision or whether it can distinguish it.

STARE DECISIS AND THE HIERARCHY OF COURTS

The expression *stare decisis* is a Latin phrase sometimes used to describe the doctrine of precedent generally; at other times it refers to the detailed ground rules governing which courts bind which other courts in the legal system. In translation it means to stand by what has been decided. Strictly speaking the phrase should be *stare rationibus decidendis* since it is the *ratio decidendi* not the decision which binds.

There is some debate in the legal literature as to when the system developed in its present form. If by this we mean its precise modern form, most of the development has necessarily taken place after the passing of the Judicature Acts. These were largely responsible for the present court structure which we have illustrated in a diagramatical form on p. 103.

The House of Lords

This stands at the apex of the system and, having both a judicial and a legislative function, it occupies an anomalous position if one thinks of the classical conception of a separation of powers. The anomaly has been mitigated to a large extent by the fact that the lay peers have not participated in ordinary appeals since *R. v. Daniel O'Connell*[41] in the nineteenth century.

From the middle of the nineteenth century the rule developed that the House of Lords was bound by its previous

THE PRESENT COURT STRUCTURE IN ENGLAND AND WALES

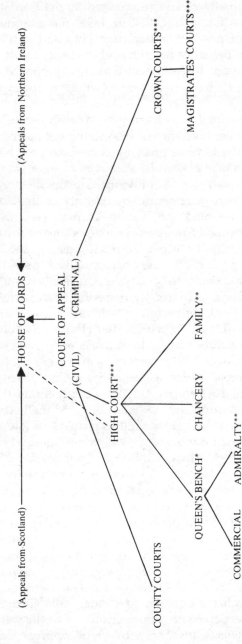

Notes

----Leapfrogging procedure.

*Under the Judicature Acts, there were also Common Pleas and Exchequer Divisions. These merged with the Queen's Bench Division in 1881.

**Under the Judicature Acts, there was a Probate Divorce and Admiralty Division. This was changed by the Administration of Justice Act 1970, which created the Family Division and transferred Admiralty to Queen's Bench and Contentious Probate to Chancery.

***Each Division of the High Court has a Divisional Court which exercises a species of appellate jurisdiction. Thus appeals from the Matrimonial jurisdiction of the magistrates' courts go to the Divisional Court of the Family Division. There can also be appeals by a procedure known as case stated from the magistrates' and Crown Courts to the Divisional Court of the Queen's Bench Division. This is irrational but historically explicable.

decisions.[42] This was finally clearly recognised by the Lords in *London Street Tramways Co.* v. *L.C.C.*[43] in 1898. Some argued that this was a rule of practice rather than law, and in 1966 Lord Gardiner L.C. on behalf of himself and the other Lords of Appeal issued a statement to the effect that they proposed in future to depart from their own decisions where it appeared right to do so.[44]

In practice the House of Lords has made sparing use of its new freedom.[45] Three cases where the 1966 statement has been relied upon illustrate the kind of pressing consideration which may force the Lords to take action. In *Miliangos* v. *Frank George (Textiles) Ltd.*[46] they overruled a previous House of Lords decision to the effect that judgments should only be given in sterling. This change enabled the law to keep in step with commercial needs in times of floating currencies and with the approach of the majority of other countries facing similar problems. In *Vestey* v. *I.R.C.*[47] they overruled a previous decision interpreting a tax statute because it had resulted in the Inland Revenue obtaining a discretionary taxing power which was in the words of Lord Wilberforce "arbitrary, unjust and unconstitutional." In *R.* v. *Shivpuri*[48] the House of Lords declined to follow their earlier decision in *Anderton* v. *Ryan*[49] in 1985 which drew a distinction between acts which were "objectively innocent" and those which were not for the purposes of section 1 of the Criminal Attempts Act 1981, commenting that the sooner an error distorting the law was corrected the better.

In other cases the Lords have managed to change the law by distinguishing their own previous decision to the point where it has little further effect. Thus, in *British Railways Board* v. *Herrington*[50] in 1972 the old Lords' decision that an occupier of land owes a minimal duty of care to trespassing children was so distinguished that it was effectively overturned. Although the process of distinguishing a previous decision may produce more or less the same result as overruling it, distinguishing may be a more acceptable approach for the Lords to take. Arguably it does not undermine the appearance of certainty and consistency in the law to the same extent as overruling. It makes for a more gradual approach to change, allowing the courts and public expectations to adjust gradually to the trend of the new law. It reflects the "step by step" approach for which the courts may feel they are best suited. Where the distinguishing approach is not open to the Lords, *e.g.* because the effect of the previous decision is too firmly established, that may indicate that any change in the law such as would follow from overruling is not one that is appropriate for the courts to make. This is a topic we consider in more depth in chapter 14.

Having said all this, we should not underestimate the significance of the 1966 statement. Although the years since have witnessed little express reliance on the statement, they have seen a marked change of attitude by the members of the Lords. They now seem much more prepared to articulate their role in developing the law—the cases discussed in the next chapter provide clear evidence of this new-found confidence.[51]

The Court of Appeal

The Court of Appeal consists of two divisions—civil and criminal—and usually sits with three members. It is bound by decisions of the House of Lords. The Civil Division is also bound by its own previous decisions. This was established in 1944 by the court's decision in *Young* v. *Bristol Aeroplane Co. Ltd.*[52] According to this case, the court is bound by its previous decisions except in three situations. These are:

(1) Where there are two conflicting decisions, a later court can choose.

(2) Where the decision is inconsistent with a subsequent House of Lords decision.

(3) Where the decision was given *per incuriam*,[53] which means a failure to advert to an earlier inconsistent decision of itself or the House of Lords.

To these has been added a fourth by *Boys* v. *Chaplin*[54] in 1968 and a fifth by *Rickards* v. *Rickards*[55] in 1989. *Boys* v. *Chaplin* held that the decision of a court of two judges on an interlocutory matter does not bind a subsequent court. On the other hand Webster J. held in *Amanuel* v. *Alexandros Shipping Co.*[56] that, notwithstanding that an *ex parte*, (*i.e.* after hearing only one side) decision of the Court of Appeal did not bind a court of first instance determining the same issue *inter partes* (*i.e* hearing

both sides), the ordinary doctrine of precedent applied equally
to *ex parte* and *inter partes* decisions of the Court of Appeal and
thus a High Court judge in another case was bound to follow
an *ex parte* decision of the Court of Appeal unless it had been
reversed by the House of Lords, was inconsistent with a
subsequent decision of the House of Lords or Court of Appeal
or was *per incuriam*. *Rickards* v. *Rickards* establishes that in a rare
and exceptional case concerning the jurisdiction of the court
and where no review by the House of Lords is possible, the
Court of Appeal is justified in not following its earlier and
otherwise binding decision, which it is satisfied has been
wrongly decided. Lord Donaldson said that the following were
some relevant considerations:

1. The preferred course must always be to follow the
   previous decision but to give leave so that the House of
   Lords might remedy the error.

2. Certainty in relation to the substantive law was usually
   to be preferred to correctness, since at least it enabled
   the public to order their affairs with confidence.
   Erroneous decisions as to procedural rules affected only
   the parties engaged in relevant litigation. Since that was
   a much less extensive group a departure from established practice was to that extent less desirable.

3. An erroneous decision involving the jurisdiction of the
   court was particularly objectionable, either because it
   would involve an abuse of power, if the true view was
   that the court had no jurisdiction, or a breach of the
   court's statutory duty, if in truth the court was wrongly
   declining jurisdiction. Such a decision, of which the
   present case was an example, was thus in a special
   category.

Where the Court sits in its Criminal Division the position is
different. It was laid down in the 1950 case of *R.* v. *Taylor*[57]
that, as criminal appeals deal with questions involving the
liberty of the subject, a full appellate court, (*e.g* seven judges in
Taylor) assembled for the purpose was entitled to overrule its
own previous decisions if they had misapplied or misin-
terpreted the law. In 1950 the criminal appeal court was the
Court of Criminal Appeal. The Criminal Division of the Court
of Appeal is the successor to that court and has followed[58] the

Taylor rule as clearly it should. Apart from this the Court of Appeal Criminal Division is bound by the same principles as the Civil Division.[59]

After the 1966 statement freeing the House of Lords, Lord Denning, until 1982 the senior judge in the Civil Division, conducted a one man crusade with the object of freeing the Court of Appeal from the shackles of *stare decisis*, of allowing it to disregard decisions of the House of Lords and its own previous decisions where justice demanded it. His first line of attack was to suggest that the Court of Appeal was not bound by a House of Lords decision which was reached *per incuriam* or was unworkable.[60] The House of Lords reacted strongly, holding that it was not open to the Court of Appeal to take this view for in a hierarchical system of courts "it is necessary for each lower tier, including the Court of Appeal, to accept loyally the decisions of the higher tiers."[61] Unabashed, Lord Denning responded in a case two years later by suggesting that the Court of Appeal was free to disregard the Lords' decisions where the reason for their ruling no longer existed[62]; *cessante ratione cesset ipsa lex* as the Latin maxim puts it. Once again the Lords reacted by holding that although they might apply the maxim and overrule their own previous decision, it was not for the Court of Appeal to do so.[63] (As a matter of fact, on the issue in question, whether judgments can only be given in sterling, the Lords did overrule their own previous decision and permitted judgments to be given in foreign currency, as the reason for the old rule—the stability of sterling—no longer applied!)

Rebuffed yet again, Lord Denning switched his attack to the question of whether the Court of Appeal was bound by its own decisions. His campaign culminated in the case of *Davis* v. *Johnson*[64] in 1977. There, a Court of Appeal of five judges held by three to two that it was not bound to follow one of its own previous decisions interpreting a 1976 statute which gave protection to "battered wives." Two of the majority judges based their decision upon narrow extensions to the *Young* exceptions. According to one of the judges, the court was free to overrule where the result would otherwise be detrimental to the victim of violence and according to the other, where the result would otherwise be against the clear intent of Parliament as expressed in the Act. Lord Denning, the third judge, considered that instead of creating further exceptions to *Young's* case, the Court should adopt the same practice as the House of Lords and be free to depart from its own previous decisions. Otherwise, he suggested, injustice could result though a party could seek to have a previous Court of Appeal decision overruled by appealing on to the House of Lords, the costs involved might deter such a course of action and even if they did not, the appeal process might take a further year, "so justice is delayed and often denied, by the lapse of time before the error (the previous Court of Appeal decision) is corrected."

The House of Lords rejected Lord Denning's approach and held that the Court of Appeal was still bound by *Young's* case. The reasons for their views are well expressed in the following extract from the speech of Lord Salmon:

> "I sympathise with the views expressed on this topic by Lord Denning M.R., but until such time, if ever, as all his colleagues in the Court of Appeal agree with those views, *stare decisis* must still hold the field. I think that this may be no bad thing. There are now as many as 17 Lords Justice in the Court of Appeal, and I fear that if *stare decisis* disappears from the court there is a real risk that there might be a plethora of conflicting decisions which would create a state of irremediable confusion and uncertainty in the law. This would do far more harm than the occasional unjust result which *stare decisis* sometimes produces but which can be remedied by an appeal to your Lordships' House. I recognise that only those who qualify for legal aid or the very rich can afford to bring such an appeal. This difficulty could however be surmounted if when the Court of Appeal gave leave to appeal from a decision it had felt bound to make by an authority with which it disagreed, it had a power conferred on it by Parliament to order the appellants and/or the respondents' costs of the appeal to be paid out of public funds. This would be a very rare occurrence and the consequent expenditure of public funds would be minimal."

To this it need only be added that as a litigant can now make a "leapfrogging" appeal from the High Court to the House of Lords in suitable cases, there is less need for the Court of Appeal to adopt a role such as Lord Denning saw fit for it. (N.B. in the *Davis* case, the litigant was appealing from a County Court decision and where this is the case the appeal must be to the Court of Appeal, no leapfrog to the Lords being available.) With the retirement of Lord Denning, it seems unlikely that anyone will convince the Court of Appeal judges unanimously to agree to abandon *Young's* case and the principle of *stare decisis*.[65] On the other hand his successor, Lord Donaldson M.R., has shown a willingness to review old principles as is demonstrated by *Rickards* v. *Rickards*.[66]

Divisional Courts

These are an anomalous species of court whose jurisdiction could perhaps be conveniently merged with that of the Court of Appeal. In civil matters they are bound by decisions of the House of Lords and the Court of Appeal (Civil Division) as well as their own.[67] Logic would require that in criminal matters they should be governed by a rule similar to that in *R.* v. *Taylor* but this does not appear to be the case.[68]

Trial Courts

The trial courts, the High Court and County Court for civil matters, the Crown Court and Magistrates Court for criminal matters, are not bound by their own previous rulings although they generally follow them.[69] Where there are two conflicting decisions of the High Court the later decision is to be preferred provided that it was reached after full consideration of the earlier decision unless the third judge is convinced that the second judge was wrong.[70] They are bound by the decisions of superior courts. Where there is a conflict between the superior courts then it is their duty "to give credence and effect to the decision of the immediately higher court, notwithstanding that it may appear to conflict with the decision of a still higher court. The decision of the still higher court must be assumed to have been correctly distinguished (or otherwise interpreted) in the decision of the immediately higher court."[71] Thus where the Court of Appeal has subsequently reached a decision appearing to conflict with an earlier Lords' decision, the High Court judge should follow the Court of Appeal, not the Lords.

Of course, if the Court of Appeal decision was then followed by a conflicting Lords decision, the problem would not normally arise as the Lords' decision would usually overrule that of the Court of Appeal.

The Judicial Committee of the Privy Council

Although this is the ultimate Court of Appeal of the colonies and those countries of the British Commonwealth which have not abolished the right of appeal to it, its decisions have never bound English courts and are merely persuasive. Since, however, the committee customarily includes a majority of English Law Lords some of the recommendations have been treated as having considerable persuasive force by the English courts. A leading case in the law of torts, *The Wagon Mound*,[72] has effectively overruled the Court of Appeal decision in *Re Polemis*.[73] Where the relevant law is English law, the Privy Council will follow the House of Lords.[74]

An interesting further question is whether Commonwealth courts are bound by Privy Council rulings from other parts of the Commonwealth. On this there is a conflict of authority[75] and which line one takes depends on one's view of the uniformity of the common law within the Commonwealth. If the view is taken that the common law is uniform then it would follow that national courts are bound.

The European Court of Justice

This is the ultimate interpreter of E.C. sources of law and will be discussed in chapter 13.

A COMPARISON WITH THE POSITION OF CASE LAW IN FRENCH AND GERMAN LAW[76]

The role of case law in France and Germany can only be understood by considering its relationship with legislation.

Both France and Germany have largely codified systems. There is a tradition in both countries of hiding judicial law-making behind the guise of interpretation. In fact Article 5 of the French Civil Code expressly forbids the judges to lay down general rules.

Despite this theory and that provision, do the judges in fact make law? The answer would seem to be that they do but they do so within a basic framework established by the codes and legislation.[77] The scope of judicial law-making is thus more limited than in the common law world and Scotland. In French administrative law, however, the Conseil d'Etat engages in overt law-making.

Another important point is that the rules laid down by the courts do not have the same authority as the legal rules contained in the codes or legislation. The rules laid down by the courts can always be rejected or modified by a later court. They are not authoritative and are not legally binding although they are frequently followed in practice. David and Brierley described the position thus: "The judicially created rule only exists and is only applied so long as the judges—that is each judge—consider it a good rule. Under these conditions it is understandable that one hesitates to speak of a truly legal rule."[78]

CONCLUSION

Case law is still an important source of English law and its authority is greater than in French and German law. Case law is a form of practical reasoning, which is basically an amalgam of reasoning by analogy and reasoning with rules, with a superstructure of techniques for identifying the scope of the *ratio decidendi* and detailed ground rules determining the relationship of courts in the legal system. Although English courts, unlike the French and German courts, accept a doctrine of binding precedent it does not bind in an inexorable sense and there is considerably scope for manœuvre within the system. Judges by reason of their different personality attributes and the exigencies of the particular case oscillate between the two poles of certainty and flexibility. In the words of Lord Denning, some are "timorous souls" and others are "bold spirits."[79]

The late Professor Julius Stone, with his learning and insight, summed up the position in this way[80]:

> "In short, a 'rule' or 'principle' as it emerges from a precedent case is subject in its further elaboration to continual review, in the light of analogies and differences, not merely in the logical relations between legal concepts and propositions, not merely in the relations between fact situations, and the problems springing from these; but also in the light of the import of these analogies and differences for what is thought by the latter court to yield a tolerably acceptable result in terms of 'policy,' 'ethics,' 'expediency' or whatever other norm of desirability the law may be thought to subserve. No 'ineluctable logic,' but *a composite of the logical relations seen between legal propositions, of observations of facts and consequences, and of value judgments about the acceptability of these consequences*, is what finally comes to bear upon the alternatives with which 'the rule of *stare decisis*' confronts the courts, and especially appellate courts. And this, it may be supposed, is why finally we cannot assess the product of their work in terms of any less complex quality than that of wisdom."

In Appendix 2 we set out a specimen law report with explanatory notes, in Appendix 1 we give details of the law reports and in the next chapter we illustrate the case law process at work. You may find it helpful to compare the theory of precedent explained in this chapter with the practice illustrated in the next.

Notes

[1] *The Common Law*, p. 1.

[2] See the wording of the oath discussed by Lord Denning in *The Road to Justice*, pp. 4 *et seq.* See also Lord Simon of Glaisdale in *Rugby Joint Water Board* v. *Shaw-Fox* [1973] A.C. 202.

[3] Denning, *op. cit.*, p. 4.

[4] See the discussion of social roles in Vilhelm Aubert's *Elements of Sociology*, Chap. III and see also Robert B. Seidman, "The Judicial Process Recon-

sidered in the Light of Role-Theory" (1969) 32 M.L.R. 516, 520, where he argues that the courts should formulate rules of conduct for "trouble" cases.

⁵ See P. Stein and J. Shand, *Legal Values in Western Society*, Chap. 2.

⁶ The early writer and judge, Bracton, in his treatise on the laws of England, stated the principle thus, "If like matters arise, let them be decided by like since the occasion is a good one for proceeding *a similibus ad similia.*" Bracton, *The Laws and Customs of England* (Thorne ed.), Vol. 2, p. 21.

⁷ See Irving M. Copi, *Introduction to Logic* (4th ed.), p. 360.

⁸ John Stuart Mill, *A System of Logic* (8th ed.), Chap. XX, pp. 364–368. Reasoning by analogy was classified by some medieval philosophers as divisible into three types:—

  (a) *unius ad alterum* which can be represented thus A————B
  (b) *duorum ad tertium* which can be represented thus

  (c) *plurium ad plura* which can be represented thus A————B, C————D
  (a) is a simple comparison which indicates a relationship of similarity in a certain respect.
  (b) is based on proportion, that is a relationship in common of two things to a third thing.
  (c) is a relationship of proportionality—A is to B as C is to D.
      All three are used in legal reasoning, but (a) and (b) are most common. See further Ralph McInerny, *The Logic of Analogy—An Intepretation of St. Thomas*, Chap. VI.

⁹ See Levi, *Introduction to Legal Reasoning*, pp. 1–8 for a brillant discussion of this process. Karl Llewellyn used the phrase "situation sense" in this context in *The Common Law Tradition*.

¹⁰ See L. Becker, "Analogy in Legal Reasoning" (1973) *Ethics* 248. See also C. Hall, "*Validity Criteria and the Problem of Choice*" (1973) *Cambrian Law Review* 45.

¹¹ See Gideon Gottlieb, *The Logic of Choice*, Chap. VI.

¹² See Professor T. B. Smith in *Judicial Precedent in Scots Law*, pp. 106–107.

¹³ The main procedure is that of "relevancy." In the quaint words of Professor David Walker in "The Theory of Relevancy," 63 *Juridical Review* 1, "The question is: do the averments of fact focused by the pleas-in-law support the conclusions of the summons? If not, the action is irrelevant." To test this the allegations of fact are accepted by the court. The leading case of *Donoghue* v. *Stevenson* [1932] A.C. 562 arose out of this procedure.

¹⁴ [1932] A.C. 562.

¹⁵ See generally Chap. 8.

¹⁶ See generally on this Julius Stone, "The Ratio of the Ratio Decidendi" (1959) 22 M.L.R. 597, 610 *et seq.*

¹⁷ Much of what follows is based on Sir Rupert Cross, *Precedent in English Law* (3rd ed.). See also the essays in *Precedent in Law* ed. by L. Goldstein.

¹⁸ 5th ed., edited by R. Campbell, Vol. II, p. 627.

¹⁹ *Essays in Jurisprudence and the Common Law*, pp. 25–26 (our italics).

²⁰ See (1959) 21 M.L.R. 123–124. He states there that "there is no actual *uniform* operation of English courts concerning the application of precedents" (p. 123).

²¹ He appears to receive some support from the judgment of Lord Simon of Glaisdale in the tax case of *Lupton* v. *F.A. & A.B. Ltd.* [1972] A.C. 634 at pp. 658–659. Lord Simon emphasises, however, that material facts found in the case need to be reassessed in the light of subsequent decisions.

²² *Op. cit.*
²³ See "The Ratio of the Ratio Decidendi" (1959) 22 M.L.R. 597. See also 69 Col. L.R. 1162 (1969).
²⁴ Patterson, *Jurisprudence*, p. 313.
²⁵ Goodhart, *op. cit.*, p. 22.
²⁶ Cross, *op. cit.*
²⁷ See *supra*, n. 13.
²⁸ See Vaughan C.J. in *Bole* v. *Horton* (1673) Vaughan 360, 382.
²⁹ See R. E. Megarry in (1944) 60 L.Q.R. 222.
³⁰ See Cairns J. in *W.B. Anderson & Sons Ltd.* v. *Rhodes* [1967] 2 All E.R. 850.
³¹ *Jurisprudence* (4th ed.), p. 192.
³² For a more detailed discussion see Sir Rupert Cross, *Precedent in English Law* (3rd ed.).
³³ *In re Harper* v. *N.C.B.* [1974] Q.B. 614.
³⁴ *Beamish* v. *Beamish* (1861) 9 H.L.C. 274.
³⁵ (1880) 9 P.D. 96.
³⁶ [1928] 1 K.B. 176.
³⁷ [1954] P. 312.
³⁸ See A. W. B. Simpson, "The Ratio Decidendi of a case and the Doctrine of Binding Precedent" in *Oxford Essays in Jurisprudence* (1st series), ed. by A. G. Guest, p. 175.
³⁹ 11th ed., p. 76.
⁴⁰ Lord Simon in *Lupton* v. *F.A. & A.B. Ltd.* [1972] A.C. 634, 658–659 appears to support Professor Williams' view here.
⁴¹ *R.* v. *O'Connell* (1844) *Reports of State Trials* (N.S.) 2.
⁴² *Beamish* v. *Beamish* (1859) 9 H.L.C. 274.
⁴³ [1898] A.C. 375.
⁴⁴ See [1966] 3 All E.R. 77.
⁴⁵ For an interesting general discussion of the factors involved see Lord Diplock in *Geelong Harbour Trust Commrs.* v. *Gibbs Bright & Co.* [1974] A.C. 810 (P.C.). See also Lord Reid, "The Judge as Law-Maker" in (1972) XII J.S.P.T.L. (N.S.) 22 at p. 25.
⁴⁶ [1976] A.C. 443.
⁴⁷ [1980] A.C. 1148.
⁴⁸ [1972] A.C. 877.
⁴⁹ [1985] A.C. 560.
⁵⁰ [1972] A.C. 877.
⁵¹ See pp. 116 *et seq.*
⁵² [1944] K.B. 718. For a more detailed discussion see Cross, *op. cit.*, p. 108.
⁵³ For a discussion of this phrase see Lord Denning M.R. in *Miliangos* v. *George Frank (Textiles) Ltd.* [1975] Q.B. 487, 503, and Lord Simon of Glaisdale in the House of Lords [1976] A.C. 477 *et seq.* See also *Williams* v. *Fawcett* [1986] 1 Q.B. 604, 616–617. As to whether failure to refer to an E.E.C. Directive made a decision *per incuriam* see *Duke* v. *Reliance Systems Ltd.* [1987] 2 W.L.R. 1225 (C.A.). The Court of Appeal distinguishes between material which *must* have caused the court to reach a contrary decision and that which *may*.
⁵⁴ [1968] 2 Q.B. 1.
⁵⁵ *The Times*, July 3, 1989.
⁵⁶ [1986] 2 W.L.R. 962.
⁵⁷ [1950] 2 K.B. 368.
⁵⁸ *R.* v. *Gould* [1968] 2 Q.B. 65. See G. Zellick, "Precedent in the Court of Appeal, Criminal Division" [1974] Crim. L.R. 222. For a recent example of the court exercising its power see *R.* v. *Ghosh* [1982] 3 W.L.R. 110, where it refused to follows its earlier decision in *R.* v. *McIvor* [1982] 1 W.L.R. 490.

⁵⁹ *R.* v. *Spencer* [1985] 2 W.L.R. 197 at 203, *per* May L.J. delivering the judgment of the court.

⁶⁰ *Broome* v. *Cassell & Co.* [1971] 2 All E.R. 187 (C.A.).

⁶¹ *Cassell & Co.* v. *Broome* [1972] A.C. 1027. See generally, Professor Julius Stone, "On the Liberation of Appellate Judges—How not to do it!" in (1972) 35 M.L.R. 449.

⁶² *Schorsch Meier GmbH* v. *Henning* [1975] 1 Q.B. 416.

⁶³ *Miliangos* v. *George Frank (Textiles) Ltd.* [1976] A.C. 443.

⁶⁴ [1979] A.C. 264.

⁶⁵ For discussion of the issues raised in *Davis*, see Rickett, "Precedent in the Court of Appeal" (1980) 43 M.L.R. 136.

⁶⁶ *The Times*, July 3, 1989. See also *Williams* v. *Fawcett* [1986] 1 Q.B. 604, 616–617.

⁶⁷ *Read* v. *Joannou* (1890) 25 Q.B.D. 300 at pp. 302–303.

⁶⁸ *Police Authority* v. *Watson* [1947] K.B. 842. But see now *R.* v. *Manchester Coroner ex p. Tal* [1984] 3 W.L.R. 643 (D.C.). *Cf.*, however, *R.* v. *Spencer* [1985] 2 W.L.R. 197 (C.A.).

⁶⁹ See Lord Goddard C.J. in *Police Authority* v. *Watson* [1947] K.B. 842, 848.

⁷⁰ *Colchester Estates (Cardiff)* v. *Carlton Industries Plc.* [1984] 3 W.L.R. 693. (Nourse J.).

⁷¹ *Miliangos* v. *George Frank (Textiles) Ltd.* [1976] A.C. 443 at p. 477 (H.L.), *per* Lord Simon.

⁷² [1961] A.C. 388.

⁷³ [1921] 3 K.B. 560.

⁷⁴ *Tai Hing Ltd.* v. *Liu Chong Hing Bank* [1985] 3 W.L.R. 317.

⁷⁵ *Fatuma Binti, etc.* v. *Mahamed Bin Salim* [1952] A.C. 1, 14 (P.C.); *cf. Negro* v. *Pietro Bread Co. Ltd.* [1933] 1 D.L.R. 490; *Morris* v. *English, Scottish & Australian Bank* (1957) 97 C.L.R. 624. See also *Australian Consolidated Press Ltd.* v. *Uren* [1969] 1 A.C. 590, 641–644 and *Abbot* v. *R.* [1976] 3 W.L.R. 462, 471.

⁷⁶ See René David and John E. C. Brierley, *Major Legal Systems in the World Today*, 3rd ed., pp. 105 *et seq.*; John H. Merryman, *The Civil Law Tradition*, 2nd ed., Chap. VI; F. H. Lawson, *A Common Lawyer Looks at the Civil Law*, pp. 83 *et seq.*

⁷⁷ David and Brierley, *op. cit.*, p. 105.

⁷⁸ *Op. cit.*, p. 106.

⁷⁹ *Candler* v. *Crane, Christmas & Co.* [1951] 2 K.B. 164, 178.

⁸⁰ "The Ratio of the Ratio Decidendi" (1959) 22 M.L.R. 597, 618 (our italics). See the accounts, in the context of Stone's exposition of "the categories of illusory reference", in Stone, *The Province and Function of Law* (1946, repr. 1968, Wm. Hein), pp. 186 *et seq.*, and Stone, *Legal System and Lawyers' Reasonings* (1964), pp. 269 *et seq.*

Chapter 8

CASE LAW IN OPERATION

In the previous chapter we examined the theory of case law, the rules for determining the binding elements of cases, the methods of distinguishing cases and the ground rules of precedent. But understanding the techniques in the abstract does not enable one to appreciate the whole. To do that one must observe the operation of the process in a particular context and over a period of time. In this chapter we shall examine the operation of the process in relation to negligence liability for defective property. The law students are likely to become familiar with this area early in their law studies and will quickly realise that the substantive law is extremely complex. Our aim is not to disentangle the complexities—that is the functions of specialist texts and articles.[1] Rather it is to examine, albeit at a superficial level, the patterns through which the case law has developed.

THE BACKGROUND

In the celebrated case of *Donoghue* v. *Stevenson*[2] in 1932 the House of Lords held that where the use of a defective product (the ginger beer bottle with the decomposed snail) caused physical damage to the consumer, the manufacturer would be liable for the damage if the defect was due to its negligence.

Previous cases had imposed negligence liability for physical damage in a number of different situations, *e.g.* where the damage was caused by a dangerous activity or where there was a special relationship between the parties such as between an owner and the person he invited onto his property. The greatness of Lord Atkin's speech in *Donoghue* lay in the fact that he was able to formulate a general principle to explain liability for damage in all these cases. The following extracts from his judgment illustrate his view of the court's function in relation to the development of principles:

"It is remarkable how difficult it is to find in the English authorities statements of general application defining the relations between parties that give rise to the duty. The Courts are concerned with the particular relations which come before them in actual litigation, and it is sufficient to say whether the duty exists in those circumstances. The result is that the Courts have been engaged upon an elaborate classification of duties as they exist in respect of property, whether real or personal, with further divisions as to ownership, occupation or control, and distinctions based on the particular relations on the one side or the other, whether manufacturer, salesman or landlord, customer, tenant, stranger, and so on. In this way it can be ascertained at any time whether the law recognizes a duty, but only where the case can be referred to some particular species which has been examined and classified. And yet the duty which is common to all the cases where liability is established must logically be based upon some element common to the cases where it is found to exist. To seek a complete logical definition of the general principle is probably to go beyond the function of the judge, for the more general the definition the more likely it is to omit essentials or to introduce non-essentials.

At present I content myself with pointing out that in English law there must be, and is, some general conception of relations giving rise to a duty of care, of which the particular cases found in the books are but instances. The liability for negligence, whether you style it such or treat it as in other systems as a species of *"culpa,"* is no doubt based upon a general public sentiment of moral wrongdoing for which the offender must pay. But acts or omissions which any moral code would censure cannot in a practical world be treated so as to give a right to every person injured by them to demand relief. In this way rules of the law arise which limit the range of complainants and the extent of their remedy. The rule that you are to love your neighbour becomes, in law, you must not injure your neighbour; and the lawyer's question, Who is my neighbour? receives a restricted reply. You must take reasonable care to avoid acts or omissions which you can reasonably foresee would be likely to injure your neighbour. Who, then, in law is my neighbour? The answer seems to be—persons who are so closely and directly affected by my act that I ought reasonably to have them in contemplation as being so affected when I am directing my mind to the acts or omissions which are called in question. There will no doubt arise cases where it will be difficult to determine whether the contemplated relationship is so close that the duty arises. But, in the class of case now before the Court I cannot conceive any difficulty to arise. A manufacturer puts an article of food in a container which he knows will be opened by the actual consumer. There can be no inspection by any purchaser and no reasonable preliminary inspection by the consumer. Negligently, in the course of preparation, he allows the contents to be mixed with poison. It is said that the law of England and Scotland is that the poisoned consumer has no remedy against the negligent manufacturer. If this were the result of the authorities I should consider the result a grave defect in the law, and so contrary to principle that I should hesitate long before following any decision to that effect which had not the authority of this House. . . . There are other instances than of articles of food and drink where goods are sold intended to be used immediately by the consumer, such as many forms of goods sold for cleaning purposes, where the same liability must exist. The doctrine supported by the decision below would not only deny a remedy to the consumer who was injured by consuming bottled beer or chocolates poisoned by the negligence of the manufacturer, but also to the user of what should be a harmless proprietary medicine, an ointment, a soap, a cleaning fluid or cleaning powder. I confine myself to articles of common household use, where every one, including the manufacturer, knows that the articles will be used by other persons than the actual ultimate purchaser—namely, by members of his family and his servants, and in some cases his guests. I do not think so ill of our jurisprudence as to suppose that its principles are so remote from the ordinary needs of civilized society and the ordinary claims it makes upon its members as to deny a legal remedy where there is so obviously a social wrong."

These extracts concentrate on Lord Atkin's statement of principles. They do not do justice to the breadth of his reasoning in the case. He dealt exhaustively with the earlier authorities showing how those establishing liability fitted with the principles and those denying liability could be distinguished. One final point to note; although his initial statement of principle is wide, his concluding statements illustrate the narrow ratio of the case relating to the duty of a manufacturer of common household items. The immediate impact of the decision was limited to that narrow context but gradually over the years the wider neighbour principle has provided a basis for extending liability for negligently caused physical damage, for overruling earlier decisions denying recovery. The process has taken time. For example, it was only in 1963[3] that a builder was clearly held liable for damage to a person resulting from his negligent construction of a house when a defective concrete canopy over the front door collapsed onto the unfortunate person.

It is important to see that *Donoghue* only holds that there is liability for the *damage* (Mrs. Donoghue's subsequent illness) caused by a defect. It does not hold that there is liability for the *defect* itself. If Mrs. Donoghue had noticed the remains of the snail before drinking and demanded compensation to remedy the defect, *e.g.* money to buy a substitute drink, there is nothing in Lord Atkin's speech to indicate that she would have been successful. Similarly, had the householder noticed the defective canopy and claimed compensation to rectify it before it fell, it is unlikely that the courts of 1963 would have been willing to impose liability. However, in the 1970s the courts began a process of developing negligence liability for defects only to change their minds in the 1980s and beat a hasty retreat back to their starting point. This chapter analyses the leading cases of the period, concentrating on the techniques used by the courts to extend and then restrict liability. The diagram on page 120 places the leading cases on a graph charting this rise and fall movement.

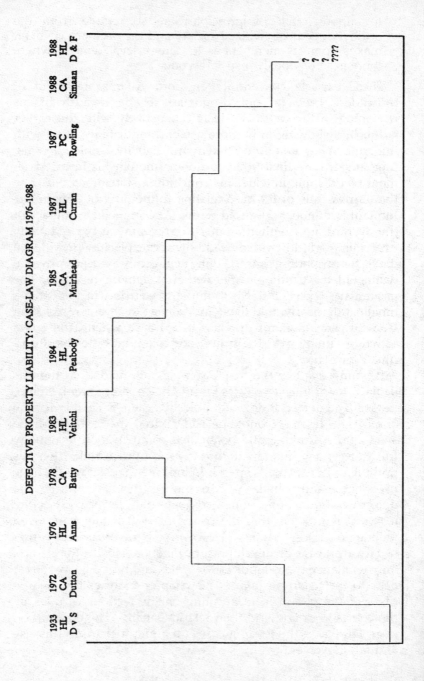

DEFECTIVE PROPERTY LIABILITY: CASE-LAW DIAGRAM 1976–1988

THE CASE LAW DEVELOPMENT

The Advance of Liability

The development begins in 1971 with the case of *Dutton* v. *Bognor Regis United Building Co. Ltd.*[4] A local council had negligently allowed a house to be built with inadequate foundations. As a result the house was *defective*. It had cracks resulting from subsidence. It was also *dangerous*. Sooner or later bits of it might collapse damaging the owner's furnishings etc., or even causing her personal injury. But it had not yet done this. It had not caused any actual *damage*. The lawyer for the council argued that although the council might be liable if the ceiling fell down and injured Mrs Dutton, they would not be liable simply because the defects in the house diminished its value. In the Court of Appeal, Lord Denning dismissed this argument saying, "(This) would mean that if the inspector negligently passes the house as properly built and it collapses and injures a person, the council are liable; but if the owner discovers the defect in time to repair it—and he does repair it—the council are not liable. That is an impossible distinction. They are liable in either case."

By terming the distinction "impossible," Lord Denning was appealing to common sense to extend liability from damage to a dangerous defect. The decision was little criticised and when very similar facts came before the House of Lords in 1977 in the case of *Anns* v. *Merton London Borough Council*,[5] Lord Wilberforce felt able to say that liability for the cost of repairing the dangerous defect followed from "normal principle." He dealt with the problem of the nature of the loss by saying "If classification is required, the relevant damage is physical damage . . . what is recoverable is the amount of expenditure necessary to restore the dwelling to a condition in which it is no longer a danger to the safety of persons occupying." The distinction between liability for damage and for dangerous defect was being blurred if not buried. *Batty* v. *Metropolitan Property Realisations Ltd.*[6], decided the following year, marked a further extension on *Dutton* and *Anns*, for in *Batty* although the house in question had not suffered any subsidence at the time of the action, it was doomed. It was bound to collapse down a hillside. The defective nature of the house, *i.e.* its position on the hillside, could not be rectified. The Court of Appeal found the builder liable and Bridge L.J. in an unreserved judgment commented that the distinction between a defect causing damage to occupant and a defect rendering house incapable of repair *"is really untenable"* Once again, an appeal to common sense without any apparent appreciation that liability was being greatly extended. (For an account of the real significance of the case, see Lord Oliver's judgment set out at the end of this chapter.)

The extension of liability reached its high water mark in the 1982 decision of the House of Lords in *Junior Books Ltd.* v. *Veitchi Co. Ltd.*[7] There, a subcontractor had negligently laid a floor in a factory with the result that the floor was *defective* but, unlike the *Anns* situation, *not dangerous* in any way. (A subcontractor works under a contract with a main contractor, helping it carry out its own contract with a developer—a factory owner in the *Junior Books* case.) Giving the leading judgment, Lord Roskill cited *Dutton, Anns* and *Batty* as demonstrating "how far the law has developed" and after noting that it was conceded that there would be liability if the floor was dangerous, said "It seems curious that if the work had been so bad that to avoid imminent danger expenditure had been incurred (the owner) could recover that expenditure, but that if the work was less badly done so that remedial work could be postponed it cannot do so." He concluded, " . . . proper control (of liability) lies not in somewhat *artificial distinctions* between physical and economic loss . . . but in establishing the relevant *principles* and then deciding whether the particular case falls within those principles." For the principle Lord Roskill adopted the two stage test used by Lord Wilberforce in *Anns*, namely,

"First one has to ask whether, as between the alleged wrongdoer and the person who has suffered damage there was a sufficient relationship of proximity or neighbourhood such that, in the reasonable contemplation of the former, carelessness on his part may be likely to cause damage to the latter, in which case a *prima facie* duty of care arises. Secondly, if the first question is answered affirmatively, it is necessary to consider whether there are any considerations which ought to negative, or to reduce or limit the scope of the duty."

Applying this principle, Lord Roskill held the subcontractor liable to the factory owner for the cost of remedying the defects. Common sense, analogy and principle were all involved in supporting this final extension of liability to defective property. But this time the extension did not go unchallenged.

The Challenge

Lord Brandon gave a powerful dissent in *Junior Books*. He argued that the effect of imposing a duty in respect of non-dangerous defects was "to create, as between two persons who are not in any contractual relationship with each other, obligations of one of those two persons to the other which are only really appropriate as between persons who do have such a relationship between them." In other words, liability for non-dangerous defects should be based on contract not tort. This theme was echoed in a powerful academic critique of *Junior Books*, the article *"Donoghue* v. *Stevenson—The not so Golden Anniversary"*[8] by Professors Smith & Burns. Both they and Lord Brandon pointed to the problems that would arise if tortious liability for non-dangerous defects was accepted. Lord Brandon asked, "by what standards of quality would the question of defectiveness fall to be decided?" The standard specified in a contract between a subcontractor and its employer, a main contractor, would be unfair on an owner who was not a party to this subcontract. Equally, the standard expected by an owner would be unfair to a subcontractor working to a lesser standard specified in a subcontract. There was no right answer but if liability for defects could only arise in contract, the question would not have to be asked.

The Retreat

The retreat began in 1984 with the case of *Peabody Fund* v. *Sir L. Parkinson & Co. Ltd.*[9] A council inspector negligently approved a defective drainage system for a housing estate. The system failed. The developer sued the council for the cost of remedying the defects. The House of Lords held the council not liable. There were obvious reasons for this finding. The system had been designed by the architect employed by the developer and clearly in such a situation the developer should look to his architect rather than the council for compensation. Furthermore, the statutory requirement for council approval was intended to protect the health of occupiers of the estate and not the pocket of the developer. However, in addition to mentioning these points, Lord Keith took the opportunity to voice the wider concern of the House of Lords about the development of the law. He said:

> "there has been a tendency in some recent cases to treat these passages (the *Anns* two stage test) as being of a definitive character. This is a temptation which should be resisted . . . the scope of the duty (of care) must depend on all the circumstances of the case . . . in determining whether a duty of a particular scope was incumbent upon the defendant it is material to take into consideration whether it is just and reasonable that it should be so."

Here we have a new, more cautious and pragmatic approach designed to lead the retreat from the advances made in the name of principle. It was soon supported by the highest appeal court in Australia in the case of *Sutherland Shire Council v. Heymen*.[10] The facts were similar to those in *Anns* but the court reinterpreted Lord Wilberforce's proximity test in *Anns* as requiring a "close relationship" and not simply one where there was "reasonable contemplation of damage." So defined, there was insufficient proximity because there was no evidence that the occupier had ever relied on the council's approval of the house foundations as assuring that the house would be free of subsidence defects.

Meanwhile, the next case to come before the English courts, *Muirhead* v. *Industrial Tank Specialities Ltd.*,[11] returned to the implications of *Junior Books*. The negligent manufacturer of water pumps was sued by the operator of a lobster farm whose lobsters had died because defects had prevented the pumps circulating adequate supplies of fresh water. In the event, the manufacturer was held liable as the defect had led to *damage* to the plaintiff's property (the lobsters). But Goff L.J. made it clear that the manufacturer would not have been liable for the *defect* alone. He distinguished *Junior Books* as "a case in which on its particular facts there was considered to be such a very close relationship between the parties that there could be liability." *Junior Books* was now to be looked upon as establishing an exception to non-liability for defects rather than a general basis for liability. The distinguishing technique was next used on *Anns* by the House of Lords in its decision in *Curran* v. *N.I. Co-Ownership Housing Association*.[12] The Association had negligently approved a house extension financed by a housing improvement grant. The extension was so defective that it had to be completely rebuilt. The owner sued the Association for the cost and failed. The court distinguished *Anns* on the ground that, unlike the council's power in that case, the Association's power in *Curran* did not give it control over the day to day execution of the work. Without such control there was insufficient proximity. Both the Smith & Burns article and the *Sutherland* decision were cited in support of this more restrictive approach.

A Privy Council decision in 1988 needs to be considered next for although it was not directly concerned with defective property, it did contain an important statement of the philosophy underlying the retreat from *Anns*. In *Rowling* v. *Takaro Properties Ltd*.[13] the issue concerned the liability of a New Zealand government minister for alleged negligent exercise of his statutory powers. The Privy Council held that there was no liability on the ground that there was no negligence, but dealing with the broader question Lord Keith said that whether a duty of care should be imposed was "a question of an intensely pragmatic character, well suited for gradual development but requiring most careful analysis." He went on to add a warning. " . . . the imposition of liability may even lead to harmful consequences. The cure may be worse than the disease. There are reasons for believing that this may be so where liability is imposed on local authorities as in the *Anns* case because there is a danger that some inspectors may react to that decision by increasing unnecessarily the depth of foundations, thereby imposing a very substantial and unnecessary financial burden on members of the community."

After *Rowling* it was fairly clear that the days of local authority liability for dangerously defective property under the *Anns* principle were numbered. However, it was *Junior Books* liability for non-dangerous defects which was the first in line for rejection. The blow was delivered by the Court of Appeal in *Simaan General Contracting Co.* v. *Pilkington Glass Ltd.*[14] A manufacturer supplied a subcontractor with glass panels for the exterior cladding of a building in Abu Dhabi. The glass should have been green but it was alleged that due to negligent manufacture, the glass turned red under the Middle Eastern sun. The main contractor, who had to bear the cost of replacing the defective glass, sued the manufacturer in tort. The relationship between the manufacturer and the main contractor appeared very similar to that between the subcontractor and the owner in *Junior Books* and yet the court had no hesitation in distinguishing that decision as limited to its particular facts. Dillon L.J. went further, saying "my own view of *Junior Books* is that it has been subject to so much analysis with differing explanations of the basis of the case that it cannot now be regarded as a useful pointer to any development of the law. Indeed I find it difficult to see that future citation from *Junior Books* can ever serve any useful purpose." Of course in theory the Court of Appeal cannot overrule a decision of the House of Lords, but this may be the practical outcome of *Simaan*.

Our catalogue of cases ends in mid 1988 with *D & F Estates Ltd.* v. *Church Commissioners*[15] in which the House of Lords returned to the problem of liability for dangerous defects. Here ceilings negligently plastered by a subcontractor were dangerously defective. They threatened to fall on the heads of the occupiers. The occupiers sued for the cost of rectifying the defects. They failed in their action. The House of Lords was unwilling to accept that there was a separate category of dangerous defect for which liability could be imposed. Either the defect caused damage before it was discovered, in which case there was liability under *Donoghue*; or it was discovered first and was then "no longer dangerous" because precautions could be taken. Once the defect had been discovered, the property was simply defective and the loss involved was not recoverable in tort. That reasoning disposed of the case before the Lords, but it left the decision in *Anns* looking rather exposed. The Lords were not in a position to overrule *Anns* because the facts in *D & F* did not raise the issue of local authority liability. So instead, they were limited to commenting upon the decision. They confessed that they could not see much of a logical basis on which it could still be supported but nevertheless suggested narrow grounds such as the nature of the council's statutory power or the notion that the defect in the property could be said to have damaged other parts of the property. Reading the speech of Lord Oliver set out at the end of this chapter should give you some appreciation of how difficult an exercise this was. It would have been far simpler if some litigant had conveniently brought the *Anns* facts before the court again. Then the decision could have been cleanly overruled with no need to devise complex qualifications. Unfortunately but not surprisingly, no litigant has been pre-pared to waste his money taking such a case to the House of Lords.

CONCLUSION

What does this advance and retreat of liability for defective property reveal about the nature of case law reasoning? In the advance we see the courts driving forward by the use of analogy. The judges argue that common sense suggests that no distinction can be drawn between liability on one set of facts and its extension to the next set of facts. Analogical arguments are backed by appeals to general principle, to tests which will encompass all liability situations. In the retreat we see a shift of approach. We see the decisions which had imposed liability being distinguished on their facts and the principles which had justified liability being re-interpreted to fit a more cautious approach. Liability must be just and reasonable on the particu-lar facts of the particular case. Pragmatism is the watchword. In the last decade both judges[16] and academics,[17] although not agreed on its virtues, have seen pragmatism as the hallmark of the English common law. Of course, it is an important charac-teristic of case law reasoning but perhaps one should remem-ber that in the 1970s the watchword was principle. The truth is that judges make use of principled and pragmatic arguments as the need arises.

Our study also shows that the reasoning is not dominated by the ratios of binding cases. The dissenting judgment of Lord Brandon in *Junior Books* turns out to be more influential than the binding judgment of Lord Roskill. The former is cited with much approval by later courts and the latter is increasingly ignored. Nor are the materials cited limited to English case law. The views of two leading academics and the judgment of an Australian appeal court play an important role in justifying the new approach. Policy, too, plays a role. The judges consider the uncertain legal consequences of allowing tortious liability for defects. They also consider the possible financial consequences of imposing liability on local authorities and thereby encouraging the use of unnecessarily deep foundations, although whether this is an argument they can properly consider is another matter. Dworkin might well disapprove.

We might end with one other comment about Dworkin's theories. Dworkin likens the formulation of judicial decisions to the writing of a chain novel. Suppose you were given the first few sections of Dickens' *A Christmas Carol*. You would have some choice as to how to write the next section but your choice would be limited by the characters and plot outlined in the sections you were given. If you were given *Junior Books* as the last section of your novel,[18] would you have written a *D & F Estates* sequel? To draw an analogy from contemporary chain soap operas, isn't the change of direction since *Junior Books* rather akin to resurrecting Bobby Ewing?[19] Perhaps not. It took five years and a gradual step by step retreat (and we have only featured the major episodes) to get from one storyline to the other. Judges have more respect for their plot than television scriptwriters.

We conclude that the bare rules of precedent discussed in the previous chapter cannot express the true nature of the case law process. The interrelationship of analogy, rule and principle—the richness of the common law—is only apparent when you study a whole pattern of case law development or when, as we would ask you to do now, you study a leading judgment or speech in depth.

EXTRACTS FROM THE SPEECH OF LORD OLIVER IN D & F
ESTATES LTD. v. CHURCH COMMISSIONERS
[1988] 2 All E.R. 992

LORD OLIVER OF AYLMERTON. My lords, I have had the advantage of reading in draft the speech prepared by my noble and learned friend Lord Bridge, and I agree that the appeal should be dismissed for the reasons which he has given. In particular, I agree with his conclusion that . . . the cost of replacing the defective plaster would, in any event, be irrecoverable.

It is, I think, clear that the decision of this House in *Anns* v. *Merton London Borough Council* (1977) introduced, in relation to the construction of buildings, an entirely new type of product liability, if not, indeed, an entirely novel concept of the tort of negligence. What is not clear is the extent of the liability under this new principle. In the context of the instant appeal, the key passage from the speech of Lord Wilberforce in that case has already been quoted by my noble and learned friend. [Lord Bridge had quoted this passage:

"The damages recoverable include all those which foreseeably arise from the breach of the duty of care . . . these damages may include damages for personal injury and damage to property. In my opinion they may also include damage to the dwelling-house itself; for the whole purpose of the byelaws in requiring foundations to be of certain standard is to prevent damage arising from weakness of the foundations which is certain to endanger the health or safety of the occupants. To allow recovery for such damage to the house follows from normal principle. If classification is required, the relevant damage is, in my opinion, physical damage, and what is recoverable is the amount of expenditure necessary to restore the dwelling to a condition in which it is no longer a danger to the health and safety of persons occupying. On the question of damages generally I have derived much assistance from the judgment (dissenting on this point, but of strong persuasive force) of Laskin C.J. in the Canadian Supreme Court case of *Rivtow Marine Ltd.* v. *Washington Iron Works* (1974)."]

A number of points emerge from this.

(1) The damage which gives rise to the action may be damage to the person or to property on the ordinary *Donoghue* v. *Stevenson* principle. But it may be damage to the defective structure itself which has, as yet, caused no injury either to persons or to other property, but has merely given rise to a risk of injury.

(2) There may not even be "damage" to the structure. It may have been inherently defective and dangerous *ab initio* without any deterioration between the original construction and the perception of risk.

(3) The damage to or defect in the structure, if it is to give rise to a cause of action, must be damage of a particular kind, *i.e.* damage or a defect likely to cause injury to health or, possibly, injury to other property (an extension arising only by implication from the approval by this House of the decision of the Court of Appeal in *Dutton* v. *Bognor Regis United Building Co. Ltd.*).

(4) The cause of action so arising does not arise on delivery of the defective building or on the occurrence of the damage but on the damage becoming a "present or imminent risk" to health or (*semble*) to property and it is for that risk that compensation is to be awarded.

(5) The measure of damages is at large but, by implication for the approval of the dissenting judgment in the Canadian case referred to (*Rivtow Marine Ltd.* v. *Washington Iron Works*), it must at least include the cost of averting the danger.

These propositions involve a number of entirely novel concepts. In the first place, in no other context has it previously been suggested that a cause of action in tort arises in English law for the defective manufacture of an article which causes no injury other than injury to the defective article itself. If I buy a secondhand car to which there has been fitted a pneumatic tyre which, as a result of carelessness in manufacture, is dangerously defective and which bursts, causing injury to me or to the car, no doubt the negligent manufacturer is liable in tort on the ordinary application of *Donoghue* v. *Stevenson*. But if the tyre bursts without causing any injury other than to itself or if I discover the defect before a burst occurs, I know of no principle on which I can claim to recover from the manufacturer in tort the cost of making good the defect which, in practice, could only be the cost of supplying and fitting a new tyre. That would be, in effect, to attach to goods a non-contractual warranty of fitness which would follow the goods into whosoever's hands they came. Such a concept was suggested, *obiter*, by Lord Denning M.R. in *Dutton's* case, but it was entirely unsupported by any authority and is, in my opinion, contrary to principle.

The proposition that damages are recoverable in tort for negligent manufacture when the only damage sustained is either an initial defect in or subsequent injury to the very thing that is manufactured is one which is peculiar to the construction of a building and is, I think, logically explicable only on the hypothesis suggested by my noble and learned friend Lord Bridge, that in the case of such a complicated structure, the other constituent parts can be treated as separate items of property distinct from that portion of the whole which has given rise to the damage, for instance, in *Anns'* case, treating the defective foundations as something distinct from the remainder of the building. So regarded this would be no more than the ordinary application of the *Donoghue* v. *Stevenson* principle. It is true that in such a case the damages would include, and in some cases might be restricted to, the costs of replacing or making good the defective part, but that would be because such remedial work would be essential to the repair of the property which had been damaged by it.

But even so there are anomalies. If that were the correct analysis, then any damage sustained by the building should ground an action in tort from the moment when it occurs. But *Anns* tells us, and at any rate, so far as the local authority was concerned, this was a ground of decision and not merely *obiter*, that the cause of action does not arise until the damage becomes a present or imminent danger to the safety or health of the occupants and the damages recoverable are to be measured, not by the cost of repairing the damage which has been actually caused by the negligence of the builder, but by the (possibly much more limited) cost of putting the building into a state in which it is no longer a danger to the health or safety of the occupants.

It has, therefore, to be recognised that *Anns* introduced not only a new principle of a parallel common law duty in a local

authority stemming from but existing alongside its statutory
duties and conditioned by the purpose of those statutory
duties, but also an entirely new concept of the tort of negligence in cases relating to the construction of buildings. The
negligent builder is not answerable for all the reasonably
foreseeable consequences of his negligence, but only for consequences of a particular type. Moreover, the consequence
which triggers the liability is not, in truth, the damage to the
building, *qua* damage, but the creation of the risk of
apprehended damage to the safety of person or property.
Take, for instance, the case of a building carelessly constructed
in a manner which makes it inherently defective *ab initio* but
where the defect comes to light only as a result, say, of a
structural survey carried out several years later at the instance
of a subsequent owner. What gives rise to the action is then
not "damage" in any accepted sense of the word but the
perception of possible but avoidable damage in the future. The
logic of according the owner a remedy at that stage is illustrated by the dissenting judgment of Laskin C.J. in *Rivtow
Marine Ltd.* v. *Washington Iron Works* and it is this: if the
plaintiff had been injured the negligent builder would
undoubtedly have been liable on *Donoghue* v. *Stevenson* principles. He has not been injured, but he has been put on notice to
an extent sufficient to deprive himself of any remedy if he is
now injured and he therefore suffers, and suffers only, the
immediate economic loss entailed in preventing or avoiding the
injury and the concomitant liability for it of the negligent
builder which his own perception has brought to his attention.
It is fair therefore that he should recover this loss, which is as
much due to the fault of the builder as would have been the
injury if it had occurred. Thus, it has to be accepted either that
the damage giving rise to the cause of action is pure economic
loss not consequential on injury to person or property, a
concept not so far accepted into English law outside the *Hedley
Byrne* type of liability, or that there is a new species of the tort
of negligence in which the occurrence of actual damage is no
longer the gist of the action but is replaced by the perception of
the risk of damage.

   I think that it has to be accepted that this involves an entirely
new concept of the common law tort of negligence in relation

to building cases. Its ambit remains, however, uncertain. So far as *Anns* was concerned with liability arising from breach of statutory duty, the liability of the builder was a matter of direct decision. No argument was advanced on behalf of the builder in that case, but it was an essential part of the rationale of the decision in relation to the liability of the local authority that there was a precisely parallel and co-existing liability in the builder. Moreover, it is, I think, now entirely clear that the vendor of a defective building who is also the builder enjoys no immunity from the ordinary consequences of his negligence in the course of constructing the building, but beyond this and so far as the case was concerned with the extent of or limitations on his liability for common law negligence divorced from statutory duty, Lord Wilberforce's observations were, I think, strictly *obiter*. My Lords, so far as they concern such liability in respect of damage which has actually been caused by the defective structure other than by direct physical damage to persons or to other property, I am bound to say that, with the greatest respect to their source, I find them difficult to reconcile with any conventional analysis of the underlying basis of liability in tort for negligence. A cause of action in negligence at common law which arises only when the sole damage is the mere existence of the defect giving rise to the possibility of damage in the future, which crystallises only when that damage is imminent, and the damages for which are measured, not by the full amount of the loss attributable to the defect, but by the cost of remedying it only to the extent necessary to avert a risk of physical injury, is a novel concept. Regarded as a cause of action arising not from common law negligence but from breach of a statutory duty, there is a logic in so limiting it as to conform with the purpose for which the statutory duty was imposed, that is to say the protection of the public from injury to health or safety. But there is, on that footing, no logic in extending liability for a breach of statutory duty to cases where the risk of injury is a risk of injury to property only, nor, as it seems to me, is there any logic in importing into a pure common law claim in negligence against a builder the limitations which are directly related only to breach of a particular statutory duty. For my part therefore, I think the correct analysis, in principle, to be simply that, in a case where no question of breach of statutory duty arises, the builder of a house or other structure is liable at common law for negligence only where actual damage, either to person or to property, results from carelessness on his part in the course of construction. That the liability should embrace damage to the defective article itself is, of course, an anomaly which distinguishes it from liability for the manufacture of a defective chattel but it can, I think, be accounted for on the basis which my noble and learned friend Lord Bridge suggested, namely that, in the case of a complex structure such as a building, individual parts of the building fall to be treated as separate and distinct items of property. On that footing, damage caused to other parts of the building from, for instance, defective foundations or defective steel-work would ground an action but not damage to the defective part itself except in so far as that part caused other damage, when the damages would include the cost of repair to that part so far as necessary to remedy damage caused to other parts. Thus, to remedy cracking in walls and ceilings caused by defective foundations necessarily involves repairing or replacing the foundations themselves. But, as in the instant case, damage to plaster caused simply by defective fixing of the plaster itself would ground no cause of action apart from contract or under the Defective Premises Act 1972.

. . . Since *Anns* there have, of course, been the decision of the Court of Appeal in *Batty* v. *Metropolitan Property Realizations Ltd.* and the decision of the House in *Junior Books Ltd.* v. *Veitchi Co. Ltd.* I do not, for my part, think that the latter is of any help in the present context. As my noble and learned friend Lord Bridge has mentioned, it depends on so close and unique a relationship with the plaintiff that it is really of no use as an authority on the general duty of care and it rests, in any event, on the *Hedley Byrne* doctrine of reliance. So far as the general limits of the general duty of care in negligence are concerned, I, too, respectfully adopt what is said in the dissenting speech of Lord Brandon in that case.

Batty v. *Metropolitan Property Realisations Ltd.*, however, is directly in point and it needs to be carefully considered because it is, in my opinion, equally difficult to reconcile with any previously accepted concept of the tort of negligence. The defendant builder in that case had previously owned the land on which the plaintiffs' house was built and was working in close conjunction with the plantiffs' vendor, who had bought the land from him. Thus the plaintiffs had a contractual relationship with the vendor, but none with the builder. There was no negligence in the construction of the house as such, nor was there any breach of statutory duty, nor had any damage yet occurred to the house. The negligence consisted solely in not appreciating what the builder ought reasonably to have appreciated, that is to say that the immediately adjacent land was in such a condition that it would ultimately bring about the subsidence of the plaintiffs' land and the consequent destruction of anything built on it. At the date of the action and of the hearing no actual damage had been occasioned to the house. All that had happened was that a part of the garden had subsided, that being the event which alerted the plaintiffs to the danger which threatened the house. That, however, was not an event in any way attributable to fault on anyone's part but merely to the natural condition of the adjoining land. So that although there had been physical damage to the garden, it was not physical damage caused by any neglect on the part of the builders. The case is thus, on analysis, one in which the claim was for damages for pure economic loss caused by the putting onto the market of a produce which, because defective, would become a danger to health and safety and thus of less value than it was supposed to be. It is not specified in the report of the case how the damages of £13,000 were calculated, but it seems that the sum must have been based on the difference between the market value of the house (which was doomed to destruction and therefore valueless) and the value of an equivalent house built on land not subject to landslips. Thus, what the plaintiffs obtained from the builders by way of damages in tort was the sum for which the builders would have been liable if they had given an express contractual warranty of fitness, a sum related directly not to averting the danger created by the builders' negligence but to the replacement of an asset which, by reason of the danger, had lost its value. The decision in *Batty's* case was based on *Anns*, but in fact went one step further because there was not in fact any physical damage resulting from the builders' negligence, although Megaw L.J. appears to have considered that what mattered was the occurrence of physical damage to some property of the plaintiffs, however caused. As in *Anns*, the cause of action was related not to damage actually caused by the negligent act but to the creation of the danger of damage, and the case is therefore direct authority for the recovery of damages in negligence for pure economic loss.

My Lords, I confess to the greatest difficulty in reconciling this with any previously accepted concept of the tort of negligence at common law and I share the doubt expressed by my noble and learned friend Lord Bridge whether it was correctly decided, at any rate so far as the liability of the builder was concerned. The case was, however, one in which the builder and the developer, with whom the plaintiffs had a directly contractual relationship, were, throughout, acting closely in concert and it may be that the actual decision, although not argued on this ground, can be justified by reference to the principle of reliance established by the decision of this House in *Hedley Byrne & Co. Ltd.* v. *Heller & Partners Ltd.*

My Lords, I have to confess that the underlying logical basis for and the boundaries of the doctrine emerging from *Anns* v. *Merton London Borough Council* are not entirely clear to me and it is in any event unnecessary for the purposes of the instant appeal to attempt a definitive exposition. This much at least seems clear: that in so far as the case is authority for the proposition that a builder responsible for the construction of the building is liable in tort at common law for damage occurring through his negligence to the very thing which he has constructed, such liability is limited directly to cases where the defect is one which threatens the health or safety of occupants or of third parties and (possibly) other property. In such a case, however, the damages recoverable are limited to expenses necessarily incurred in averting that danger. The case cannot, in my opinion, properly be adapted to support the recovery of damages for pure economic loss going beyond that, and for the reasons given by my noble and learned friend Lord Bridge, with whose analysis I respectfully agree, such loss is not in principle recoverable in tort unless the case can be brought within the principle of reliance established by *Hedley Byrne*. In the instant case the defective plaster caused no damage to the remainder of the building and in so far as it presented a risk of damage to other property or to the person of any occupant that was remediable simply by the process of removal. I agree, accordingly, for the reasons which my noble and learned friend Lord Bridge has given, that the cost of replacing the defective plaster is not an item for which the builder can be held liable in negligence. I too would dismiss the appeal.

Notes

[1] See, *e.g.*, Michael Jones, *Torts* (2nd ed., 1989).
[2] [1932] A.C. 562.
[3] *Sharpe* v. *Sweeting (E.T.) & Son Ltd.* [1963] 1 W.L.R. 665.
[4] [1972] 1 Q.B. 373 (C.A.).
[5] [1978] A.C. 728 (H.L.).
[6] [1978] Q.B. 554 (C.A.).
[7] [1983] 1 A.C. 520 (H.L.).
[8] (1983) 46 M.L.R. 147.
[9] [1985] A.C. 210 (H.L.).
[10] (1985) 60 A.L.R. 1 (H.C.).
[11] [1986] Q.B. 507 (C.A.).
[12] [1987] A.C. 718 (H.L.).
[13] [1988] 1 All E.R. 163 (H.L.).
[14] [1988] 2 W.L.R. 761 (C.A.).
[15] [1988] 3 W.L.R. 368 (H.L.).
[16] Lord Goff, *The Search for Principle*, Maccabaean Lecture in Jurisprudence 1983.
[17] Atiyah, *Pragmatism and Theory in English Law*, sees pragmatism as both a strength and weakness.
[18] When the last edition was written in 1983 *Junior Books* was the last section of the novel and the equivalent of this chapter traced the extension of negligence liability through to that case. Fortunately, the authors predicted that "we may be due for a period of caution, a restriction of *Veitchi*" but they would be the first to confess that the speed and extent of the retreat was not foreseeable!
[19] Bobby Ewing was a character in the 1980s soap *Dallas*. The character was killed off at the end of one season but, after bad ratings in the following season, the scriptwriters resurrected the character by the device of treating the previous season's episodes as part of a bad dream by one of the other characters. It is said that the viewing public did not find this explanation easy to accept. "Ratings" and "peer acceptability" should not be lightly dismissed when considering what happened to *Junior Books*.

Chapter 9

LEGISLATION

AN OUTLINE OF THE LEGISLATIVE PROCESS

Until the nineteenth century, Parliament was primarily a deliberative body and in practice legislation was not a very productive source of law. However, with the rapid changes in society created by the Industrial Revolution and with the growth of modern government, legislation has become the most productive source in fact, as well as the most important source in English legal theory. The crucial fact still remains, however, that Parliament has other tasks to perform apart from legislation. These political tasks limit the time it can spend on legislation and the effective control it can exert over its detailed provisions.

Although legislation is now the principal expression of policy in legal form, the sources of that policy are diverse. The most important sources in practice are the manifestos of the political parties as revised by the party when in power and the deliberations of the permanent civil servants in the departments of state. To these can be added public opinion, which Sir Robert Peel defined in 1820 as "that great compound of folly, weakness, prejudice, wrong feeling, right feeling, obstinacy and newspaper paragraphs." In the development of public opinion, pressure groups consisting of interest groups and cause groups are active.[1] Pressure groups are an essential part of the modern political scene. Added to these are the Law Commissions which on less controversial matters play an advisory role to Parliament and act as a major source of reform ideas. In the formulation of those ideas and in the consultative process, pressure groups again exert influence. The legislative process represents a constant interaction between these bodies.

A distinction is drawn between *public general acts, local acts* and *private acts*.[2] The most common and important are *public general acts*. These apply to everyone and everywhere within their scope. *Local acts* are a species of public act which is limited to a particular locality. The most important distinction is between public and private acts. *Private acts*, which are not to be confused with private members' bills which lead to public acts, confer a *privilegium*, that is an exception from the general law or a provision for something which cannot be obtained by means of the general law. Their operation is in respect of a person or body of persons, including individuals, local authorities, statutory companies or private corporations.[3] They are also governed by different procedures, being drafted by parliamentary agents (specialist outside practitioners) and originating by petition. They are formally advertised and the procedure in Committee is quasi-judicial with the petitioners and their opponents being heard and evidence being given.

Sometimes a new statute is passed which re-enacts the contents of earlier statutes with only such modifications as are necessary to produce a coherent whole.[4] This is called a *consolidating act*. The Law Commission is actively engaged in work on consolidation which is a time-consuming but necessary process. Where an act attempts to sum up the existing legislation and common law and equity on a particular topic it is called a *code*. Codification is an important but controversial topic which will be dealt with in chapter 11.

Lastly we have *delegated legislation*. This is legislation by subordinate law-making bodies which has been sanctioned by Parliament. The relevant bodies must act within their powers which the courts scrutinise carefully. If the courts find that the powers have been exceeded, the delegated legislation is invalid. Delegated legislation consists mainly of statutory instruments made by government departments. Statutory instruments are usually required to be laid before Parliament

for a prescribed period and in the absence of a negative ruling
they become law. Sometimes the converse applies in that they
do not take effect unless approved. In the preparation of
delegated legislation there is usually consultation with outside
bodies such as the relevant interest groups.

MECHANICS OF ENACTMENT

The actual mechanics involved in the enactment of a government public bill are as follows.[5] The civil servants who are
responsible for formulating the principles behind a particular
Act of Parliament brief the departmental lawyers who in turn
draft instructions to the Office of Parliamentary Counsel to
prepare a draft bill. The latter are a band of draftsmen and
women recruited from the Bar and solicitors and trained in the
mysteries of their art. They are nominally under the control of
the Prime Minister but are very much a law unto themselves.
They normally have to work to a pretty tight timetable and
usually work in pairs. The senior of the two takes full responsibility for the drafting of the bill and any amendments and
advises the ministers and parliamentary officials as to matters
arising during the passage of the bill through Parliament. The
draft bill is discussed in departmental committees but normally
there is no outside scrutiny until the bill is introduced into
Parliament. In this latter respect there is a contrast with
legislation resulting from recommendations of the Law Commission which often appends a draft bill to its reports.

The main structure of a bill is as follows:

Long Title
Preamble (if any)
Enacting formula
Short title
Definitions (sometimes, perversely, this section appears in
the middle or at the end)
Principal provisions
Administrative provisions
Transitional provisions
Repealing clauses

The date of coming into effect

Schedules

(A copy of the Human Organ Transplants Act 1989 (with annotations) is set out in Appendix 1. You may find it useful to refer to this now. Further details appear in Appendix 2).

At present 10 Fridays in a session are available for consideration of private members' bills. Priority for the use of this time is regulated by ballot. Apart from the ballot there is provision for a member to introduce a private bill under what is known as "the Ten Minute Rule." Without government support a private member's bill has little chance of enactment.

The procedure for a public (non money) bill is begun by the bill's introduction and first reading in either the House of Commons or the House of Lords. Bills with financial implications are almost invariably introduced into the House of Commons. This first reading consists of the Clerk reading the short title to the bill and is intended merely to give notice of the proposed measure. No questions are put at this stage. The bill is then printed and a second reading follows in which the general principles of the bill are discussed. The bill is normally sent to one of the Standing Committees for detailed discussion and amendment of its provisions. Sometimes this discussion takes place before a Committee of the whole House. Alternatively, a bill may be referred to a Select Committee or to a Joint Committee consisting of members of both the Commons' and Lords' Select Committees. Next follows the Report stage before the House. If the bill has been amended in Committee, members will consider it in its revised form. Following the Report stage, the bill is then read for a third time and follows a similar routine in the other House. Sometimes there is reference back on particular points between the two Houses. After this, the bill receives the Royal Assent and becomes law, unless there is a provision for a later commencement date. It has become increasingly common to introduce different parts of an act at different times.[6]

LEGISLATION AND LANGUAGE

Whereas case law emanates from the exigencies of particular fact situations and the solution of particular problems, legislation usually speaks in general terms. Legislative rules relate to classes of persons, classes of behaviour and classes of situation. The drafter of legislation, therefore, is faced with a dilemma; not only must a proposed rule be general enough to cover all foreseeable instances falling within the policy of the statute, it must contain sufficient detail to ensure that its meaning is clear. Breadth of scope and precision are not always compatible objectives. In practice, different legal systems employ different styles of drafting to attempt to cope with the problem. The French often prefer to use general principles, whereas in the past English drafting has tended to err on the side of excessive detail, so that statutes sometimes emerge as labyrinths of rules, definitions, amplifications and cross references. The result is sometimes difficult for a lawyer to understand and frequently unintelligible to the layperson. There are some areas of the law, such as tax and criminal law, where detail is required in the interests of the subject. Arguably, however, such a style is inappropriate to all areas of law. In some areas of law, such as family law for example, Parliament may wish to leave the courts a discretion to administer law as they think best having regard to the circumstances of the individual case.

In attempting to produce a clear and unambiguous text, the legislative drafter is of course subject to the normal rules and natural limitations of the English language. The main sources of linguistic uncertainty are ambiguity, vagueness and generality. Ambiguity is sometimes classified into three categories—lexical, syntactic and contextual. Lexical ambiguity arises from the range of possible meanings attributable to a single word. Sometimes a word may have several related meanings attaching to it. The word "purpose," for example, can refer to aim, intention or policy. Sometimes the same word sound has two or more quite distinct meanings. The word "conveyance" can refer to a transfer of land or to a vehicle. The first type of lexical ambiguity can raise considerable problems whereas the second seldom does. In legislation, lexical problems will usually be resolved by syntax and context. Syntactic ambiguities arise from the actual structure of sentences, *e.g.* the definition of anthropology as "the science of man embracing woman." Contextual ambiguities are those which concern the relationship of one word or phrase or sentence to others in a particular context. An obvious and common example is inconsistency between two or more statutory provisions. Whereas lexical ambiguity can often be resolved by reference to syntax, and syntactic ambiguity by reference to context, contextual ambiguity has to be resolved by reference to the purpose of the particular legislation.

A term is vague when there are borderline cases where there is no definite answer as to whether the term applies or not. These are the cases which fall within a word's penumbra of uncertainty or fringe of application, *e.g.* does "aeroplane" refer to a flying boat? Unlike ambiguity, vagueness is often a constructive uncertainty. The legislature may wish to maintain flexibility and use vague words as a means of doing so. Many value words such as "fair" and "reasonable" contain a value element.

Like vagueness, generality is not necessarily a problem. It is also a technique which can be used creatively to confer discretion. Generalisation is a process which is vital to both thinking and communication. However, legislative classes do not exist in nature, ready made with clear cut edges,[7] and the main problems are the formulation of suitable class characteristics and the identification of a member of the class.

CLEAR AND PROBLEM CASES

In spite of the difficulties arising from the English style of drafting, many cases are clear cases.[8] They fall squarely within a legislative category and rule. In such cases the process of interpretation resembles logical deduction. The major premise is the rule, the particular facts are identified as falling within the rule, and the rule is applied to the particular facts. In many cases, the problems do not arise as a result of the legislation, but the inevitable difficulties involved in fact finding. Once the facts are known, the case usually solves itself. As a result many cases do not come to court, or if they do they are pretty open and shut. There is a great tendency amongst legal academics to concentrate on problem cases. They are regarded as more interesting. One should, however, avoid the conclusion that

because they are more interesting and tend to be the cases
which appear in the Law Reports, they are the most common
in practice. This is not true. However, the study of the problem
case is useful from the point of view of legal education if one
bears this in mind.

A problem case may arise for a variety of reasons. First, the
legislative drafter may have failed to reduce uncertainty to the
level at which it will not affect the legislative purpose.
However, even the most careful and skilful drafter cannot
eliminate statutory doubt altogether. The inherent limitations
of language discussed above, the passage of the bill through
Parliament and the various amendments which have been
made, the unusualness of the fact situation which has arisen
and changed social conditions, all occasion grounds for doubt.
In our system, such doubts are usually resolved by the courts.
Since the interpretation by the courts is regarded as authoritative and impartial, Miers and Page assert that the attitudes and
practices of the judiciary provide a model of authoritative
interpretation which constitutes a standard to be complied
with.[9] Although judicial interpretation is confined to relatively
few cases, it has a normative significance for interpretation
generally.

INTERPRETATION OF LEGISLATION BY THE COURTS

The role of the courts with regard to legislation has changed in
the last 600 years. Originally the judges were members of the
King's Council and took part in the formulation of the legislative policy and sometimes in the drafting of legislation. "Do
not gloss the statute for we know better than you, we make
them", said one medieval judge to counsel.[10] The earliest
approach to legislation was therefore pretty free ranging; it was
only later that a more rigid concept of separation of powers
developed.[11] By the end of the seventeenth century, however,
such a doctrine had developed and this inevitably had an
influence on the judges' perception of their role with regard to
legislation. From this time onwards, the judges concentrated
on interpreting the wording of the legislation. This sometimes

led to unfortunate results and caused them to seek on occasion for a secondary meaning to avoid such results. The topic of judicial interpretation of statutes has received attention by law reform bodies in recent years. So far the recommendations have not been enacted, but some have been anticipated by the practice of the courts.

Traditionally, the courts have approached the question of interpretation in terms of the application of certain canons of construction and presumptions. The logical status of these is problematic. They are not rules in a strict sense. They do not bind the courts. They are too general to be called principles and indeed they have little or no ethical content. As a result they are sometimes called canons or maxims to emphasize the high level of generality. They have been called pointers or approaches in recent years.[12] A distinction can perhaps be drawn between ascertaining a meaning and justifying a meaning which has been ascertained. The primary utility of the canons and presumptions is probably justificatory, to justify an interpretation which has been arrived at by a general consideration of the facts of the case, the statutory rule and its purposes.[13] However, let us now look at the canons in more detail.

The Ordinary Meaning Approach to Interpretation

The obvious starting point for all interpretation is the statutory text itself. Unless the context otherwise requires the words used by Parliament should be given their ordinary or usual meaning. Adherence to ordinary meaning is arguably the fairest means of ascertaining and interpreting Parliament's intention.[14]

In its original formulation as the so-called "Literal Rule" this approach emerged at about the same time as Parliament itself was established as the supreme law-making body. This can be seen in the words of Tindal C.J.:

"The only rule for the construction of Acts of Parliament is that they should be construed according to the intent of the Parliament which passed the Act. If the words of the statute are in themselves precise and unambiguous, then no more can be necessary than to expound those words in that natural and ordinary sense. The words themselves alone do, in such a case, best declare the intention of the lawgiver."[15]

It is assumed that there is generally a plain meaning and it is the court's function to give effect to it even though the result is absurd or unjust.[16] The remedy against such absurdity or injustice is thought to lie in the hands of the legislature. The judges' role is simply to interpret the laws Parliament has made according to the supposed intention of Parliament, this intention being most reliably ascertained by giving the words Parliament has used their ordinary, plain or natural meaning.[17]

While adherence to ordinary meaning has much to recommend it as a starting point for interpretation, expressed in such a way the approach lays itself open to criticism. Not only does it adopt what many today would regard as too narrow a view of the judicial function, its direction to apply *the* ordinary meaning of words also implies a misunderstanding of the complexity of language itself. Simple, straightforward results must not be expected from a concept which does not itself possess those qualities. In fact it is not always clear what constitutes a word's ordinary or normal meaning. Ordinary meaning is often equated with "core" meaning. However, the element of vagueness present in most words means that there is often no clearly defined boundary between a word's core and its penumbra of fringe meanings. It is inevitable that there will occasionally be disagreement as to what the ordinary meaning of a word actually is. It is unfortunate that the phrase "ordinary meaning" implies a simple either/or choice; either something is an ordinary meaning or it is not. For this reason some writers prefer to talk of "obvious" meaning.[18] The latter term readily lends itself to description in terms of degrees of obviousness.

Similarly, it is not immediately clear what usage of a word is to be taken as representative of the usage of society as a whole. The chosen standard of speech should not correspond to slang usage, nor should it necessarily correspond to the customary usage of the judicial community. It may well be that an appropriate dictionary definition is the best guide to a word's "standard sense." Evidence of meaning so derived will of course be subject to contrary indications in the relevant statutory context. Where legislation is aimed at one particular group in society, for example legislation dealing with the regulation of a specific professional group, then obviously the ordinary meaning of the statutory language should be taken as the ordinary meaning of that particular speech community. This has not always been done. It is only within the last two decades that certain members of the judiciary have shown an awareness of the need to take account of linguistic register. In the case of *Maunsell* v. *Olins* Lord Simon of Glaisdale displayed a more relative approach to ordinary meaning[19]:

> "Statutory language, like all language, is capable of an almost infinite gradation of 'register,'—*i.e.* it will be used at the semantic level appropriate to the subject matter and to the audience addressed (the man in the street, lawyers, merchants, etc.). It is the duty of a court of construction to tune in to such register and so to interpret the statutory language as to give to it the primary meaning which is appropriate in that register (unless it is clear that some other meaning must be given in order to carry out the statutory purpose or to avoid injustice, anomaly, absurdity or contradiction). In other words, statutory language must always be given presumptively the most natural and ordinary meaning which is appropriate in the circumstances."

This was again emphasised in the House of Lords case, *Stock* v. *Jones (Frank) (Tipton) Ltd.*[20]:

"Nowadays," said Lord Simon, "we should add to 'natural and ordinary meaning' the words 'in their context and according to the appropriate linguistic register'."

Lord Simon's recognition that ordinary meaning is to be ascertained only after a consideration of the context seems to indicate a welcome modification of the traditional approach to ordinary meaning. A similar recognition of the importance of context is reiterated in numerous modern cases. Time and again the courts have stressed that statutes are to be read as a whole and meaning given to the disputed passage only after such a reading. While it would clearly be inaccurate to imply that all cases adopting the traditional literal approach assumed an excessively narrow and isolationist view of meaning,[21] the modern judicial tendency does seem to be towards a more frequent and extensive reference to context. A conception of ordinary meaning which includes context as an integral part of its determination would avoid many of the criticisms justifiably aimed at a more restrictive formulation. However, so long as disagreement exists between judges over the extent to which contextual materials *outside* the act can be considered in its interpretation, criticism cannot be avoided altogether. Early cases rarely went beyond a consideration of the act itself. The majority of modern cases adopting the ordinary meaning approach also stop at a consideration of the act read as a whole. Few have regard for context in its widest sense and consider the consequences of an interpretation.

Interpretation to Avoid Absurdity, etc.

In its more traditional application the ordinary meaning approach stopped short of a consideration of the consequences of a particular construction. Parliament alone was considered responsible for eliminating undesirable consequences by amending the law where necessary. Not all judges, however, take such a limited view of their role. Sometimes ordinary meaning is departed from and a secondary, less usual meaning adopted in cases where application of the ordinary meaning principle would lead to some absurdity, incongruity, repugnance or inconsistency. This practice was clearly recognised in 1836 by Parke B. in the case of *Becke* v. *Smith*:[22]

"It is a very useful rule in the construction of a statute to adhere to the ordinary meaning of the words used, and to the grammatical construction, unless that is at variance with the intention of the legislature to be collected from the statute itself, or leads to any manifest absurdity or repugnance, in which case the language may be varied or modified so as to avoid such inconvenience, but no further."

A further classic statement of this approach was given by Lord Blackburn in 1877 in *River Wear Commissioners* v. *Adamson*[23] when he said:

" . . . I believe that it is not disputed that what Lord Wensleydale used to call the golden rule is right, *viz.*, that we are to take the whole statute together, and construe it all together, giving the words their ordinary signification, unless when so applied they produce an inconsistency, or an absurdity or inconvenience so great as to convince the Court that the intention could not have been to use them in their ordinary significance, and to justify the Court in putting on them some other signification, which, though less proper, is one which the Court thinks the words will bear."

It is somewhat unclear what degree of absurdity, etc., is necessary before the ordinary or primary meaning will be departed from. Sometimes the judges have said there must be a "manifest" absurdity; sometimes the absurdity is described as "great" or "obvious."[24] The House of Lords have laid down an anomalies test:[25]

" . . . a court will only be justified in departing from the plain words of that statute where it is satisfied that:
(1) there is a clear and gross balance of anomaly
(2) Parliament, the legislative promoters and the draftsmen could not have envisaged such anomaly and could not have been prepared to accept it in the interest of a supervening legislative objective; . . .
(4) the language of the statute is susceptible of the modifications required to obviate the anomaly."

This approach, sometimes known as the "golden rule," bears an obvious relationship to both the ordinary meaning and purposive approaches to interpretation. *Prima facie* the statutory words will be given their ordinary meaning.[26] If these words, read in their proper context, are considered by the judge to be unequivocal that will be the end of the matter. The ordinary meaning will be applied regardless of the consequences of that application, for as in all interpretation the courts are bound by what appears to be the clear intention of Parliament. Departure from ordinary meaning will only be allowed where the statutory words are also capable of bearing some secondary, less usual meaning. There must be some doubts as to which of these meanings Parliament intended. Where application of the ordinary meaning would lead to an absurdity or inconsistency, then the less usual meaning will be preferred. In other words, in such a case the reasonableness of the consequences of the alternative construction will be a proper consideration in the ascertainment of meaning.[27]

It is clear that in such an analysis the court is not simply construing the statutory rule in its immediate context but also in the broader context of its consequences. While terms such as inconsistency, incompatibility and illogicality imply some discrepancy revealed by the statutory text itself, reference to absurdity seems to imply a value judgment linked closely with the reasonableness of the result.

Something approximating to the "golden approach" is found in other legal systems. As yet the English cases do not go as far as their American counterparts. There the cases are more various and it seems that in the construction of a statute considerations of what causes injustice[28] or unfairness can have a potent influence on the courts' interpretation.[29] Similarly, the courts will assume an intention not to discriminate unjustly between different classes of the same kind.[30] There is even a doctrine expressed in the language of presumption that the legislature is to be presumed not to have intended a rule attended with inconvenience,[31] hardship[32] or oppression.[33] In seeking to avoid absurdity the "golden" approach resembles the French *"interprétation logique"* but the French approach seems to take in a wider range of considerations including statutory analogies and general principles of law; in short, reference is made to the whole "logic" of the French legal system.[34]

Interpretation by Reference to the Statutory Purpose

Nowadays it is common for judges to attempt an interpretation that best accords with what they perceive to be the statutory purpose.[35] This is commonly called the purposive approach and bears some resemblance to two distinct continental approaches to interpretation—the historical and teleological approaches.[36] The first of these seeks primarily to ascertain the intention of the draftsman by research into the legislative history of the statute. The second is an interpretation by reference to the end or purpose (*telos* in Greek) or social goal of the legislation.

Interpretation by reference to the statutory purpose is nowadays generally recognised by judges to be "the better practice of the courts."[37] But such an approach to interpretation is not new. The so-called "mischief approach," on which the current judicial practice is based, was laid down as early as 1584 by the Barons of the Exchequer in *Heydon's Case*[38]:

> "And it was resolved by them, that for the sure and true interpretation of all statutes in general (be they penal or beneficial, restrictive or enlarging of the Common Law), four things are to be discerned and considered:
> 1st—What was the Common Law before the making of the Act,
> 2nd—What was the mischief and defect for which the Common Law did not provide,
> 3rd—What remedy the Parliament hath resolved and appointed to cure the disease of the commonwealth,
> and, 4th—The true reason of the remedy; and then the office of all the Judges is always to make such construction as shall suppress the mischief, and advance the remedy, and to suppress subtle inventions and evasions for continuance of the mischief, and *pro privato commodo*, and to add force and life to the cure and remedy, according to the true intent of the makers of the Act, *pro bono publico*."

Obviously this statement of the mischief approach is in need of modification if it is to recognise the changes which have occurred in the 400 years since its formulation. Its language is archaic.[39] Reference to "mischief" implies that legislation is only designed to deal with some evil and not to further positive social goals.[40] More important, however, is the point that in its original form the mischief approach reflects a different constitutional balance than would be acceptable today.[41] Not only did the doctrine of separation of powers develop sometime later, but this early formulation assumes statute law to be subsidiary and supplemental to the existing common law.[42] The legislature today has assumed a far greater function as a source of law. The volume of legislation has increased vastly and covers subjects not touched upon by the common law, for example, bankruptcy, town planning, social welfare and revenue law. A direction to consider the existing common law is often irrelevant.

These difficulties have largely been dealt with by the more up-to-date formulation of this approach in terms of a prefer-

ence for constructions promoting the general underlying legislative purpose.[43] Other difficulties have been resolved by subsequent judicial explanation. The failure of *Heydon's Case* to lay
down any clear test as to the significance of the actual words
used by Parliament has been remedied by Lord Simon's two-
tiered approach to interpretation in *Maunsell* v. *Olins*[44]:

> "The rule in *Heydon's Case*, 3 Co. Rep. 7a itself is sometimes
> stated as a primary canon of construction, sometimes as
> secondary, (*i.e.* available in the case of an ambiguity): *cf.*
> *Maxwell*, pp. 40, 96, with *Craies on Statute Law*, (7th ed.,
> 1971), pp. 94, 96. We think that the explanation of this is
> that the rule is available at two stages. The first task of a
> court of construction is to put itself in the shoes of the
> draftsman—to consider what knowledge he had and,
> importantly, what statutory objective he had—if only as a
> guide to the linguistic register. Here is the first consideration
> of the mischief. Being thus placed in the shoes of the
> draftsman, the court proceeds to ascertain the meaning of
> the statutory language. In this task the first and most
> elementary rule of construction is to consider the plain and
> primary meaning, in their appropriate register, of the words
> used. If there is no such plain meaning (*i.e.* if there is an
> ambiguity), a number of secondary canons are available to
> resolve it. Of these, one of the most important is the rule in
> *Heydon's Case*. Here, then, may be a second consideration of
> the mischief."

A conflict between the statutory purpose and what would
otherwise appear to be the plain meaning of words may arise
in Lord Simon's initial stage of interpretation. Arguably, such a
conflict would operate in a similar way to the so-called golden
approach. It would put the court on guard to look for ambiguities in the legislative text. The court must presume that
Parliament intended to enact provisions consistent with the
legislative purpose. In this respect the purposive and golden
approaches are related. The absurd or repugnant results that
lead a court to depart from the primary meaning of words are
usually "absurd" or "repugnant" for the very reason that they
are inconsistent with the supposed legislative intention. Presumably with this in mind the English and Scottish Law
Commissions have stated that the golden rule "on closer
examination turns out to be a less explicit form of the mischief

rule."[45] It is now clear, therefore, that the "ground and cause of the making of the statute" is referred to *before* deciding whether the statutory words are clear and unambiguous. The mischief or purposive approach has thus insinuated itself into the literal approach.[46]

In essence interpretation by reference to the statutory purpose enjoins a court to look to the object or purpose of an act and to construe doubtful passages in accordance with that purpose. At the time of *Heydon's Case* the "four-corners" rule prevailed. As Lord Diplock explained in the *Black Clawson Case*,[47] when the mischief approach was first propounded the judges needed to look no further than the act itself:

> "Statutes in the sixteenth century and for long thereafter in addition to the enacting words contained lengthy preambles reciting the particular mischief or defect in the common law that the enacting words were designed to remedy. So, when it was laid down, the 'mischief' rule did not require the court to travel beyond the actual words of the statute itself to identify 'the mischief and defect for which the common law did not provide,' for this would have been stated in the preamble. It was a rule of construction of the actual words appearing in the statute and nothing else. In construing modern statutes which contain no preambles to serve as aids to the construction of enacting words the 'mischief' rule must be used with caution to justify any reference to extraneous documents for this purpose."

Today, evidence of purpose is not always apparent from the facts of the act. Adoption of a purposive approach raises the question of how far beyond the act the court can go in determining what that purpose was. Lord Diplock's speech illustrates the hesitance with which some courts approach extrinsic materials. By no means all such materials are permitted to be used as formal evidence of Parliament's intentions. The reasons for and consequences of this rule of exclusion will be discussed below. It only remains here to say that the effectiveness of interpretation by reference to the statutory purpose depends greatly upon the availability of reliable evidence of that purpose.

The Evolution of a Unitary Approach

Over the years certain changes have occured in judicial formulation of the three traditional approaches to interpretation. Judges have become increasingly aware of the importance of context in ascertaining meaning and with this awareness the once diverse approaches have begun to merge. It is now no longer possible to pigeon-hole judgments neatly into one or other of the traditional categories if it ever was. The ordinary meaning of words will now be determined after the statute has been read as a whole in its appropriate context. The purpose or object of a statute is commonly regarded as part of the appropriate context. It is a small step to argue that the ordinary meaning must accord with statutory purpose. This of course differs from the view adopted in the *Sussex Peerage Case* and still held by some judges today[48] that consideration of the statutory purpose only becomes relevant if the statutory words are "unclear." As we have seen Lord Simon in *Maunsell* v. *Olins* made it clear that purpose is relevant at a more fundamental stage, that of deciding whether the statutory words are in fact clear at all. This latter view corresponds with that now adopted by the leading academic writers, that "Today there is only one principle or approach, namely, the words of an Act are to be read in their entire context in their grammatical and ordinary sense harmoniously with the scheme of the Act, the object of the Act and the intent of Parliament."[49] This approach is essentially an ordinary meaning approach, but ordinary meaning in total context. As Professor Driedger stated, it is "a revamped version of the literal rule which requires the general context and purpose to be taken into consideration before any decision is reached concerning the ordinary (or, where appropriate, the technical) meaning of statutory words."[50] The late Sir Rupert Cross also agreed that the traditional canons had been fused and attempted a restatement similar to that above.[51] Such restatements of the judicial approach are preferable to the traditional three-fold statement of the canons of statutory interpretation not only in terms of linguistic theory but also as accurate reflections of the evolving modern judicial practice.

Context as an Aid to Interpretation

Nowadays, few would disagree that without a proper regard for context the courts cannot make a rational assessment of

statutory meaning. Words derive clear meaning from their
context. This is perhaps the most important ground rule
regarding interpretation. The question is, what is to be the
extent of the context considered by the courts? Clearly an act
must be read as a whole. One assumes that in drafting one
clause of a bill the draftsman had in mind the language and
substance of other clauses. Parliament is, therefore, regarded
as having a comprehension of the whole act.[52] More complicated is the question whether the court can look at extrinsic
materials. A distinction can be drawn between the relevance of
materials and their admissibility. For various policy reasons,
the relevance of material is not always a ground for its legal
admissibility.

It is generally recognised that at some initial stage a judge
might wish to inform himself about the general, legal and
factual background of the enactment.[53] There does not seem to
be any specific limitation on the sources to which the court
might refer to obtain this background information.[54] On the
other hand, not all this information can be referred to explicitly
by the judge as the basis of his interpretation.

Intrinsic Material

Most statutes contain definition sections. Where such a
section is used, it may alter the ordinary meaning of words for
a particular statute. It may extend it or restrict it. Where such
sections appear in the statute they must be applied, provided
that in their terms they are not subject to the qualification
"unless the context otherwise requires."

Preambles to an act were formerly very common and were
used as a useful source of the legislature's intention. Now they
are much less common. In *Attorney-General* v. *Prince Augustus of
Hanover*[5] Lord Normand said that it was permissible to have
recourse to a preamble as an aid to interpretation, but it was
not of the same weight as other relevant enacting words. Thus
general words in the statute are not to be cut down merely
because they go further than the preamble has indicated.[56]

The long title to an act is admissible as an aid to interpretation if the wording of a provision is ambiguous.[57] On the other

hand, the short title may not be relied upon.[58] Headings in a statute are admissible,[59] but probably only to resolve an ambiguity.[60] Marginal notes cannot be referred to as an aid to interpretation as they are regarded as mere catch words.[61] On the other hand, marginal notes may be referred to to ascertain the mischief with which the act is dealing.[62] Formerly, one could not refer to punctuation in an act and indeed many early statutes had no punctuation. However, the modern tendency is to have regard to it, provided that it does not alter the plain intention of the statute.[63]

Presumptions of Intention

Quite apart from the so-called canons and the rules regarding intrinsic material there are various presumptions which the courts employ as an indicator of parliamentary intention. Presumptions can be classified into two main groups—those relating to form and those relating to substance.[64] The former relate to questions of language, grammar, syntax and logic. The latter are more specifically legal in nature. In the first category fall presumptions such as a change in word implies a change in meaning and that one part of a statute is not intended to contradict another part. The cluster of presumptions which are usually expressed in Latin—*ejusdem generis, noscitur a sociis,* and *expressio unius est exclusio alterius*—all indicate that words must take their meaning from their context.[65]

A useful example of the *ejusdem generis* principle is *Brownsea Haven Properties Ltd.* v. *Poole Corporation*[66] in 1958. The principle is based on the logician's approach to classification and definition by *genus et differentia.* Logicians divide the world into broad categories called *genera* which are characterised by some essential attribute and the *genera* into species which have merely incidental differences. The *ejusdem generis* principle provides that where there is a list of particular species which fall under one *genus* and these are followed by general words, the potential scope of the latter words is cut down to make them fit into the genus. In the *Brownsea* case the Court of Appeal considered a statutory provision which authorised a local authority to make orders concerning road traffic "in all times of public processions, rejoicings, or illuminations, and in any case when the streets are thronged or liable to be obstructed . . . " The local authority had made an order that certain streets should carry only one-way traffic for a period of six months. The court held that this order was invalid since "in any case" had to be read *ejusdem generis* with the earlier words and could not, therefore, cover dislocations due to ordinary traffic. *Expressio unius est exclusio alterius* means that the expression of one thing results in the exclusion of another. An old example of this will suffice. The Poor Relief Act 1601 imposed rates on occupiers of "lands, houses . . . and coalmines." The word "land" might in its ordinary meaning have been wide enough to cover all mines but the specific reference to coalmines means that land was not intended to cover mines in this case.[67] *Noscitur a sociis* simply means that a word takes its meaning from the other words with which it is associated. Some writers do not regard these as presumptions, but merely as common sense guides.

The second category of presumption relates to the substance of legal rules. There is the presumption against interference with vested rights. As a particular facet of this there is the presumption that an act should not be given retrospective effect. There is a presumption that the jurisdiction of the court should not be ousted, that an act should accord with international law and treaty obligations and that there should be no crime without a guilty mind. Numerous other examples could be given.[68] Many of these presumptions are subject to exceptions. For instance, where an act is declaratory in nature, the presumption against construing it retrospectively is inapplicable.[69] Many conflict with each other in relation to particular enactments. As the American writer Karl Llewellyn said, they tend to travel in pairs of opposites.[70] Even the content of some is doubted today.[71]

Extrinsic Material

Some words and phrases used in statutes are the subject of general definitions in the Interpretation Acts, the latest of which is 1978. These definitions apply unless the context otherwise requires.

It seems to be generally agreed that resort can be had to a dictionary to ascertain the ordinary meaning and indeed a secondary meaning of words used in a statute. The Oxford Dictionary is regularly referred to.[72] In addition, where a particular phrase has appeared in an earlier statute which deals with the same subject matter, the courts refer to previous decisions on the earlier statute, although with caution. Such statutes are sometimes called *in pari materia*.

It used to be the rule that the courts would not allow access to pre-parliamentary reports. (This category includes reports of the Law Commissions, the Law Reform Committee and Royal Commissions.) However, the position now is that such reports can be looked at to ascertain the purpose of the legislation, but not to construe the particular words used.[73] This distinction seems somewhat arbitrary and artificial. Nevertheless it remains the law despite recent attempts by some judges to extend reference to pre-parliamentary reports to ascertain the meaning of statutory words.[74]

Normally the court will not allow access to Parliamentary debates. Indeed, until recently there were limitations on the extent to which the judges could even have access to *Hansard*. However, by resolution of the House of Commons on October 31st 1980, a general permission was granted and it is now no longer necessary to petition the House for leave to place *Hansard* before the court. It is thought that this will not necessarily increase the extent to which the courts will allow it to be cited. Indeed the courts' reluctance to do so has recently been re-affirmed by the House of Lords.[75] The main argument against citation of *Hansard* are its cost, unavailability, the irrelevance of much of what is reported and the dubious worth of statements as to particular provisions as a guide to their meaning. On the other hand, the rule has become artificial since the courts allow greater access to textbooks of leading authors. It is common for modern textbooks to refer to *Hansard* and other Parliamentary materials when dealing with new legislation.[76]

Where an English statute adopts an international convention, the correct approach is to interpret the English text in the

normal manner appropriate for the interpretation of an international convention, unconstrained by technical rules of English law and precedent, but on broad principles of general
acceptation.[77] As Lord Scarman pointed out in *Fothergill* v.
Monarch Airlines[78] the reason for adopting a broad approach is
to ensure uniformity. Frequently, the text to the convention
will be included in a Schedule to the Act.

Where an English statute implements an E.E.C. directive
then it is permissible to have resort to the English text of the
directive to resolve any ambiguity. Also by virtue of section 3
of the European Communities Act 1972, the English courts are
bound by decisions of and by the principles laid down by the
European Court. This is discussed in chapter 13.

One final matter which must be touched upon is the question of the effect of previous cases interpreting the relevant
statutory provisions. There are three main possibilities. First
the previous court may have interpreted the particular provision. Here the *ratio decidendi* of the earlier case is binding if the
court is a higher court but a distinction is drawn between the
principle and the actual words used by the court. Only the
former is binding. The court after all is not the legislature.[79]
Secondly the previous court may have interpreted the same
provisions in an earlier act which has been re-enacted in the
present act. Here the later court will generally follow the earlier
case although it is not strictly bound.[80] However, in the case of
codification and possibly now consolidation the correct
approach is only to resort to such authorities if the wording of
the provision is unclear.[81] In practice, however, previous cases
are often referred to. Thirdly the previous court may have
interpreted the same phrase in a different act. Here the
position was discussed by Lord Diplock in *Carter* v. *Bradbeer*[82]
where he said:

> "A question of statutory construction is one in which the
> strict doctrine of precedent can only be of narrow applica-
> tion. The *ratio decidendi* of a judgment as to the meaning of
> particular words or combinations of words used in a particu-
> lar statutory provision can have not more than a persuasive
> influence on a court which is called on to interpret the same
> word or combination of words appearing in some other
> statutory provision. It is not determinative of the meaning of

that other provision. This is because the inherent flexibility of the English language may make it necessary for the interpreter to have recourse to a variety of aids or canons of construction, which are not merely lexicographical, in order to select from what may be a number of different meanings which the words as a matter of language are capable of bearing, the precise meaning in which the legislature intended them to be understood."

We shall consider in a moment the main reform proposals put forward by law reform bodies. The main policy factors regarding the admissibility of extrinsic materials seem to be availability, relevance, reliability, the time and expense which access to such materials would result in, and the greater uncertainty. These factors curtail to some extent the natural desire for freedom of citation of materials.

CURRENT JUDICIAL PRACTICE

A survey was carried out in 1980 by Ann Farrar of cases on interpretation of statutes in the New Zealand Law Reports of 1958 and 1978.[83] This revealed an increase of both ordinary meaning and purposive approaches in 1978, with the latter approach showing the greater increase. The number of cases adopting an interpretation which would avoid an absurdity remained relatively constant. The increase in cases adopting an ordinary meaning approach did not indicate a revival of the old literal rule but reflected the trend towards a more informed construction based on an understanding of the broader statutory context. This, together with the increased regard for statutory purpose, is consistent with a trend towards a more unitary approach to interpretation although as yet Driedger's amalgamated approach is an overstatement of judicial practice in New Zealand.

In both years, in approximately half the cases no clear approach based on meaning or purpose was adopted. In these cases several factors formed the basis of judicial decision-making, among them reliance on precedent, the exercise of discretion, the application of a definition, policy and common sense. A sizeable proportion of the cases seemed to involve an issue of application rather than interpretation. Over the 20 year period the number of cases involving an exercise of discretion increased noticeably, this being consistent with current trends of legislative drafting in New Zealand.

Although these findings are based on New Zealand cases, it is likely that a similar result would be obtained in this country. Indeed, in the next chapter we consider recent cases on a provision of the homeless persons legislation which indicate that, if anything, the English courts have made less explicit use of the canons and have been influenced by factors such as the scheme and policy of the Act and a common sense approach. However the ordinary meaning and purposive approaches were implicit in these cases.

REFORM PROPOSALS

The increasing number of cases calling for interpretation of statutory provisions and the difficulties that have arisen through certain methods of drafting and interpretation have led many to call for reform, both of the preparation and interpretation of legislation. In 1969 the English and Scottish Law Commissions produced the first detailed consideration of interpretation ever attempted by a law reform body.[84] A number of recommendations were made, none of which have so far been implemented by legislation. Of the three traditional approaches to interpretation, the Commissions favoured the mischief approach and recommended the enactment in a new Interpretation Act of a more up to date version mandating the courts to adopt an interpretation which would promote the general legislative purpose underlying the provision.[85] As regards the general question of context, the Commissions did not favour allowing widespread use of *Hansard*, but instead favoured a relaxation of the extrinsic evidence exclusion rule regarding such documents as White Papers and Reports.[86] They were also prepared to recommend the preparation in selected cases of explanatory memoranda to accompany an act and to be available to the courts.[87]

In 1975 the Renton Committee published its Report on the Preparation of Legislation. The Committee agreed with the

Law Commissions that a comprehensive new Interpretation Act should be prepared which should include a provision mandating a construction promoting the general legislative purpose. It did not think that any general change in the law concerning the admissibility of extrinsic materials should take place.[88] In particular the Report criticised the Law Commissions' proposal for explanatory memoranda.[89]

In February 1980 Lord Scarman, who as Sir Leslie Scarman had been Chairman of the English Law Commission at the time of their Report, introduced an Interpretation Bill in the House of Lords. The bill basically enacted the Law Commissions' draft clauses. After severe criticisms of the bill on its second reading, Lord Scarman withdrew it. Later in 1981 he introduced a modified and more limited version. The bill in its new form passed through the House of Lords, but was rejected on the motion for a second reading in the House of Commons.[90]

The first clause of the bill specified various aids to interpretation and set out the contextual matters to be included among the materials at present considered in ascertaining the meaning of a provision. The initial inclusion of pre-parliamentary reports among these materials was dropped from the later bill. The second clause set out principles to be applied in the interpretation of acts where more than one construction is reasonably possible. Most important of these was an embodiment of the purposive approach. On the whole its inclusion received a cool response from the House of Lords. Many of the Lords regarded the provision as saying nothing more than what is presently the law or the better practice of the courts.[91] Some thought that being declaratory the provision could do no harm, while others felt there was no need for legislation at all.[92] Perhaps the strongest criticism of the clause relates to what is left unsaid. Does the principle override the literal meaning in all cases or only where it is doubtful?[93] Furthermore, to direct the courts to favour an interpretation promoting the underlying legislative purpose begs the question of how the courts are to ascertain that purpose. The debate tends to be circular unless some firm decision is taken to relax the extrinsic evidence rules. The Law Commissions' recommendation of the explanatory memoranda had at least the advantage of breaking the vicious circle and it is interesting to see that the proposal is currently under consideration in Australia.[94]

The question of resolving the admissibility of such documents is arguably more important than any attempt to codify
the correct judicial approach. What is conceived as the correct
approach of the judiciary necessarily changes as society
changes. In the nineteenth century many judges saw their task
as the formulators of general principles which could then be
applied in a formal, deductive way with little reference to the
justice in the particular case. It was an age of formalism. By the
1960s and 1970s there was a breaking away from formalism and
a greater awareness of policy factors and the exigencies of
particular cases. While there have been signs recently of a
retreat by certain Law Lords from policy, in case law it still
remains as the dominant source of legislation and the problem
is the accurate identification of the legislative policy.

Notes

[1] See generally John Farrar, *Law Reform and the Law Commission*, Chaps. 4, 5
and 6.

[2] Sir Courtenay Ilbert, *Legislative Methods and Forms*, p. 26.

[3] Erskine May, *Parliamentary Practice* (19th ed.), p. 857.

[4] See, generally, Lord Simon of Glaisdale in *Maunsell* v. *Olins* [1975] A.C. 373,
392C–F.

[5] This is based on the Statute Law Society pamphlet, *Statute Law Deficiencies*,
Part II.

[6] For a more detailed discussion of the parliamentary process, see D. R. Miers
and A. C. Page, *Legislation*, pp. 113 *et seq.* and pp. 131 *et seq.*

[7] See G. Williams, "Language and the Law," 61 L.Q.R. 71, pp. 189 *et seq.*

[8] For discussion of clear and problem cases see R. B. Seidman, "The Judicial
Process Reconsidered in the Light of Role Theories" [1969] M.L.R. 516, 520–
521.

[9] D. R. Miers and A. C. Page, *Legislation*, p. 180.

[10] Y.B. 33 and 35 Edward 1 (Rolls Series) 83 (1305).

[11] See 1 Blackstone's Comm. 87. *Cf.* J. Bentham's critique in *A Comment on the
Commentaries*, Section XII.

[12] See Lord Reid in *Maunsell* v. *Olins* [1975] A.C. 373, 382E where he said,
"They are not rules in the ordinary sense of having binding force. They are
our servants, not our masters. They are aids to construction, presumptions
or pointers. Not infrequently one 'rule' points in one direction, another in a
different direction. In each case we must look at all relevant circumstances
and decide as a matter of judgment what weight to attach to any particular
'rule'."

[13] A useful analysis of the justificatory role of the canons is to be found in A.
Ross, *On Law and Justice* pp. 152 *et seq.*

14 See *Black-Clawson International Ltd.* v. *Papierwerke Waldhof-Aschaffenburg* [1975] A.C. 591.
15 *Sussex Peerage Case* (1844) 11 Cl. & Fin. 85.
16 See, *e.g.* Lord Esher M.R. in *R.* v. *The Judge of the City of London Court* [1892] 1 Q.B. 273, 290.
17 This view of the judicial function has recently been reaffirmed by Lord Diplock in *Duport Steels Ltd.* v. *Sirs* [1980] 1 W.L.R. 142, 157.
18 *e.g.* G. Williams "The Meaning of Literal Interpretation—Part I" [1981] N.L.J. 1128. See also N. MacCormick *Legal Reasoning and Legal Theory*, p. 203.
19 [1975] A.C. 373, 391E.
20 [1978] 1 All E.R. 948, 952.
21 See, *e.g.*, the attitude adopted by Lord Esher M.R. in *R.* v. *The Judge of the City of London Court* [1892] 1 Q.B. 273, 290.
22 (1836) 2 M. & W. at p. 195.
23 (1877) 2 App.Cas. 743, 764–765.
24 *e.g. Brown* v. *The Russian Ship Alina* (1880) 42 L.T. 517; *R.* v. *The Judge of the City of London Court, loc. cit.; Becke* v. *Smith, loc. cit.* Compare the use of "manifest" as a synonym for "great" by Jessel M.R. in *Brown* v. *The Russian Ship Alina* and Lord Esher in *R.* v. *The Judge of the City of London Court* with that of Parke B. in *Becke* v. *Smith* where "manifest" seems to refer to something demonstrable or obvious.
25 *Stock* v. *Frank Jones (Tripton) Ltd., loc. cit.* at p. 955c *per* Lord Simon of Glaisdale.
26 *Nokes* v. *Doncaster Amalgamated Collieries* [1940] A.C. 1014, 1022.
27 *Per* Lord Reid in *Gartside* v. *I.R.C.* [1968] A.C. 553, 612.
28 See, *e.g., Denver* v. *Holmes* 156 Colo. 586, 400 P 2d 907.
29 For discussion of the American approach in general see *American Jurisprudence*, Vol. 73, p. 429.
30 See, *e.g., Kellum* v. *Hohnson* 237 Miss. 580, 115 So. 2d 147.
31 *e.g. Randal* v. *Richmond & D.R. Co.* 107 N.C. 748, 12 S.E. 605.
32 *e.g. People* v. *Frank G. Heilman Co.* 263 Ill. App. 514.
33 *e.g. State* v. *Standard Oil Co.* 188 La 978, 178 So. 601.
34 See R. David and H.P. De Vries, *The French Legal System*, pp. 88–91.
35 *e.g.* Lord Scarman in *Hanlon* v. *Law Society* [1980] 2 All E.R. 199, 213, Lord Wilberforce in *Maunsell* v. *Olins, supra*; Lord Diplock in *Fothergill* v. *Monarch Airlines* [1980] 2 All E.R. 696, 705.
36 See David and De Vries, *op. cit.*, pp. 91 *et seq.*
37 H.L. Deb. (March 9, 1981), Col. 1 *per* Lord Simon of Glaisdale.
38 (1584) 3 Co. Rep. 7a.
39 See Law Com. No. 21 p. 49.
40 *Ibid.*
41 *Ibid.*, p. 19.
42 *Ibid.*, p. 20.
43 For examples of this modern formulation see Law Com. No. 21; Clause 2 (*a*) of the 1981 Interpretation Bill and the various Commonwealth enactments of the purposive approach, *e.g.* s.5(*j*) Acts Interpretation Act 1924 (N.Z.).
44 *Supra*, at p. 395 A–C.
45 Law Com. No. 21, p. 19.
46 R. Cross, *Statutory Interpretation*, p. 170. *Cf.* the second edition by Bell and Eagle, Chap. 8 for more conservative views.
47 *Loc. cit.* at p. 638.
48 *e.g.* Lord Dilhorne in the House of Lords Debate, February 13, 1980, Col. 298.
49 E. A. Dreidger, *The Construction of Statutes* (1974) p. 67.
50 D. Lloyd, *Introduction to Jurisprudence*, 5th ed. p. 1144.

51 See R. Cross, *Statutory Interpretation Cf.* the second edition (*op. cit.*) Chap. 8.
52 *Per* Lord Reid in *I.R.C.* v. *Hinchy* [1960] A.C. 748, 766.
53 Law Com. No. 21, para. 47.
54 *Ibid.*, para. 48.
55 [1957] A.C. 460, 467.
56 *Per* Brandon J., *The Norwhale* [1975] 2 All E.R. 501, 507.
57 See, *e.g. Fielding* v. *Morley Corp.* [1899] 1 Ch. 1, 3 and *Brown* v. *Brown* [1967] P. 105, 110.
58 *Vacher & Sons Ltd.* v. *London Society of Compositors* [1913] A.C. 107.
59 *D.P.P.* v. *Schildkamp* [1971] A.C. 1, 28.
60 *R.* v. *Board of Trade ex p. St. Martins Preserving Co.* [1965] 1 Q.B. 603, 619.
61 *Per* Lord Reid, *Chandler* v. *D.P.P.* [1964] A.C. 763, 789.
62 *R* v. *Kelt* [1977] 3 All E.R. 1099, 1110–2. See, too, *Prior* v. *Sovereign Chicken Ltd.* [1984] 1 W.L.R. 921 at 929, *per* Lawton L.J.; *Hailbury Investments Ltd.* v. *Westminster City Council* [1986] 1 W.L.R. 1232 at 1242, *per* Lord Bridge.
63 See, *e.g.*, *Hanlon* v. *Law Society, loc. cit.* p. 221.
64 *Cf.* R. Cross, *Statutory Interpretation* (2nd ed.), Chap. 7.
65 See M. Zander, *The Law-Making Process* (2nd ed.), p. 129.
66 [1958] Ch. 574.
67 *Lead Smelting Co.* v. *Richardson* (1762) 32 Burr. 1341.
68 See *Maxwell on the Interpretation of Statutes* (12th ed.).
69 See Craies, *Statute Law* (1971), p. 387.
70 See W. Twining, *Karl Llewellyn and the American Realist Movement.*
71 For instance the traditional presumption that tax statutes should be strictly construed has now been largely abandoned.
72 *e.g.* Cozens Hardy M.R. in *Camden (Marquis)* v. *I.R.C.* [1914] 1 K.B. 641, 647.
73 *Black-Clawson International Ltd.* v. *Papierwerke Waldhof-Aschaffenburg, loc. cit.*
74 See *Davis* v. *Johnson* [1978] 1 All E.R. 1132: *Fothergill* v. *Monarch Airlines, loc. cit.*, pp. 705–706; and the recent attempts to alter the exiting law by means of the 1980 and 1981 Interpretation Bills.
75 *Hadmor Productions* v. *Hamilton* [1982] 1 All E.R. 1042, 1055 *per* Lord Diplock where it was unanimously affirmed that "recourse to the reports of proceedings in either House of Parliament [Hansard] during the passage of a Bill . . . is not permissible as an aid to [the Act's] construction."
76 *e.g.* Lord Denning's reference to such a text in *R.* v. *Local Commissioner for Administration, etc.* [1979] 2 W.L.R. 1. See also Samuels, 'The Interpretation of Statutes' [1980] Stat. L.R. 86, 98.
77 *Per* Lord Wilberforce in *James Buchanan* v. *Babco* [1977] 3 All E.R. 1048, 1052.
78 *Loc. cit.* See, too, *Government of Belgium* v. *Postlethwaite* [1987] 3 W.L.R. 365 at 383.
79 See Lord Reid in *Paisner* v. *Goodrich* [1957] A.C. 65, 88. See Denning L.J. in the Court of Appeal [1955] 2 Q.B. 343, 346.
80 See *ex p. Campbell* (1869) L.R. 5 Ch. 763, 766 and Denning L.J. in *Royal Crown Derby Porcelain Ltd.* v. *Raymond Russell* [1949] 2 K.B. 417, 429.
81 See Lord Simon in *Farrell* v. *Alexander* [1976] 2 All E.R. 721, 733–6.
82 [1975] 3 All E.R. 158, 161.
83 A. A. Farrar, "Judicial Approaches to Meaning in the Interpretation of Statutes," an unpublished LL.M. thesis for the University of Canterbury, New Zealand. For a recent survey of New Zealand cases, see J. F. Burrows *Recent Development in Statutes and their Interpretation*, New Zealand Law Society Seminar May–July 1988.
84 Law Com. No. 21.
85 *Ibid.*, pp. 48 *et seq.*
86 *Ibid.*, pp. 30–31.

[87] *Ibid.*, pp. 36–42.

[88] Report of the Renton Committee on the Preparation of Legislation (1975), Cmd. 6053. See paras. 19.15, 19.17 and 19.23.

[89] *Ibid.*, para. 19.24.

[90] For general discussion on the bill see F. Bennion "Another Reverse for the Law Commission's Interpretation Bill" (1981) 131 N.L.J. 840. For an earlier plaintive note by Lord Scarman see his speech in *Tuck* v. *National Freight Corporation* [1979] 1 W.L.R. 37 at 55.

[91] *Per* Lord Simon of Glaisdale, H.L. Deb. March 9, 1981, Col. 78.

[92] *e.g.* Viscount Dilhorne, House of Lords Debate, February 13, 1980, Col. 198.

[93] See F. Bennion, *op. cit.*, p. 841.

[94] See "New Guidelines For the Interpretation of Commonwealth Laws" pp. 1–2, a pamphlet issued by the Attorney-General of Australia in 1981. See Ann Farrar and John Farrar "Legislation" in *A Career in Law*, Sydney, The Federation Press, ed. by J. F. Corkery. Chap. 7.

Chapter 10

LEGISLATION IN OPERATION

The purpose of this chapter is to illustrate some aspects of legislation and its interpretation by reference to one particular statutory provision, section 60 of the Housing Act 1985. This section comes within the part of the Act concerned with housing homeless persons. We have set out this section along with other inter-related provisions of the Act and its accompanying Code of Guidance in an appendix to this chapter. All these provisions were first introduced by a 1977 statute and have been re-enacted as part of the wider 1985 legislation. We shall begin by explaining the broad scheme of the provisions relating to homeless persons and the role played by the courts in their interpretation. Then we shall examine some of the interpretation problems that have arisen in relation to the section. Finally we shall take a wider look at what can be learnt from examining this one piece of legislation in operation.

THE SCHEME OF THE HOMELESSNESS PROVISIONS[1]

The legislation places a duty on housing authorities such as District Councils or London Boroughs, to provide permanent housing for those homeless or threatened with homelessness who have a priority need for accommodation. There are four categories of priority need;[2] pregnant women, those with dependant children, the specially vulnerable whether through old age, illness or disability and, finally, the victims of an emergency such as a fire or flood. Thus for example, the young married couple who have to live apart because of the long housing waiting lists will be entitled to permanent accommodation if they have or are expecting a child.

The duty to provide permanent housing is subject to one important qualification: section 65 provides that where an authority is satisfied that a person has become homeless or threatened with homelessness intentionally, its duty is limited to giving advice and assistance including temporary accommodation if necessary. Section 60 defines "intentionally homeless" as being where a person has deliberately done or failed to do something in consequence of which he has lost or is threatened with the loss of accommodation which it would otherwise have been reasonable for him to continue to occupy.[3] Some further explanation is provided by the Code of Guidance for authorities issued by the government. It provides, for example, that a person who has lost his accommodation "because of wilful and persistent refusal to pay rent, would in most cases be regarded as having become homeless intentionally."[4] The authorities make the decision whether a person is intentionally homeless. Section 62 provides that they shall make any enquiries necessary to satisfy themselves on this matter. There is no provision entitling a person to appeal against their decision. However, it is always possible to ask a court to "judicially review" the decision of a public authority. In the earlier chapter on Classification,[5] we briefly explained the difference between this public law procedure of review and the ordinary private law procedures of appeal, noting in particular that a court "reviewing" an authority's decision will not substitute its own decision for that of the authority as it would under the ordinary appeal procedure. Rather it has the power to hold the authority's decision invalid and to require it to reconsider the question. The court may invalidate the decision on the ground of unreasonableness, *e.g.* where the decision is totally at variance with the facts, procedural irregularity, *e.g.* failing to allow the aggrieved person to put his case, or, finally, a mistake in construing the limits of its power.[6] It is this last ground that will bring before the courts questions of statutory interpretation. At the time of writing — Spring 1989—section 60 and the equivalent section under the 1977 legislation have been considered by the higher courts in over seventy cases many of which have reached the Court of Appeal. A number of problems have given rise to these cases and we will now examine four of these in more detail.

THE PROBLEMS

The Immigrant Problem

This problem is easy to state, less easy to solve. Should immigrants who leave permanent accommodation in their home country, arrive in the United Kingdom perhaps staying first in temporary accommodation with relatives and then becoming homeless, be regarded as intentionally homeless for the purposes of the Act? This is a particular problem for authorities in the vicinity of international airports, for it is in their areas that immigrants will often find themselves to be homeless and it will then be their duty to permanently house them unless they are found "intentionally homeless."

The problem was first considered by the higher courts in *De Falco* v. *Crawley Borough Council*,[7] a case concerning Italian immigrants who had become homeless after spending two months in temporary accommodation following their arrival in the United Kingdom. Crawley B.C. found them to be intentionally homeless on the basis that they had deliberately left their permanent accommodation in Italy. The immigrants argued that this finding should be invalidated because the authority had failed to observe the wording of the Code of Guidance which at that time stated "In assessing whether a person has become intentionally homeless it will be relevant to consider the most immediate cause of that homelessness rather than events which may have taken place previously." Following this guidance, the authority should have considered not the immigrants' deliberate decision to leave Italy but rather the fact that they were forced to leave their temporary U.K. accommodation. The Court of Appeal upheld the authority's decision. They rejected the immigrants' argument, stating that although the authority had to have regard to the Code, it was entitled to depart from it in its interpretation of the statute if it thought fit. Here it was justified in so departing from it. Lord Denning said of the relevant paragraph of the code, "(it) may be all very well for people coming from Yorkshire . . . but it should not . . . be applied to people coming from Italy, or any other country of the Common Market." The Code has now been altered to take account of this decision.[8]

Does the *De Falco* interpretation solve the problem for housing authorities? Only in part. In the first place, it means that the authorities will be faced with the difficult task of deciding whether the immigrant acted deliberately and unreasonably in leaving his home country accommodation; it appears that the economic and social conditions of the home country may have to be considered.[9] Secondly, it does not solve the problem of the immigrant who finds permanent U.K. accommodation for himself only to lose it when he subsequently brings his family to the United Kingdom. This is what happened in the case of *Islam* v. *London Borough of Hillingdon*.[10] There, an immigrant from Bangladesh had managed to find permanent single room accommodation for himself but when after six years he was finally able to bring his family to the United Kingdom, his landlord evicted them from the accommodation. The Court of Appeal led by Lord Denning upheld the authority's decision that the immigrant was intentionally homeless.[11] Lord Denning took the view that the immigrant had technically "occupied" his wife's home in Bangladesh as a result of his occasional visits there over the six year period of separation, and that consequently both he and his wife could be said to have deliberately left that home. Lord Denning commented:

> "The moral of this case is that men from overseas should not bring their wives and children here unless they have arranged permanent and suitable accommodation for them to come to. The applicant is homeless intentionally. He is not entitled to permanent accommodation. He will not take priority over young couples here who are on the waiting list for housing accommodation."

However, the House of Lords reversed this decision, holding that the meaning given by Lord Denning to the word "occupation" was artificial and quite inconsistent with its ordinary meaning according to which the immigrant had occupied only his permanent accommodation in the United Kingdom. Lord Bridge commented:

> "I should be hard put to it to formulate any defensible principle to justify denying the benefits conferred by the (Act) to immigrants who . . . have acquired under the relevant legislation controlling immigration the unrestricted right not only to live and work in this country, but also to bring their families to live with them here."

Islam illustrates that there are difficulties left unsolved by the *De Falco* decision: subsequent case law has concerned immigrants from Ghana, Canada and Australia along with victims of harassment in Northern Ireland. It also illustrates the policy conflict underlying the interpretation question. It is easy to sympathise with the view of Lord Wilberforce in *Islam* that the difficulties should be solved by a reconsideration of the Act, but whether the legislature would find it any easier than the judges to resolve the policy conflict is more debatable.

Causal Link Problems

De Falco established that authorities could examine not only the immediate cause of homelessness, *e.g.* loss of temporary accommodation, but also prior events, *e.g.* leaving home country accommodation. But what if at the time a person loses his later temporary accommodation, his previous permanent accommodation is no longer available to him? This was the problem that arose in *Dyson* v. *Kerrier District Council*.[12] Dyson was a tenant of a flat in Huntingdon. She lived there with her young baby. In September 1978 her sister left that area to live in Cornwall. In November, Dyson gave up her flat and moved to be next door to her sister in Cornwall. She was only able to rent her flat there for the winter period. In May 1979 she had to leave that flat to make it available for holidaymakers. Was she intentionally homeless?

Look at the wording of section 60 set out in the appendix. You will see that it is drafted in the present and future tenses.

In particular it provides that a person is intentionally homeless if he does something "in consequence of which he ceases to occupy accommodation which is available for his occupation." In May, Dyson's old Huntingdon flat had been let to someone else. It could not be said to be accommodation "which is available" for her. On the strict wording of the Act her decision to leave her old flat could not therefore be regarded as rendering her intentionally homeless the following May. However, the Court of Appeal took the view that this was not what the wording meant. What the section required was a link between cause and effect. There was this link between Dyson's conduct in November and her homelessness the following May. The court held therefore that although the statute was drafted in the present and future tenses, it should be read as referring to the past tense. Dyson was intentionally homeless because she had done something in consequence of which she had ceased to occupy accommodation which was available for her occupation.

Dyson interpreted the section as requiring a causal link between the prior intentional vacation of accommodation and the present homelessness, a link clearly established in that case. But the concept of a causal link is not always simple to apply, as the case of *Din* v. *London Borough of Wandsworth*[13] shows. Din could not pay rent and rates on his house. His local housing authority advised him to await eviction and then to apply for help. Rather than doing this, Din anticipated the inevitable, left the house and took his family to live with a relative. A few months later the relative asked them to leave and it was at this point that Din applied for help. The authority decided that he was intentionally homeless because he had voluntarily left his old house and this had caused his present homelessness. Din argued that the cause of his homelessness should be assessed as at the time of his application for help. At that time his decision to leave his old house no longer had a causal connection with his homelessness; he would have been homeless by then even if he had remained in his house and awaited eviction.

In the House of Lords, Lord Bridge accepted this argument, commenting that "it offends common sense to hold that the cause of his homelessness after that date (the date on which he would have been evicted anyway) was that he chose to leave of his own volition before that date." He concluded that the approach of the authority, *i.e.* refusing help to those threatened with eviction until a court order for possession has been made against them, was wrong. "It must involve a great expenditure of unnecessary legal costs." However, his was a dissenting judgment. The majority found Din to be intentionally homeless. According to Lord Wilberforce, the plain wording of the section required the question of intention to be determined at the time when Din vacated his original house. To take into account the hypothetical fact that he would have been evicted anyway would require an unacceptable reconstruction of the statutory wording. In policy terms Lord Wilberforce justified his conclusion as follows:

"[The Act] confers great benefits on one category of persons in need of housing (those with a priority need) to the detriment of others (those on the normal waiting list). This being so, it does not seem unreasonable that, in order to benefit from the priority provisions, persons in the first category should bring themselves within the plain words."

Rent Arrears

Din's argument assumed that had he actually been evicted for non-payment of rent or rates he would not have been classed as intentionally homeless. The Code would seem to support this view. It provides[14] that if a person has lost his home "because of wilful and persistent refusal to pay rent, [he] would in most cases be regarded as deliberate." In Din's case there did appear to be "real difficulties" as opposed to a "wilful and persistent refusal." However, the cases which actually deal with this problem appear to have interpreted the section in a rather different way from the draftsman of the Code.

In *Robinson* v. *Torbay Borough Council*[15] the person concerned was a tenant of a private housing association. In both 1978 and 1979 he fell into rent arrears but both times he paid them off when threatened with legal action. However, the association obviously concluded that he was unreliable and in 1980 they terminated the tenancy, rendering Robinson homeless. The local housing authority concluded that he was intentionally homeless. On behalf of Robinson, it was argued that he had not intended to be evicted and did not appreciate that his delayed payments might result in his eviction. Certainly it was not clear that his non-payment was wilful and persistent. Nevertheless, the authority's decision was upheld by the court. Construing the section, the judge held that the word "deliberately" applied to the conduct of the tenant and not to the end result and hence it was irrelevant that the tenant did not intend to get evicted. It was sufficient said the judge "if his conduct is such as to drive his landlord to evict him, and if the fair-minded bystander can say of the person evicted, 'well, I'm sorry, but he asked for it,' then I think the test of intentional homelessness . . . is satisfied." The Code has since been amended to provide that "full knowledge of the likely consequences" of the conduct is also required before a person such as Robinson can be found intentionally homeless.[16]

Family Responsibilities

What happens if a person has given up accommodation because of the intentional conduct of some other member of the family unit? To what extent is the "innocent" member of the family to be held responsible for the conduct of the others? This problem arose in *Lewis* v. *North Devon District Council*.[17] Mrs. Lewis and her child lived with a farm worker in his tied cottage. He decided to leave his job and that meant that they both had to leave the cottage. He was found to be intentionally homeless, but was she? The housing authority considered that she was, arguing that the section should be construed as reading, "if [s]he or a person who resides with her/him deliberately does something as a consequence of which [s]he ceases to occupy accommodation, etc." On review, the judge refused to interpret the section as including the underlined additional wording. It was Mrs. Lewis's conduct only which was relevant. However, the judge upheld the authority's decision on the basis that Mrs. Lewis had acquiesced in her man's decision to leave his job and hence become homeless.

The judge illustrated this principle further with the example of a case where the husband spent all the rent money on drink.

> "If the wife acquiesced to his doing this then it seems to me that it would be proper to regard her, as well as him, as having become homeless intentionally. . . . If on the other hand she had done what she could to prevent the husband spending his money on drink instead of rent then she had not failed to do anything and it would not be right to regard her as having become homeless intentionally."

This line of reasoning has been followed in other cases. Thus a tenant evicted because neighbours had complained about the bad language, noise and rubbish for which her son was responsible was found to be intentionally homeless because she had acquiesced in her son's conduct.[18] The mother of a rebellious son or the wife of a hard drinking man is clearly in a difficult position.

INTENTIONAL HOMELESSNESS—A WIDER PERSPECTIVE

So far we have examined just some of the cases in four problem areas. Our perspective has been narrow. There are other cases and problems we could have discussed in relation to the section. Rather than examine the particular cases any further, we wish to widen our viewpoint, to use the cases and problems so far discussed to illustrate, first, some of the general features of the judicial approach to statutory interpretation, secondly some of the difficulties facing the legislative draftsman and finally some of the extra-legal considerations which may determine the practical impact of legislation.

Statutory Interpretation

In the cases discussed in this chapter, the judges did not engage in any lengthy analysis of how they should interpret statutes. There is no mention of the principles, approaches or indeed controversies which we discussed in the last chapter although no doubt they were implicit. Rather, the judges simply got on with the job. How? What techniques did they use in determining the precise application of the rather general wording? If we return to the cases we can see some common features of their approach.

The Scheme of the Section or Act. Rather than interpreting statutory words or phrases in isolation, judges will often seek to interpret the scheme of the section or Act as a whole and construe the particular words in that context. In *Dyson*, the judge concluded that the section was dealing with cause and effect, requiring a causal link between the conduct and the homelessness. With that as a basis for interpretation he was able to read the present tense used in the section as including the past tense. To a limited extent it is perhaps fair to say that he rewrote the statute. In *Lewis*, the judge looked at the scheme of the Act in coming to the conclusion that authorities were required to consider the family as a whole unit. Consequently in applying the intentional homelessness test to one member of the family he took into account the conduct of other members.

The Common Sense Approach. In their analysis[19] of the way in which judges in the House of Lords write their speeches, Rawlings and Murphy point to the fact that they frequently justify their interpretation in terms of common sense. We can see at least two examples of this in our cases. In *Robinson*, the judge invoked the supposed views of the fair-minded bystander in coming to the conclusion that intentional homelessness could be interpreted as applying to the person evicted for failure to pay rent. Resort to the fair-minded bystander or the Reasonable Man is in effect an appeal to common sense notions. Lord Bridge made a similar appeal in his dissenting judgment in *Din*. Common sense with "no profound philosophical analysis" demonstrated that the connection between conduct and homelessness was broken by the fact that the applicant would have lost his accommodation anyway even if he had not voluntarily left it. As we have seen, the majority did not share the same common sense. Common sense is a rather variable notion and Bertrand Russell once described it as the metaphysics of barbarians. It is not a particularly reliable yardstick with which to measure the consequences of interpretation.

Policy. In other chapters[20] we have noted the nature of policy arguments and the controversy as to their role in judicial decisions. In the context of statutory interpretation the debate centres around whether or not judges should seek to implement the policy or purpose of the legislation. In our cases, policy arguments seem to have been mainly used at a secondary level, to support an interpretation rather than to dictate it. Thus in *Din*, Lord Bridge supported his dissenting interpretation by referring to the injustice of disqualifying a person who had left accommodation prematurely and to the undesirability of authorities refusing help until a person has been evicted by a court order. Lord Wilberforce, giving the leading majority speech, also ended by referring to a policy consideration, namely that failure to disqualify such a person would involve "greater expense for a hard pressed authority, and greater pressure on the housing stock."

Obviously in any situation of this kind there are likely to be competing policy considerations. *Din* illustrates this. So do the immigrant cases. In *De Falco*, Lord Denning supported his conclusion that the immigrants were deliberately homeless in choosing to leave Italy by reference to the problems that would otherwise arise for authorities in the area of an airport. In typical vein he ended by trusting that such authorities, unlike Canute, would be able to keep their feet "dry against the new advancing tide [of immigrants]." The opposing view was put by Lord Bridge in *Islam*:

"I should be hard put to it to formulate any defensible principle to justify denying the benefits conferred by the [Act] to immigrants who have acquired under the relevant legislation controlling immigration the unrestricted right not only to live and work in this country but to bring their families to live with them here."

In this, as in other cases, the policy and purpose of the legislation seem to depend very much on whether you take the viewpoint of the hard pressed authorities or the unfortunate homeless.

The Limits of Interpretation. The legislative scheme, common sense and policy all assist the judges to interpret the legislation but it is clear that there are limits to how far they should go in the process of creative interpretation. In the Court of Appeal in *Islam*, Lord Denning took the view that the applicant was technically occupying his wife's home in Bangladesh even though he was actually resident in the United Kingdom at the time. His interpretation was rejected by the House of Lords. Lord Lowry said that, he was "using the word [occupy] in an artificial sense . . . quite inconsistent with its ordinary meaning." Judges should interpret legislation only within the confines of its possible ordinary meanings. Similarly in *Lewis*, the judge rejected the authority's attempt to interpret the section as providing that a person is intentionally homeless if he *or the person with whom he resides* does something resulting in homelessness. Such a construction involving the addition of the underlined words was just not possible. The judicial addition of the past to the present tense in *Dyson* is just about as far as a judge can legitimately go.

Legislative Drafting

In many of the cases we have discussed the judges clearly had a choice as to how to interpret the section. That is demonstrated by the number of dissenting judgments and reversed decisions. References to the scheme of the legislation, common sense or policy can be seen as steps in the exercise of choice. But could this have been avoided by more precise legislative drafting, by a statutory wording which gave no choice? In most situations this is simply not possible—for two reasons. First, the legislator cannot anticipate all possible fact situations that may be potentially governed by the statute. As a result the aim of the legislation must remain to some extent indeterminate, to be determined only when the facts arise. Secondly, as we noted in chapter 6, the language in which the legislation is expressed will normally be somewhat "open textured" or general in phrasing. Both these inherent obstacles to precise, "no choice" legislation are clearly illustrated by our example.

Inability to Anticipate Facts. It seems probable that the drafters of the Act did not anticipate all the various fact situations which arose in the problem areas we have discussed. The legislative history of the Act and in particular the provision that is now section 60 was perhaps unfortunate in this respect.[21] The 1977 statute was originally a private member's bill for which a Department of Environment draft was substituted. In its original form it contained no "intentionally homeless" qualification to the duty to house. The provision was introduced during its passage through Parliament to meet the fears of some housing authorities and to secure all party support. It represented more of a compromise than a clear policy. However, even if it had emerged from extensive deliberations of, say, the Law Commission, the very nature of the social problem concerned would make it likely that some fact situations would not have been anticipated or, if anticipated, would not have been solved but left rather to those responsible for applying the Act.[22]

Open Textured Language. The wording of section 60 is open textured. The repeated use of such words as "intentionally," "deliberately," "reasonable," "good faith" all confer on those who apply the Act a wide degree of legitimate choice. In the Parliamentary debates there was dispute between those M.P.s who favoured giving the Authorities a wide discretion by the use of such language and those who favoured a more clearly defined legal duty and qualification. The precise drafting approach has a disadvantage: it cannot enable us to anticipate all fact situations and it may therefore make it more difficult for us to deal with those we failed to anticipate. As Professor Hart[23] has said, by using this kind of technique "we shall indeed succeed in settling in advance, but also in the dark, issues which can only be reasonably settled when they arise and are identified." How would you draft section 60 to deal with the immigrant problem supposing that you had antici- pated it in general terms? Would you have drawn any distinc- tion between immigrants from the E.E.C. on the one hand and the Commonwealth on the other?[24] Would you have referred to the housing conditions in the countries from which they came? Would you really have wished to determine these questions before seeing the variety of fact situations that could arise? Clearly the Government was satisfied with the approach taken, for when it came to re-enact the provisions in the 1985 legislation the substance was left unchanged although the opportunity was taken to improve the drafting style (see the comparison of section 62 and its predecessor section set out in the appendix).

Informal Codes and Flexibility. The person who drafted the act met the problems we have just discussed by adopting a "wait and see" approach, by drafting the statute in general terms but providing for the Government to issue a Code of Guidance to assist authorities in the application of the Act. The original code contained relatively little guidance as to the application of the section, sometimes using mere synonyms for the statutory phrasing, *e.g.* "wilful and persistent" for "deliberate." Further- more, as we have seen from the *De Falco* case, the courts have taken the view that authorities are free to depart from it if they think fit. The Code, said Lord Denning, "should not be regarded as a binding statute." But the fact that it does not have the force of a statute is in one sense a strength rather than a weakness. It means that it can be amended in the light of experience without the recourse to Parliament which would be necessary were it part of the statute. In the appendix we have highlighted in bold those sections of the Code which were added when it was amended in 1983 and, as you will see, some of the additions were designed to deal with problems revealed by the case law discussed in this chapter. Whether it is constitutionally desirable for the way in which the law is to be applied to be altered in this way by executive revision of a Code rather than legislative revision of a statute may be debatable. The fact of the matter is that it is difficult to find parliamentary time to revise statutes in the light of experience. A Code is one means of achieving the necessary flexibility.

The Role of the Courts

Lawyers acting for the homeless have used the courts to challenge local authorities' decisions on intentional homelessness and many other aspects of the legislation. Not only has this imposed a heavy case load on the courts but it also led to the feeling that the courts were being used to undermine the scheme of the legislation which was to give the decision-making power to the local authorities. In 1985 the House of Lords finally issued a stern warning in the case of *Puhlhofer* v. *Hillingdon London Borough Council*[25] Giving the judgment of the court, Lord Brightman said:

> "I think that great restraint should be exercised in giving leave to proceed by judicial review. The plight of the homeless is a desperate one. But it is not, in my opinion, appropriate that the remedy of judicial review should be made use of to monitor the actions of local authorities save in the exceptional case. . . . Where the existence or non-existence of a fact is left to the judgment of a public body and that fact involves a broad spectrum ranging from the obvious to the debatable to the just conceivable, it is the duty of the court to leave the decision of that fact to the public body to whom Parliament has entrusted the decision-making power save in a case where it is obvious that the public body, consciously or unconsciously, are acting perversely."

Despite this warning, challenges to authorities' interpretation of the law have continued to flow and the difficulty in drawing the law/fact distinction, which we noted in chapter 4, means that courts cannot escape being asked to consider facts as well.

Extra-Legal Considerations

The impact of legislation is often influenced as much by extra-legal considerations such as the broader economic and social policies of the Government or the attitudes and resources of those charged with applying the law, as it is by purely legal considerations such as the principles of statutory interpretation. This is certainly true of the homeless persons legislation. A study published in 1981 by Shelter[26] suggests that some authorities used the intentionally homeless proviso to avoid housing applicants who would probably not have been regarded as intentionally homeless by the courts. Unless such applicants choose to challenge the authorities by judicial review, it is the authorities' attitude rather than the courts' interpretation which will determine the way in which the law is applied.

The authorities themselves face difficult problems. There may be a potential conflict between their role as landlords and their role as housing providers. As landlords they may evict a tenant for rent arrears or bad behaviour. What is the point of doing that if they will only have to rehouse the homeless tenant under the provisions of the Act? Finding the tenant to be intentionally homeless provides one solution to this dilemma. However, above all the authorities' problems stem from a shortage of housing stock and finance to build more houses. The original 1977 legislation contained no financial provision to enable authorities to fulfil their new housing duties. Some would say that Government policies since the Act have tended to discourage rather than encourage authorities to provide more housing. However, there is now a recognition that many of the problems can only be solved by extra-legal methods rather than by revising the Act or Code of Guidance.[27] Thus, the Government have recognised that housing investment programmes must take account of the greater demands placed on some authorities by the homeless. Changes in the immigration rules and more publicity warning immigrants of housing problems may help alleviate that particular problem. New social security provisions may prevent rent arrears from arising and solve that particular problem.

These direct measures will obviously reduce the problems but not all of them will disappear; they are too deep rooted for that. Perhaps we should also remember that even where a person is clearly intentionally homeless under the section, his problem still remains. As Lord Bridge remarked in *Din*, if the authority puts the family on the street by finding it intentionally homeless, "the most likely outcome must surely be that the family will be broken up and the children taken into care." Solving the problem under section 60 merely creates a new legal and social problem for a different area of the welfare system.

APPENDIX

HOUSING ACT 1985

S.60

(1) A person becomes homeless intentionally if he deliberately does or fails to do anything in consequence of which he ceases to occupy accommodation which is available for his occupation and which it would have been reasonable for him to continue to occupy.

(2) A person becomes threatened with homelessness intentionally if he deliberately does or fails to do anything the likely result of which is that he will be forced to leave accommodation which is available for his occupation and which it would have been reasonable for him to continue to occupy.

(3) For the purposes of subsection (1) or (2) an act or omission in good faith on the part of a person who was unaware of any relevant fact is not to be treated as deliberate.

(4) Regard may be had, in determining whether it would have been reasonable for a person to continue to occupy accommodation, to the general circumstances prevailing in relation to housing in the district of the local housing authority to whom he applied for accommodation or for assistance in obtaining accommodation.

S.62

(1) If a person (An "applicant") applies to a housing authority for accommodation or for assistance in obtaining accommodation, and the authority have reason to believe that he may be homeless or threatened with homelessness, they

shall make such inquiries as are necessary to satisfy the authority whether the person who applied to them is homeless or threatened with homelessness.

(2) If they are so satisfied, they shall make any further inquiries necessary to satisfy themselves as to—

    (a)   whether he has a priority need, and

    (b)   whether he became homeless or threatened with homelessness intentionally:

and if they think fit they may also make inquiries as to whether he has a local connection with the district of another local housing authority in England, Wales or Scotland.

S.63.

(1) If the local housing authority have reason to believe that an applicant may be homeless and have a priority need, they shall secure that accommodation is made available for his occupation pending any decision which they may make as a result of the inquires under section 62.

(2) This duty arises irrespective of any local connection he may have with the district of another local housing authority.

[NB Sections 62 & 63 replace s.3 of the 1977 Act set out below. If you compare the 1985 draft with the earlier one you will see that although the content is the same, the expression has been greatly improved.

    S.3(1) If—

    (a)   a person applies to a housing authority for accommodation or for assistance in obtaining accommodation, and

    (b)   the authority have reason to believe that he may be homeless or threatened with homelessness,

the authority shall make appropriate inquiries.

    (2) In subsection (1) above "appropriate inquiries" means—

    (a)   such inquiries as are necessary to satisfy the authority whether the person who applied to them is homeless or threatened with homelessness, and

(b)   if the authority are satisfied that he is homeless or threatened with homelessness, any further inquiries necessary to satisfy them—

        (i)   whether he has a priority need, and

        (ii)   whether he became homeless or threatened with homelessness intentionally.

(3) If the authority think fit, they may also make inquiries as to whether the person who applied to them has a local connection with the area of another housing authority.

(4) If the authority have reason to believe that the person who applied to them may be homeless and have a priority need, they shall secure that accommodation is made available for his occupation pending any decision which they may make as a result of the inquiries (irrespective of any local connection he may have with the area of another housing authority).]

S.65(1) This section has effect as regards the duties owed by the local housing authority to an applicant where they are satisfied that he is homeless.

(2) Where they are satisfied that he has a priority need and are not satisfied that he became homeless intentionally, they shall . . . secure that accommodation becomes available for his occupation.

(3) Where they are satisfied that he has a priority need but are also satisifed that he became homeless intentionally, they shall—

(a)   secure that accommodation is made available for his occupation for such period as they consider will give him a reasonable opportunity of securing accommodation for his occupation, and

(b)   furnish him with advice and such assistance as they consider appropriate in the circumstances in any attempts he may make to secure that accommodation becomes available for his occupation.

CODE OF GUIDANCE

2.14. Section 60 sets out the circumstances in which, for

the purposes of the Act, a person is to be regarded as having become homeless or threatened with homelessness intentionally. There are three requirements, all of which must be satisfied:

(a)   the applicant, if homeless, must have deliberately done, or failed to do, something in consequence of which he ceased to occupy accommodation which was (at that time) available — or, if threatened with homelessness, something of which the likely result was that he would be forced to leave such accommodation;

(b)   it must have been reasonable for him to continue to occupy the accommodation; and

(c)   he must have been aware of all the relevant facts (an act or omission in good faith on the part of someone unaware of any relevant facts is not to be regarded as deliberate).

2.15   A person who chooses to sell his home, or who has lost it because of wilful and persistent refusal to pay rent, would in most cases be regarded as having become homeless intentionally. **Authorities should in such cases be satisfied that the person has taken the action which has led to the loss of accommodation with full knowledge of the likely consequences.** Where, however, a person was obliged to sell because he could not keep up the mortgage repayments, or got into rent arrears, because of real personal or financial difficulties or because he was incapable of managing his affairs on account of e.g. old age or mental illness, his acts or omissions should not be regarded as having been deliberate. **Where homelessness is the result of serious financial difficulties arising, for example, from loss of employment or greatly reduced earnings the applicant should not normally be regarded as intentionally homeless. A spouse or cohabitee should not automatically be held to be jointly responsible for the rent or mortgage arrears incurred by the other partner; the authority should make inquiries with a view to establishing whether responsibility for the arrears was shared in practice before treating the applicant as intentionally homeless. An** owner occupier inescapably faced with foreclosure, who sells before the mortgage recovers possession throughout the courts, should not on that account be treated as intentionally homeless.

2.16 In the opinion of the Secretaries of State, a battered woman who has fled the marital home should never be regarded as having become homeless intentionally because it would clearly not be reasonable for her to remain; nor would it be appropriate that a homeless pregnant woman be treated as intentionally homeless simply because she is pregnant. If people can no longer afford to remain in their accommodation (e.g. because of a drop in income) and no further financial help is available, it should not be regarded as unreasonable for them to leave. In general authorities should not treat as intentionally homeless those who have been driven to leave their accommodation because conditions had degenerated to a point when they could not in all the circumstances reasonably be expected to remain — perhaps because of overcrowding or lack of basic amenities or severe emotional stress. But in considering whether it would have been reasonable for people to remain where they were, authorities may have regard to the general housing conditions of the area; e.g. whether there are many people in the area living in worse conditions than the applicants. **A person who loses tied accommodation because the employment has ended through no fault of his own should not be treated as intentionally homeless. Where the person has voluntarily resigned from the job, he should not be treated as intentionally homeless if the circumstances indicate that it would not have been reasonable for him to continue in employment.**

2.17 Examples of people who might be regarded as unaware of relevant facts are those who get into rent arrears, being unaware that they are entitled to rent allowances or rebates or other welfare benefits; and those who left rented accommodation on receipt of notices to quit (or distraint warrants), being unaware of their legal rights as tenants.

2.18 **The courts have established that in assessing whether a person has become homeless intentionally, it is**

**open to an authority to look beyond the most immediate cause
of that homelessness. In particular, where homelessness arises
from loss of accommodation of a temporary nature, it may
therefore be relevant to consider the circumstances in which
the previous accommodation was given up.** [NB the earlier
version of 2.18 was to the contrary viz 'In assessing whether a
person has become homeless intentionally it will be relevant to
consider the most immediate cause of that homelessness rather
than events that may have taken place previously.] It would
however be inappropriate to treat as intentionally homeless a
person who gave up accommodation to move in with relatives
or friends who then decided after a few months that they could
no longer continue to accommodate him; **each case must be
considered individually. Authorities are asked to exercise care
in dealing with loss of accommodation arising from a move to
seek work.**

Notes

[1] For those interested in studying the Act in depth there are two excellent
studies: *Homeless Persons: The Housing Act 1985* by Arden and *Homelessness* by
Hoath.

[2] In the case of pregnant women and the vulnerable, those who might
reasonably be expected to live with them are also regarded as having a
priority need.

[3] s.60(3) further provides that conduct in good faith by a person unaware of a
relevant fact is not to be treated as deliberate.

[4] Code of Guidance, para. 2.15.

[5] *Ante*, Chap. 3.

[6] *R. v. London Borough of Hillingdon ex p. Puhlhofer* [1986] A.C. 484. See further
Arden, Chap. 3.

[7] [1980] 1 All E.R. 913.

[8] See the amendment to para. 2.18 of the Code set out in the Appendix.

[9] *R. v. Hammersmith & Fulham London Borough Council* (1983) *The Times*, March
10, 1983.

[10] [1983] 1 A.C. 688.

[11] [1981] 2 All E.R. 1089.

[12] [1980] 1 W.L.R. 1205.

[13] [1983] 1 A.C. 657.

[14] Code of Guidance, para. 2.15.

[15] [1982] 1 All E.R. 726.

[16] See the Appendix, where the relevant amendment to para. 2.15 of the Code
is highlighted.

[17] [1981] 1 W.L.R. 328.

[18] *Smith* v. *Bristol City Council* (1981) L.A.G. Bul. 287.

[19] (1981) 44 M.L.R. 617, 623–633.

[20] Chaps. 6, 7 and 16.

[21] See, further, Partington, *The Housing (Homeless Persons) Act 1977*, Current Law Statutes reprint 1978.

[22] See Smith "An Academic Lawyer and Law Reform" (1981) 1 L.S. 125, where the author comments that the "most constant source of difficulty and difference of opinion" in the work of the Criminal Law Revision Committee concerned the "degree of particularity into which legislation should go."

[23] *The Concept of Law*, p. 126.

[24] E.C. Regulation 1612/68 provides that a worker who is a national of a Member State and is employed in another Member State shall enjoy all the rights awarded to national workers in matters of housing.

[25] [1986] A.C. 484.

[26] Widdowson, *Intentional Homelessness*.

[27] Wilkinson (1982) 132 N.L.J. 708.

Chapter 11

CODES AND CODIFICATION

BENTHAM AND THE HISTORY OF CODIFICATION IN ENG-LAND AND WALES

We have seen in chapter 9 that in English law a code is a species of statute which attempts to sum up the existing legislation and common law and equity on a particular topic. By code we mean here a formal code, not an informal code such as a Code of Guidance. In England we owe our main theories of codification to the legal philosopher, Jeremy Bentham, who wrote during the late eighteenth and early nineteenth centuries. Indeed we probably owe to him the word "codification."[1]

According to Bentham in his *General View of a Complete Code of Laws*, the object of a code is to ensure that everyone may consult the law affecting him in the least possible time.[2] Whatever is not in the code ought not to have the force of law.[3] The style should reflect force, harmony and nobleness.

> "With this view, the legislator might sprinkle here and there moral sentences, provided they are very short, and in accordance with the subject, and he [the legislator] would do no ill if he were to allow marks of his paternal tenderness to flow down upon his paper, as proof of the benevolence which guides his pen."[4]

The code should speak a language familiar to everyone; it should be simple and clear.[5] The code having been prepared, all unwritten law should be forbidden. Judges should merely interpret the code and if they see an error or omission they should notify the legislature and suggest a correction which should be adopted by legislation.[6] Once in a hundred years the code should be revised to remove obsolete terms.

Bentham's views, typical of his age, overrated the power of government and underrated the difficulties involved.[7] His attitude to the past was that it was from the folly not the wisdom of our ancestors that we have so much to learn.[8] His plans aimed at finality and paid insufficient attention to legal development and social change.

He was not, however, the first English writer to favour a code. Bacon in the early seventeenth century had favoured drastic consolidation; James I toyed with codification and in the interregnum some lawyers favoured root and branch reform including codification. Indeed to the Parliament of Saints the Ten Commandments would suffice. Nothing came of these great plans.[9]

Bentham, however, for all his extremism, or perhaps because of it, was more influential. The second part of the nineteenth century was a prolific period of law reform. The major reforms were, however, in procedure and the court structure, not so much in the form of law.

In India there were successful experiments with codification but little came of the codification movement in England. Sir James Fitzjames Stephen who had drafted some of the Indian codes prepared drafts which were never enacted in this country. Eventually, however, Judge Chalmers' Bills of Exchange Bill and Sale of Goods Bill were enacted and put on the Statute Book in 1882 and 1893 respectively. Also Sir Frederick Pollock's Partnership Bill was eventually enacted in 1890 after 10 years of machinations in Parliament. These can be regarded as codes. So too in a loose sense can the property legislation of the 1920s but this was primarily consolidation and reform rather than restatement. More recently we have had the Theft Act 1968 which again was primarily reform.[9]

The Law Commissions have codification as a major item on their agenda, being charged with the duty of (at least) considering it under the Law Commissions Act 1965.

CHOOSING AN APPROPRIATE MODEL

One of the most difficult questions facing English lawyers tackling codification is what form the code should take.[10] The two basic paradigms are the French and German civil codes respectively. The former is more in the form of a statement of general principles leaving the courts with a necessarily creative role in fact if not in theory. The German code, however, is more on the lines of Bentham's ideas and is more detailed. In fact the aim was to provide a complete answer to any legal problem within the conceptual framework of the code.

The codes drafted for India incorporated hypothetical factual examples so that the code is at once a statute and a collection of decided cases, the latter with the advantage that they were decided by the legislature.

Another idea, put forward in 1865, was that a code should be more elaborate and consist of the rules, examples of the application of the rules and then the reasons for the rules.

It would seem that there is and should be no single paradigm of a code and that differing forms and styles might be required by different legal traditions and even by different areas of law. In some areas of law such as crime there is a need for certainty; in others such as commercial law there is a need for flexibility.

INTERPRETATION AND THE ROLE OF THE JUDGE

The courts start with a presumption in the case of a consolidating Act that no significant changes were intended. Indeed the Consolidation of Enactments (Procedure) Act 1949 lays down a special simplified procedure for such Acts provided that they do not effect changes in the existing law which in the opinion of a Joint Committee of both Houses, the Lord Chancellor and the Speaker ought to be the subject of a separate Act.[11]

The presumption and the procedure do not apply to a codifying Act.[12] The basic principle here was laid down by the House of Lords in *Bank of England* v. *Vagliano*[13] in 1891. In the words of Lord Herschell the principle is:

" . . . in the first instance to examine the language of the
statute and to ask what is its natural meaning un-influenced
by any considerations derived from the previous state of the
law and not to start with enquiring how the law previously
stood and then, assuming that it was probably intended to
leave it unaltered, to see if the words of the enactment will
bear an interpretation in conformity with this view . . . I am
of course far from asserting that resort may never be had to
the previous state of the law for the purpose of aiding in the
construction of the provisions of the code. If for example
such a provision be of doubtful import, such resort will be
perfectly legitimate."

Thus, one can still look at the previous law in cases of
ambiguity or where words have acquired a technical meaning.[14]

Clearly this is not what Bentham intended. Such is the
conservative approach of English lawyers, it is thought, that
even if the code expressly forbade resort to such materials
lawyers would still in practice resort to them for guidance.

Lord Scarman, the first Chairman of the English Law Commission, has emphasised that if more and more of English law
is codified the role of the judges will change. "They will lose
their priestly character as oracles drawing from within upon
the experience of themselves and their predecessors in office to
declare the law; they will stand forth as the authoritative
interpreters of the code."[15] Clearly much will depend on the
form that future codification takes and the change in role need
not necessarily result in a change in status.

THE PROS AND CONS OF CODIFICATION

We saw earlier how codification is a matter of controversy. Let
us now examine the controversy.[16]

The main argument traditionally used, and frequently used
by the Law Commissions, is the great bulk or unwieldiness of
the present law. It is argued that a code would produce in its
place systematic, compact and accessible law. The law would
be more accessible to the public, even if not necessarily

completely intelligible to them. Case law produces gaps, uncertainties and irrational distinctions which a code would remove. Also it has been argued that the common law has not in recent times been able to adapt itself quickly enough to changing conditions. This has been particularly true in the field of contract. There is some substance in all these arguments.

Against these are a number of arguments which were put forward in the nineteenth century and have been reiterated recently. First it is said that a code is necessarily incomplete and cannot provide for all future cases. The easiest way of meeting this criticism is to recognise its partial truth and compare this with the gaps under the existing law. Then it is argued that a code is difficult to alter. In this country there is no reason why this should be so. Parliament will not abdicate its legislative functions once a code has been enacted, the judges will continue to interpret it and the Law Commissions will presumably continue in business.

Next, it is said that the common law is more malleable. Although there is some force in this criticism it is tempered to a certain extent by the doctrine of precedent. Again, it is said that a code is more likely to engender competition of conflicting rules and principles than the common law. This obviously depends on the quality of draftsmanship and might arise if the drafting of codes for different areas of law was in different hands and was not adequately supervised.

Another argument is that the legal textbooks perform the function of a code but these are clearly not authoritative unless and until they are archaic.

It is also argued that a code in order to approach completeness must consist of rules so minute and numerous that no man can learn or retain them, and that, in any event, it is impossible to provide completely for particular future cases. The answer to this is that one has a choice as regards the subject-matter of a code and, as regards its form; it should not aim at a comprehensive specification of cases but at providing a series of rules applicable to cases.

More fundamental criticisms are those made by Savigny, who attacked the codification movement in Germany in the nineteenth century and argued that a code will not adjust to the customs and experience of the community, the Volksgeist, and will destroy continuity in legal development. Apart from the inherent vagueness of the concept of the Volksgeist, there is no reason why a code which restates the English law developed over centuries and which is kept up to date by a body such as the Law Commission should not meet the changing needs of society.

Last, we have the brunt of Professor Hahlo's powerful criticism in an article in the *Modern Law Review* in 1967, dramatically entitled, "Here Lies the Common Law: Rest in Peace."[17] It did not seem unlikely to him (to employ his double negative) that as a result of codification the influence of English law outside the United Kingdom would decrease. It will suffer a loss of status from being the senior member of the Anglo-American common law family to becoming one of a large number of codified systems. He asked rhetorically, "Will America succeed England as chief custodian of the common law?" Professor Gower, by way of rejoinder,[18] argued that America had nearly overtaken England in legal development already because of its use of Restatements of the law and the model and uniform codes. We could be more helpful to other members of the Anglo-American family by our work in law reform and codification than by leaving our law in its present form.

To sum up the debate, the truth would appear to be that the arguments for and against codification are of such a high level of generality that they cannot be established or refuted scientifically. At the end of the day the choice seems to be one of policy both as to whether and what to codify and the form the code should take.

Although the Law Commission is obliged to consider codification by the terms of the Act which set it up it seems recently to have been having second thoughts, certainly as far as its projected code of the law of contract is concerned. It appears to be proceeding slowly with its work on the criminal and landlord and tenant codes and on reform and consolidation of family law with a view to a family code. These are clearly desirable. Since Parliament remains the ultimate watershed it has to be convinced that the end-product is necessary. There are at present no special procedures for codification measures and therefore parliamentary control is an effective fetter on reforming zeal.

CODIFICATION IN OPERATION—THE SALE OF GOODS ACT 1979

In earlier chapters we have studied case law and legislation in operation. Here we shall more briefly consider codification in operation, taking as our example the Sale of Goods Act.

It appears that the Sale of Goods Act 1893 (now consolidated in the Sale of Goods Act 1979) was more the result of a move for legal rationality from certain members of the profession than the response to pressure from the commercial community. In this respect it seems to have differed from the Bills of Exchange Act 1882 which was promoted by the banking community.[19] Both acts were drafted by Mackenzie Chalmers who was a skilled draftsman and on the whole they have stood the test of time.

The Sale of Goods Act 1893 codified the case law relating to contracts for the sale of goods. At one time there was some doubt about whether it superseded the equitable rules but it now appears to have done so.[20] There cannot be equitable interests in goods in respect of matters governed by the Act. Generally, security arrangements *e.g.* where goods are used as security for a loan are not governed by the Act and, therefore, equitable interests by way of security can be created.

The act creates a simple division of contractual terms into conditions and warranties. A condition is a term the breach of which gives a right to treat the contract as repudiated whereas breach of a warranty only results in a claim for damages. A problem has arisen due to the subsequent recognition under the general law of contract of a third species of term—the innominate term whose character is determined in the light of subsequent developments.[21] It has been difficult for the courts to accommodate this within the scheme of the code. This shows the need as Bentham indicated for periodic revision and updating of the code by the legislature.

Certain concepts such as description, merchantability and fitness for purpose which were simply stated in the 1893 Act have given rise to complications in the cases. There has been much case law and attempts were made to reform merchantability and fitness for purpose by statute in 1973 which have not proved particularly successful. The English reforms have not been very practical and it is interesting to compare them with recent Canadian proposals which specify a duration of liability and impose an obligation to maintain adequate spare parts.[22]

Certain concepts used in the Act overlap in practice and this can create difficulties. This is particularly true of the concepts of ascertainment of unascertained goods, appropriation and passing of property.[23] Ascertainment and appropriation are often fulfilled by the same act. Whether or not this passes the property in the goods depends on the parties' intentions. This gives rise to uncertainty. There are complex problems where goods are sold out of bulk consignment but these are largely due to the fact that English law does not generally recognise separate property in unascertained parts of a bulk. Some of these problems have been solved by a case law gloss which recognises ascertainment by exhaustion where the other parts of the bulk have been separated. The whole of this indicates that a code on a commercial matter will be based on the commercial practice of the particular period which may well change drastically with new methods of transport, communications and documentation.

The 1893 Act recognised freedom of contract so it was possible for parties to exclude liability for breach of the conditions implied by the Act. This freedom was abused and was curtailed by statute in 1973 and the present legislation is the Unfair Contract Terms Act 1977 which unfortunately was not consolidated in the 1979 Act.[25]

In practice much buying and selling is done on standard terms which in substance, if not in form, supersede the Act. Manufacturers for instance continue to operate consumer "warranty" or "guarantee" systems and commercial men often devise their own system for dealing with contractual disputes. Where these break down, the tendency is to arbitrate rather than litigate although the costs are not necessarily cheaper.

The lessons to be drawn from this are not simple. It may be that the Act stultified the growth of legal rules and principles by fossilisation of legal development and oversimplification. On the other hand the Act is clear and readily accessible. It is possible for a businessperson and a consumer to ascertain their legal rights fairly easily from the wording. The Act tends to be the one piece of law that laypeople know something about. Reform has been and is taking place. Where the law is codified reform necessarily has to take account of the relevant interest groups. What is particularly interesting but somewhat disconcerting is that businesspeople feel the need to by-pass the Act and substitute their own systems. The lessons to be derived from this are complex and are not just limited to codification.[26]

Notes

[1] Murray's *Dictionary*.
[2] See the Bowring edition of Bentham's Works, Vol. 3, p. 193.
[3] *Ibid.*, p. 205.
[4] *Ibid.*, p. 208.
[5] *Ibid.*, p. 209.
[6] *Ibid.*, p. 210.
[7] See Sir C. Ilbert, *Legislative Methods and Forms*, p. 123.
[8] *The Book of Fallacies* (Bowring ed.), Vol. 2, p. 401.
[9] See John Farrar *Law Reform and the Law Commission*, Chap. I.
[10] *Ibid.*, pp. 57 *et seq.* and pp. 97 *et seq.*
[11] See Erskine May, *Parliamentary Practice* (19th ed. by Sir David Lidderdale), pp. 524–525. Greater latitude is allowed to bills to consolidate with amendments to give effect to recommendations of the Law Commissions, *op. cit.*, p. 525. See also Lord Simon of Glaisdale in *Maunsell* v. *Olins* [1975] A.C. 392C–E.
[12] See Odgers, *Construction of Deeds and Statutes* (5th ed.), by G. Dworkin, p. 335.
[13] [1891] A.C. 107, 144.
[14] Odgers, p. 335.
[15] *Codification and Judge Made Law*, p. 11.
[16] The following summary of the arguments is taken from *Law Reform and the Law Commission*. See also Bruce Donald, "Codification in Common Law Systems" (1973) 47 A.L.J. 160.
[17] (1967) 30 M.L.R. 241. See also Professor Aubrey Diamond's "Codification of the Law of Contract" in (1968) 31 M.L.R. 361.
[18] (1967) 30 M.L.R. 262.
[19] See the valuable discussion in R. B. Ferguson, "Legal Ideology and Commercial Interest" (1977) 4 B.J.L.S. 18.
[20] *Re Wait* [1927] 1 Ch. 606, but see Sir Frederick Pollock's criticism in (1927) 43 L.Q.R. 293.
[21] See P. S. Atiyah, *Sale of Goods* (6th ed.), pp. 43–46.
[22] See Report on Sale of Goods by the Ontario Law Reform Commission—draft s. 5.13(1)(C).
[23] See R. M. Goode, *Commercial Law*, pp. 166 *et seq.* for a valuable discussion.
[24] *Wait & James* v. *Midland Bank* (1926) 31 Com. Cas. 172.

[25] See W. V. H. Rogers & M. G. Clarke, *The Unfair Contract Terms Act 1977*.
[26] See H. Beale & T. Dugdale, "Contracts between Businessmen: Planning and the Use of Contractual Remedies" (1975) 2 B.J.L.S. 45.

Chapter 12

DOCTRINE

GENERAL COMPARISONS OF APPROACH

We have seen that the common law is largely the product of the judiciary. On the continent, until the codifications of the nineteenth century, learned writings (which are usually referred to as doctrine) were a fundamental source of law. In England learned writers have traditionally played a subordinate role and their writings have never enjoyed the status afforded to continental doctrinal writings before the codifications. The position on the continent since codification seems to be that doctrine still enjoys high prestige but is now really an important secondary source in areas governed by the codes and other legislation.[1] This latter role should not be underestimated since, as David and Brierley[2] point out, doctrine creates the legal vocabulary and ideas used by legislators, and influences the methods of statutory interpretation.

Scots law seems to invest certain learned writings with very high authority and it is possibly true to say that these enjoy something of the status of the pre-codification continental doctrine.[3] Not all the works of such writers are necessarily regarded as having this institutional status and the position of writings by subsequent authors varies according to reputation. Scots lawyers are loath to invest them with institutional status.

THE POSITION OF DOCTRINE IN ENGLISH LAW

The position of learned writings in English law has varied at

200

different periods of legal history.[4] Certain classical authors are recognised as authorities and there has gradually been a relaxation of the strange, necromantic rule allowing only the citation of dead authors.

In this chapter we shall look at four great writers who wrote at critical stages in the development of English law—Bracton, Coke, Blackstone and Pollock—assess their authority at the present day and then we shall attempt to describe the modern practice.

Bracton wrote at an early stage in English legal history when the common law was only just beginning to acquire autonomy as a system and there were distinct traces of a Roman law influence in his work. Coke marks the end of the early period and an attempt to preserve the learning of the past in the service of the future. Blackstone presents an accurate and elegant restatement of the common law as it had developed by the mid eighteenth century, prior to the movement for reform. Pollock manifests the preservation of the old learning blended with a wide general culture and an interest in the rational development of the law, while at the same time avoiding the excesses of Bentham. Let us now look at each of them in turn.

Bracton[5]

Bracton was an ecclesiastic who served as a judge in the thirteenth century. He is an important figure in the early common law. His principal treatise was an exposition of the laws and customs of England unrivalled either in literary style or completeness until Blackstone's *Commentaries* in the eighteenth century. His work was influenced to some extent by Roman law but the precise extent is a matter of conjecture. The book shows that even at this early date English law had become based on the forms of actions (*i.e.* specific formulae into which a cause of action must be fitted) and decided cases. Indeed Bracton states expressly "If like matters arise let them be decided by like, since the occasion is a good one for proceeding *a similibus ad similia*."[6] At this time there were no published reports so he had to rely on his knowledge of the plea rolls—the formal record. After his death Bracton's reputation fluctuated. With the growth of a legal profession centred around the Inns of Court and learned only in its own system, the common law eschewed general principle and became in Pollock and Maitland's words "an evasive commentary upon writs and statutes."[7] In the sixteenth century Bracton was known to and cited by Coke to liberalise the common law. Sir Matthew Hale in his *History of the Common Law* put the authority of Bracton's treatise on a level with that of the records of the courts[8] and Blackstone also recognised it as authoritative.[9]

Coke[10]

Sir Edward Coke was first a law officer of the crown, then a judge, then later a politician. During his lifetime he was an important figure in the constitutional struggles of the early seventeenth century, but we are only concerned here with his writings as a source of law.

Coke was learned in the law and a skilful pleader although his writings are often verbose and lacking in form. His most important works are his *Reports* and his *Institutes*. In his day there was no agreement as to the form a report should take. Coke's reports come in all shapes and sizes—ranging from summaries of the law to very detailed reports of important cases, all containing his own comments. The *Institutes* met the need of the time for the old law to be restated in modern form. There are four *Institutes*. The first is his commentary on Littleton (an earlier writer of considerable reputation) which deals with land and some of the law of obligations and procedure. The second deals with statutes, the third with criminal law and the fourth with the jurisdiction of the courts.

Parts of Coke's writings are unreliable from the point of view of strict historical scholarship, but all of them have been influential. His knowledge of the ancient law has never been rivalled; he communicated his research in English instead of the Latin and law French of the original materials.

The authority of his writings can be judged from the following judicial remarks:

(a) in *Garland* v. *Jekyll* (1824) 2 Bing. 296 Best C.J. said, "The fact is Lord Coke has no authority for what he states on the particular point, but I am afraid we should get rid of a good deal of what is considered law in Westminster Hall if what Lord Coke says without authority is not law."

(b) *Garland* v. *Jekyll* was referred to by Darling J. in *R.* v. *Casement* [1917] 1 K.B. 98, 141 when he delivered the judgment of the Court of Criminal Appeal. He said:

> "It has been said to us that we should not follow Lord Coke because Stephen in his commentaries and other writers have spoken lightly of the authority and learning of Lord Coke. It may be that they have done so. Of course they have all the advantage. They are his successors. If Lord Coke were in a position to answer them, it may be that they would be sorry that they had entered into argument with him . . . he has been recognised as a great authority in these courts for centuries."

Blackstone[11]

Blackstone was the first Professor of English Law at Oxford and published his lectures under the title of *Commentaries on the Laws of England* in 1761. In 1770 he was made a judge.

From the point of view of style the *Commentaries* are admirable. The books were aimed beyond the legal profession to the educated public at large. Blackstone's classification follows Roman law to some extent. Thus the order is the nature of law, rights of persons, rights of things, private wrongs and public wrongs.

From the point of view of substance the work has been criticised. There is a lack of profundity and critical acumen.[12] Bentham in particular resented its complacency.[13] Nevertheless the work was a success, particularly in the colonies and the United States where it was the only available source of the common law for many frontier lawyers and judges. Blackstone's *Commentaries* are regarded as authoritative because of their clear style, comprehensiveness and accuracy. Despite Bentham's strictures the *Commentaries* facilitated reform because of their clear statement of the existing law.

Pollock[14]

Sir Frederick Pollock lived from 1845 until 1937. He was an academic lawyer who came from a family of eminent practising

lawyers. His knowledge was prodigious and his literary style
was graceful. The writer of *The Times* obituary described him as
"perhaps the last representative of the old broad culture." He
was the author of leading textbooks on the law of contract,
tort, possession and partnership and was the draftsman of the
Bill which became the Partnership Act 1890. His principal
contribution was to show students and practitioners that English law was no mere collection of precedents and statutes but
a system of rules, principles and standards which was logically
coherent and yet eminently practical because it was the product of long experience.[15]

Lord Wright wrote of him in the *Law Quarterly Review*—"the
writings of a lawyer like Pollock, constantly cited in the courts
and quoted by the judges, are entitled to claim a place under
his category of unwritten law, even in a system like ours which
does not normally seek its law from institutional writers."[16]

THE STATUS AND INFLUENCE OF DOCTRINE

We have mentioned above four leading writers. There are
others such as Glanvil, Hale, Hawkins, Fry and Lindley who
could also be mentioned. Can we make meaningful general
remarks about them? It seems that unlike certain Roman jurists
who enjoyed what is known as the *jus respondendi*,[17] they do
not enjoy the status of a primary source of law and there is no
English equivalent of the Roman law of citations to determine
their standing amongst each other.[18] The earlier English writers
are sometimes the only source of knowledge or information
about the old law but even where this is not the case they are
accepted as a valuable secondary source. Nevertheless as Lord
Goddard C.J. said in *Bastin* v. *Davies* the court "would never
hesitate to disagree with a statement in a textbook, however
authoritative or however long it has stood, if it thought it right
to do so."[19] The formal, precedent-based nature of English
common law leaves limited scope for the influence of the
academic lawyer.[20]

However, to be contrasted with the characteristically robust
attitude of Lord Goddard is the undoubted influence that

doctrine played in the development of contract principles in the nineteenth century. This has been summed up well by Professor Patrick Atiyah when he wrote[21]—

"These writers were academics, unlike all their predecessors. They were learned men, and men given to theorizing, not in the pejorative sense which the word still bears among legal practitioners, but theorizing in a more acceptable tradition; they were theorists in the sense that they sought to construct a theoretical and systematic framework of legal principle into which specific legal decisions could be fitted. They were also deeply versed in Roman law, and Pollock, at least, was well acquainted with modern civil law countries such as France and Germany, as well as with some of the developments in the United States. When these men came to write about the law of contract, they were not content to follow the traditional English practitioner's method of jumbling cases around without any sort of rational order or classification, or at best following a classification deriving from the forms of action. They found 'no literary tradition of expounding the law of contract in a form which invites the reader to proceed in the solution of problems by applying general principles of substantive law, principles under which the messy business of life is subsumed under ideal aseptic types of transaction, the types themselves being analysed and their legal consequences presented in a systematic form.' They found it necessary to set about creating a new shape to the law of contract. In one sense, it was they who actually created the general law of contract which we still know today, for it was they who formulated it and made explicit much of which had been implicit in the cases."

THE CITATION OF MODERN WRITERS

The old rule of practice was that the works of living authors could not be cited but could be plagiarised by counsel by incorporation into their own submissions to the court.[22] Various reasons have been given for this[23]—the fear that living authors would change their minds and render the law uncertain; the growth of law reporting rendered it unnecessary to cite secondary sources; and the notion that the passage of time would result in the elimination of errors by subsequent editors. Sir Robert Megarry, who speaks with considerable knowledge and experience in these matters, in his *Miscellany-at-Law*[24] adds the further reason that:

"there are a number of living authors whose appearance and demeanour do something to sap the confidence in their omniscience which the printed page may have instilled; the dead, on the other hand, so often leave little clue to what manner of men they were save the majestic skill with which they have arrayed the learning of centuries and exposed the failings of the bench."

The old rule has become honoured more in its breach than its observance. There is an interesting exchange between counsel and the Bench in *R.* v. *Ion* (1852) 2 Den. 475, 488.

"Metcalfe (counsel) . . . In the 11th edition of a work, formerly edited by one of your Lordships, *Archbold on Criminal Pleading* by Welsby, Mr. Welsby, who may be cited as authority, comments on the words 'utter or publish' . . .
Pollock C.B.—Not yet an authority.
Metcalfe.—It is no doubt a rule that a writer on law is not to be considered an authority in his lifetime. The only exception to the rule, perhaps, is the case of Justice Story.
Coleridge J.—Story is dead.
Cresswell J.—No doubt the cases are carefully abstracted by Mr. Welsby in the passage you refer to.
Lord Campbell C.J.—It is scarcely necessary to say that my opinion of Mr. Welsby is one of sincere respect."

The reporter, Denison, appends a footnote to the effect that the rule seemed to be more honoured in the breach than in its observance and he refers to a number of writers who had been cited in their lifetime.

There are numerous conflicting passages in the reports on the application of the rule[25] but certainly the practice has now developed of citing living authors. It may be as Hood Phillips maintained that the judges allow themselves more latitude than they do counsel.[26] In 1947 Lord Denning wrote in the Law Quarterly Review[27] that "the notion that (academic lawyers') works are not of authority except after the author's death has long been exploded. Indeed the more recent the work, the more persuasive it is." This view has not been universally accepted but there seems to be an increasing tendency to accept academic writings as a convenient secondary source of law or alternatively as a source of suggestions of what the law should be where there is a gap or the law is unclear. As Lord Denning said, such books "are written by men who have studied the law as a science with more detachment than is possible to men engaged in practice." Certainly, the views of Professors J. C. Smith and Glanville Williams are frequently cited in criminal cases. Indeed, the critical reception given by the latter to a House of Lords decision on criminal attempts was cited by the House a year later when it overruled that particular case.[28] However, against this is the evidence that only few of the Law Lords regularly read the leading law journals, *e.g.* the L.Q.R. or M.L.R.,[29] and one might hazard a guess that judges in lower courts have far less time available for such reading.

Sir Robert Megarry, who has been both a writer and a judge, expressed the matter a little more cautiously in *Cordell* v. *Second Clanfield Properties Ltd.*[30] when he said:

"the process of authorship is entirely different from that of judicial decision. The author, no doubt, has the benefit of a broad and comprehensive survey of his chosen subject as a whole, together with a lengthy period of gestation and intermittent opportunities for reconsideration. But he is exposed to the peril of yielding to preconceptions, and he lacks the advantage of that impact and sharpening of focus which the detailed facts of a particular case bring to the judge. Above all, he has to form his ideas without the aid of the purifying ordeal of skilled argument on the specific facts of a contested case. Argued law is tough law. This is as true today as it was in 1409 when Hankford J. said: 'Homme ne scaveroit de quel metal un campane fuit, si ceo ne fuit bien batu, quasi diceret, le ley per bon disputacion serra bien conus'; (Just as it is said 'A man will not know of what metal a bell is made if it has not been well beaten (rung)' so the law shall be well known by good disputation) and these words are none the less apt for a judge who sits, as I do, within earshot of the bells of St. Clements. I would therefore give credit to the words of any reputable author in a book or article as expressing tenable and arguable ideas, as fertilisers of thought, and as conveniently expressing the fruits of research in print, often in apt and persuasive language. But I would do no more than that; and in particular, I would expose those views to the testing and refining process of argument. Today, as of old, by good disputing shall the law be well known."

The current Scottish position appears to be that where there is a statement of the law in an institutional work which has not been contradicted the judges will look upon that statement as representing the law of Scotland.[31] The authority of such a statement has sometimes been said to be equivalent to that of a decision of the Inner House of the Court of Session to the same effect. There seems to be consensus between Lord Normand[32] (extrajudicially) and Professors Smith[33] and Walker[34] on this point although Professor Walker adds that the evaluation of any such statement depends largely on whether the legal context has changed, whether the passage has been approved of or criticised, and on its consistency with the law on related topics.

In conclusion, therefore, it must be admitted that even with the latest shift in practice we still seem to differ to some degree from continental systems in our treatment of learned writings. As with interpretation of legislation it is possible that we may be influenced by the continental practices adopted by the European Court.

Details about legal literature appear in Appendix 2 at the end of this book.

Notes

[1] René David and John Brierley, *Major Legal Systems in the World Today* (3rd ed.) p. 147.

[2] For the continental practice generally see David and Brierley, *op. cit.*, and J. H. Merryman, *The Civil Law Tradition* 2nd ed., Chap. IX. It may, however, be dangerous to generalise as the amount of codification and legislation and the nature of legal literature differ from one civil law jurisdiction to another. These have some bearing on the precise weight to be afforded to doctrine.

[3] For Scots law see Lord Macmillan, "Scots Law as a Subject of Comparative Study" in *Law and Other Things*, p. 111; The British Commonwealth series Vol. II—*Scotland* by T. B. Smith, pp. 32–33; and *Principles of Scottish Private Law* (2nd ed.), Vol. 1, by D. M. Walker, pp. 27–28.

[4] See Sir P. Winfield, *The Chief Sources of English Legal History*, p. 254. See also D. L. Carey Miller, "Legal Writings as a Source in English Law" (1975) 8 C.I.L.S.A. 236.

[5] See further Sir William Holdsworth, *Some Makers of English Law*, Lecture 1.

[6] See Bracton, *Laws and Customs of England* (Thorne ed.), Vol. 2, p. 21.

[7] Pollock and Maitland, *History of English Law*, Vol. 1, p. 204.

[8] *History of the Common Law*, p. 189.

[9] *Commentaries*, Vol. 1, p. 72.

[10] See Holdsworth, *op. cit.*, Lecture VI.

[11] *Ibid.*, pp. 240 *et seq.*

[12] Max Radin, *Handbook of Anglo-American Legal History*, p. 287.

[13] See *Fragment on Government*.

[14] Holdsworth, *op. cit.*, pp. 279 *et seq.*

[15] *Ibid.*, p. 286.

[16] (1937) 53 L.Q.R. 152.

[17] *i.e.* the privilege of giving *responsa* with the Emperor's authority. See *Digest* 1.2.2, 49 and Barry Nicholas, *An Introduction to Roman Law*, p. 31.

[18] See on this Carey Miller, *op. cit.* and Gray, *Nature and Sources of Law*.

[19] [1950] 2 K.B. 579, 582. See also *Button* v. *D.P.P.* [1966] A.C. 591.

[20] See Atiyah and Summers, *Form and Substance in Anglo-American Law*, at p. 403 where the authors contrast the limited influence of academics under the formal English system with their considerably more powerful role under the more substantively based American common law system.

[21] P. S. Atiyah, *Rise and Fall of Freedom of Contract*, pp. 682–683.

[22] See, *e.g.*, *Greenlands Ltd.* v. *Wilmshurst* (1913) 29 T.L.R. 685, 687, *per* Vaughan Williams L.J. and *Tichborne* v. *Weir* (1892) 67 L.T. 735, 736, *per* Lord Esher M.R.

[23] See Carey Miller, *op. cit.*

[24] *Miscellany-at-Law* (1955), p. 328.

[25] See, *e.g.*, the authorities cited by Megarry and Carey Miller, *op. cit.*

[26] *A First Book of English Law* (7th ed.), p. 238.

[27] (1947) 63 L.Q.R. 516.

[28] *R.* v. *Shivpuri* [1987] A.C. 1, overruling *Anderton* v. *Ryan* [1985] A.C. 560.

[29] See Paterson, *The Law Lords*, p. 14.

[30] [1968] 2 Ch. 9, 16.

[31] See Lord Benholme in *Drew* v. *Drew* (1870) 9 M. 163, 167 and Lord Inglis in *Kennedy* v. *Stewart* (1889) 16 R. 421, 430.

[32] *The Scottish Judicature and Legal Procedure*, p. 40.

[33] Smith, *op. cit.*, p. 32.

[34] Walker, *op. cit.*, p. 27.

Chapter 13

EUROPEAN INFLUENCES

For centuries the common law has developed in isolation from
other systems of law, relatively uninfluenced by rival
approaches and methods. It has been exported to much of the
Commonwealth but the movement has been largely one way;
few foreign ideas have been imported. Now this is changing.
The close political ties between the United Kingdom and
continental Europe, developed in modern times, have exposed
the common law system to new ideas.[1]

THE EUROPEAN CONVENTION OF HUMAN RIGHTS

This Convention, signed by the United Kingdom in 1950, has
exposed us to the concept of over-riding human rights, rights
which prevail over all other sources of law. Unlike some other
European states, the United Kingdom has not given these
rights direct force within the legal system by domestic enactment. Consequently our courts will still follow our case law
and legislation even where it conflicts with the rights contained
in the Convention. Thus when in 1979 an English judge had to
consider the legality of telephone tapping, he followed the
English common law in holding that the arrangements for
police "taps" were lawful whilst recognising that they probably
contravened the right of privacy established by Article 8 of the
Convention.[2]

Still, the Convention has had a powerful indirect influence. When our law appears to depart from the provisions of the Convention, a case may be brought against the United Kingdom before the European Court of Human Rights and if we are found to be in breach there may be considerable political pressure both in Europe and in the United Kingdom for our law to be brought into conformity with the Convention. Thus in *The Sunday Times* thalidomide case,[3] the Human Rights Court ruled that English court decisions prohibiting the paper from publishing its thalidomide articles because of the possible law suit between the thalidomide parents and the drug's distributors infringed the paper's right to freedom of expression under Article 10 of the Convention. This ruling was followed by United Kingdom legislation, the Contempt of Court Act 1981, intended to bring our own domestic law into line with the Convention. In a different context the Court has held that the 1970s United Kingdom legislation which permitted the operation of union closed shops infringed the rights of employees to freedom to association under Article 11.[4] This ruling combined with domestic political considerations had led to amending provisions in the Employment Act 1982 which greatly restrict the circumstances in which a closed shop may be operated. Again, when in 1984 the Court held that police tapping was an interference with the right to privacy unless it was carried out subject to adequate safeguards, the United Kingdom responded by passing the Interception of Communications Act 1985 which seeks to provide those safeguards by limiting tapping to situations where the Home Secretary has issued a warrant.

Even where United Kingdom legislation has been enacted following a Court ruling, a difference of method remains. Whilst the Convention rights are expressed in broad terms of principle, the United Kingdom legislation tends to be detailed and technical in nature and to talk in terms of duties rather than rights. Take the new closed shop provisions; they specify in great detail the circumstances in which a closed shop may be lawful, leaving the individual employee's rights to be deduced as a consequence, rather than positively stating what rights to freedom of association he has. As a result there is some doubt whether this legislation or indeed the contempt or telephone tapping legislation fully satisfies the requirements of the Convention. This is the challenge to our legal method, that of reconciling our narrow approach to the role of legislation with the broad ideas embodied in the Convention and indeed in many European constitutions.[5]

THE EUROPEAN COMMUNITY (E.C.)

The influence of the Human Rights Convention is significant but its potential is yet to be fully realised. This is not true of the E.C. The United Kingdom joined the Communities by the Treaty of Accession in 1972 under which it accepted the framework and rules of the main institution, the E.C., which had been established by the six founding states 14 years earlier under the Treaty of Rome. Unlike the Human Rights Convention, the influence of the E.C. treaty is not indirect, affecting the state alone and not its legal system. Because the E.C. system deals with social and economic issues formerly solely within the province of national laws, many of the Community laws are regarded as having a direct legal effect within the member states. To enable community laws of this kind to have an internal effect under our constitutional principles, the United Kingdom Parliament passed the European Communities Act 1972. To assess the nature and significance of the E.C. system we must now examine in more detail the institutions, their law making powers and in particular the role of the European Court of Justice (E.C.J.) before returning to the more general problems of method.

INSTITUTIONAL FRAMEWORK[6]

The heart of the community is the Commission. This body has the executive function of enforcing the treaty but it also has a policy making function in formulating further laws to give effect to the intention of the treaty. The political interests of the member states are represented through the Council of Ministers—one from each member state. Many of the laws formulated by the Commission can only be implemented with the approval of the Council. The European Parliament has primarily an advisory role, being consulted by the Commission on major policy questions. It has also limited supervisory powers, having some control over the Community budget and being able in the last resort to call for the resignation of the Commission. The fourth institution is the E.C.J., responsible for deciding legal disputes arising from the working of the Community. We will return to consider the E.C.J. in more detail after we have discussed the sources of community law.

SOURCES OF LAW

The articles of the Rome treaty provide the main primary source of law for the community and many of them are regarded as fully effective within the member states, creating rights and duties for individuals within those states. Thus, article 119 which provides that "Each member state shall . . . ensure . . . the application of the principle that men and women shall receive equal pay for equal work" has been held to give a woman the right to claim from her United Kingdom employer the same wages as were paid to the male predecessor in her job despite the fact that she has no such right under United Kingdom domestic legislation.[7]

Clearly it was not possible to create a complete legal code through the articles alone; some issues would require more detailed treatment based on further investigation and others would only arise for consideration as the aims of the community were developed. To meet this problem the Treaty gives the Council and the Commission power to issue delegated legislation in the form of Regulations, Directives and Decisions. These are known as the secondary sources.

Regulations are stated to be directly applicable in the member states and like many of the articles they create rights and duties for individuals within the states. Thus, they are means of achieving uniformity of law within the community states. On many issues complete uniformity may not be possible or desirable, given the different national traditions and systems of law. For example, it would be difficult to draft a regulation establishing a uniform legal procedure for determining what amount to equal work. A state with an inquisitorial tradition might want to determine the question in a different way from one with an adversarial tradition like the United Kingdom. To meet this kind of difficulty, a Directive may be issued. A Directive requires each member state to achieve a particular result within a set time limit, but leaves the choice of method to the state. Directives are thus intended to achieve approximation and harmonisation of member states' laws but not uniformity.[8] A good example is the 1975 Directive[9] defining equal work for the purposes of Article 119 as including "work to which equal value is attributed" and requiring states to see that measures were taken to enforce that provision. The United Kingdom could have chosen to meet this requirement by introducing an inquisitorial process under which jobs would be evaluated by a special administrative body, or by the traditional adversarial process, *e.g.* by leaving the parties to argue their case before an industrial tribunal. In the event, the United Kingdom failed to do anything within the time limit and that is what a state cannot choose to do; Directives are binding on the state and consequently, in 1981 the E.C.J. held the United Kingdom to be in breach of the treaty.[10] In 1983 the United Kingdom finally responded by introducing a mixed process under which the parties can argue their case before an industrial tribunal which will itself be advised on the equal value point by an independent investigator.

The final secondary source is Decisions. A Decision is binding only on the states or individuals to whom it is addressed. It does not create rights or duties for anyone else. Unlike a Directive addressed to state, a Decision does not give any choice; it merely states what is to happen. It is often simply a means of applying the provisions of a more general Article or Regulation to a specific situation and individual.

Regulations, Directives and Decisions are used in support of each other. A good example is provided by the programme for completing the internal market by 1992. The programme aims to establish a market "without internal frontiers in which the free movement of goods, persons, services and capital is ensured."

The 1992 deadline for achieving the goal was thought to be so important that it was incorporated into the E.C. Treaty itself by a further amending treaty, the Single European Act of 1985. But the core of the 1992 programme consists of 300 proposed Directives with their associated Regulations and Decisions. Some of these will bite before 1992, *e.g.* 1990 is the date set for mutual recognition of professional qualifications. Of course, the "Achilles heel" remains implementation by the member states and controversy surrounds the extent to which centralised enforcement by the Commission is desirable.

THE ROLE OF THE E.C.J.

The Court consists of judges nominated by each of the member states. Its main jurisdiction is threefold. First, it may review the delegated legislation, holding it invalid if it is not in conformity with the Treaty provisions or general principles of law relating to its application such as the broad concepts of proportionality and equality. Secondly, it decides cases concerning alleged infringement of the Treaty by member states, *e.g.* the United Kingdom in breach of the Equal Valuation of Work Directive. The Court itself does not apply any sanction for breach; that is left to the Council. Thirdly, the Court rules on the interpretation of community law when asked to do so by national courts. Such a request should be made whenever the interpretation of the Treaty or delegated legislation is unclear. Thus in the 1980s United Kingdom courts have referred questions concerning the interpretation of Article 119 and its accompanying Directives to the Court on a dozen or so occasions. Once the Court has ruled on interpretation, it is left to the national court to apply the interpretation to the facts of the case. Thus the function of the Court is not to act as a Supreme Court hearing appeals from national courts; rather it is simply to ensure uniformity of interpretation throughout the community.

THE COURT AND ITS LEGAL METHOD

We will now examine two aspects of the Court's approach to its task; first, its procedure and secondly, its method of interpreting Community law. Finally, we will conclude by considering the challenge presented to English legal method.

The Procedure of the Court

Arguably it is the procedure of the Court which provides the greatest contrast of approach. Whilst English courts follow an oral, adversarial procedure, the E.C.J. follows the continental model of a largely written, inquisitorial procedure.[11] The parties to a case and other affected bodies first submit written arguments to the Court. A judge is then appointed to investigate further by collecting relevant evidence, hearing and questioning witnesses. Only then will the Court hear the oral arguments of the parties, but without any of the adversarial characteristics of an English oral trial, *e.g.* there is no cross-examination by the parties' lawyers. After the oral stage comes another feature unknown to English procedure, the opinion of the advocate-general. There are a number of advocates-general attached to the Court and one of them will give an opinion in each case. Their role, which is based on French practice, is threefold; to propose a solution to the case; to relate that solution to the existing law and thirdly to outline probable future developments in the law. Their submissions are an invaluable supplement to the rather terse judgment which the Court itself then delivers. This judgment is given as the unanimous opinion of the Court and it is divided into two parts—the "motifs" (reasons) and the "dispositif" (ruling). As you will see from the example in Appendix 1, it is the opinion of the advocate-general and not the judgment of the Court which more resembles the style of an English court judgment.

Interpretation of Community Law

In its brief judgments the Court rarely says much about its approach to interpretation. However, one of its judges dealt with this question fully in a conference paper delivered in 1976. In that paper[12] Judge Kutscher identified four methods of interpretation which the Court adopts; the literal, historical, comparative and teleological. The first method is similar to the literal approach in English law but the problems confronting the Court are greater because the texts to be interpreted are in several languages. The advocates-general in particular may examine and compare the expressions used in the different texts but the problem is unlikely to be resolved by linguistic interpretation alone. Resort to other methods will be necessary. The historical method refers to the examination of the legislative history of the provision concerned to discover the intention of the draftsman. It involves a process rather similar to that undertaken by English courts when they seek to identify the legislative context of a particular statute (see page 154 *ante*). Like English courts, the E.C.J. is also cautious in the use it makes of "Travaux Préparatoires" (the proposals, drafts, etc., which have led to the provision) and places little or no reliance on the opinions of individual legislators or officials. The reason for this caution are summed up by one advocate-general as follows:

> "What members of the Council do when they adopt a regulation is agree on a text. They do not necessarily have the same views as to its meaning. That is to be sought, if necessary, by judicial interpretation of the text. It cannot be sought by inquiry from individual members of the Council. *A fortiori* it cannot be sought by ascertaining the view of the particular members of Parliament or of the Commission . . . however much they may have been concerned in the preparation of the text.[13]

Such reasons are of course very similar to those expressed by English courts when holding that reports of Parliamentary debates cannot be used when interpreting English statutes.[14]

If the first two methods bear some resemblance to those of an English court engaged in statutory interpretation, the latter two do not. The comparative method involves a comparison of the relevant laws of the member states to discover the general principles of law into which the interpretation of a particular provision must be fitted. For example, in one leading case[15] the Court had to decide to what extent investigatory powers given to the Commission by a Regulation were to be limited by the general principle that communications between a lawyer and his client are privileged, *i.e.* need not be disclosed to anyone else. The Regulation made no reference to any such qualification, but after comparing the different national laws on the point, the Court held that such a principle formed part of Community law and interpreted the Regulation as subject to it. Obviously this comparative method may raise problems. In our case, the national laws differed considerably in their approach to the question of privilege. The function of the Court, however, is not simply to find the lowest common denominator of all the laws but rather to attempt the more difficult task of finding the most appropriate principle to be applied. Teleological interpretation involves a similar process of discovering principles but this time by examining the broad nature of the Treaty. Thus in the first case[16] holding that Article 119 created rights to equal pay enforceable by individuals, the Court referred to the broad social and economic aims of the Treaty to support its interpretation.

Judge Kutscher made little reference to precedent. An English court interpreting legislation will be greatly influenced by and indeed may be bound by previous cases interpreting the statute. Not so the E.C.J. Like other continental courts it is not bound by its previous decisions. They may be influential and are frequently cited by the advocates-general, although less so by the Court. But just as influential are likely to be the writings of jurists analysing and commenting upon the provision. In the lawyer's privilege case, it was Judge Kutscher's conference paper itself which formed an important part of the advocate-general's argument. This attention to "doctrine" in the sense of jurists' writings is again a typical feature of continental legal method and one which we have discussed further in chapter 12.

The Challenge for English Legal Method

Shortly after the United Kingdom joined the community, Lord Denning stressed that when interpreting community laws, English judges must follow the European method. "No longer must they argue about precise grammatical sense. They must look to the purpose and intent . . . they must divine the spirit of the Treaty and gain inspiration from it. If they find a gap, they must fill it as best they can."[17] The recent decision of the House of Lords in *Pickstone* v. *Freemans plc.*[18] well illustrates the new approach. Mrs Pickstone worked as a warehouse operative. She was paid the same as the male warehouse operatives but less than a male warehouse checker. She claimed that she did work of equal value to that of the checker and that her lower pay was therefore in breach of the Equal Pay Act 1970. This provided a woman was entitled to be paid the same as a man where "(*a*) the woman is employed on like work with [the] man . . . (*b*) where the woman is employed on work rated as equivalent with that of [the] man . . . (*c*) where a woman is employed on work, which not being work to which (*a*) or (*b*) applies, is . . . of equal value to that of [the] man." Construed literally, this provision did not help Mrs Pickstone. She was paid equally with the man on like work in conformity with provision (*a*) and since (*a*) applied to her, it appeared she had no right to claim under (*c*). However, Parliament had added (*c*) to the Act in 1983 and in the debates a government minister has stated that this was being done to meet the requirements of the "Equal Value" Directive and the subsequent E.C.J. decision ordering the United Kingdom to comply. The Lords took the view that the provision had to be construed "purposively in order to given effect to the manifest broad intention of Parliament." They examined the history of the provision, took account of the need to construe it in conformity with Community requirements and, departing from their normal practice, considered the Parliamentary debates. They concluded that Mrs. Pickstone could claim under head (*c*).

Pickstone shows how successfully our judges can respond to the challenge of a new method of interpretation. Perhaps the extent of that challenge should not be exaggerated. In the process of developing the common law our judges have frequently resorted to principles derived from a comparison of analogous cases and from the general spirit of the common law, *i.e.* methods similar to the comparative and teleological methods of the European Court.[19] The fact that they do not apply these methods to the interpretation of statutes is not because the methods are unfamiliar or the judges lack the ability, but rather because the judges are limited by their constitutional role as subordinate to the legislature and by the fact that our own domestic legislation is not usually drafted to contain a clear statement of aim upon which a teleological interpretation could be based. Given their constitutional freedom under the European Communities Act to interpret community law in the European way and, given appropriately drafted legislation of the European type, there is no reason why our judges should not be able to respond to the challenge. Indeed it may be that our legislature will learn from the experience and that, as Lord Scarman has commented:

"since membership of the European Communities has introduced into our law a style of legislation which by means of the lengthy recital (or preamble) identifies the material to which resort may be had in construing its provisions, Parliament will consider doing likewise in statutes where it would be appropriate, *e.g.* those based on a report by the Law Commission, a Royal Commission or other law reform body.[20]

European Community law presents a real challenge at a different level, in the demands it makes on the legal profession. They must be able to advise their clients as effectively on the complexities of Community law as they do on domestic law. They must understand the nature and tactics of litigation before the European Court as well as they understand those considerations in the domestic context. In the future it may be as important for them to understand how the European Court will review the legality of community delegated legislation on the basis of such principles as proportionality and equality as to understand how an English court will review our own delegated legislation on the basis of *ultra vires*, *i.e.* exceeding statutory powers. The arrival of the Single Market in 1992 will increase both the pressures and opportunities to become familiar with the European legal method. This then is the real challenge of the community. Not so much a challenge to the common law method but rather a challenge to lawyers, practitioners, teachers and students alike to understand the role of a different method and system of law operating alongside our own and having an increasingly complex relationship with it.

Notes

[1] For a collection of 12 essays describing the influence of Europe on English domestic law see: Furmston, Kerridge & Sufrin (eds.), *The Effect on English Domestic Law of Membership of the European Communities and of Ratification of the European Convention on Human Rights*, Nijhoff 1983. In this chapter we have drawn in particular on Essay 1, *Influences on Judicial Reasoning*, by David Feldman, and to a lesser extent on essays 9, 10 and 12.

[2] *Malone* v. *M.P.C. (No. 2)* [1979] Ch. 344. Malone subsequently took his case to Europe. The Human Rights Commission has ruled in his favour, (1981) 4 E.H.R.R. 330, and the European Court of Human Rights upheld that ruling: *Malone* v. *United Kingdom* (1984) 7 E.H.R.R. 17.

[3] *Sunday Times* v. *United Kingdom* (1979) 2 E.H.R.R. 245.

[4] *Young, James and Webster* v. *United Kingdom* [1981] I.R.L.R. 408. EHRR ref.

[5] Lord Scarman has indeed suggested that this challenge can only be met fully by introducing a new constitutional settlement embodying fundamental rights: Scarman, *English Law, the New Dimension*, Parts II and VII.

[6] See generally Lasok and Bridge, *Law and Institutions of the European Communities* (1987, 4th ed.).

[7] *Macarthys Ltd.* v. *Smith* [1981] 1 All E.R. 111.

[8] Directives are normally only binding on the state. They do not create rights and duties for individuals within the state. However, the European Court has held that once the time limit has expired, a Directive which is sufficiently precise may give individuals rights against the state and possibly against other individuals although there is no decision on this latter point. Underlying this view is in part the feeling that by giving a Directive such an effect against the state, the pressure on the state to introduce implementing legislation may be stregthened. This would be a reason for allowing an individual to enforce a Directive against the state but not another individual although in some circumstances this wider enforcement might be considered desirable for reasons of consistency, *e.g.* it would be odd if an individual could enforce the equal work conditions Directive if his employer was a state airline but not if it was a private airline. See further Bebr, *Development of Judicial Control of the European Communities*, Nijhoff 1981, pp. 584–588, 596–602.

[9] Directive 75/117.

[10] *European Commission* v. *United Kingdom*, Case 61/81, [1982] E.C.R. 2601.

[11] See Lasok and Bridge, *Law and Institutions of the European Communities*, Chap. 9.

[12] *"Methods of Interpretation as seen by a Judge at the Court of Justice,"* Judicial and Academic Conference 1976.

[13] *National Panasonic (U.K.) Ltd.* v. *E.C. Commission* [1981] 2 All E.R. 1. (E.C.J.).

[14] See, *e.g.*, *Black-Clawson International Ltd.* v. *Papierwerke Waldhof-Aschaffenberg A.G.* [1975] A.C. 591 (H.L.).

[15] *A.M. & S. Europe Ltd.* v. *E.C. Commissiion* [1983] 1 All E.R. 705 (E.C.J.).

[16] *Defrenne* v. *Sabena* [1981] 1 All E.R. 122 (E.C.J.).

[17] *H. P. Bulmer* v. *J. Bollinger S.A.* [1974] Ch. 401.

[18] [1988] 2 All E.R. 803.

[19] See Warner, "Some Aspects of the European Court" (1976) 14 J.S.P.T.L.(N.S.) 15 where the author, a past advocate-general, makes this comparison

between the Court interpreting the treaty articles and an English court developing the common law. In other respects, too, he suggests that the differences of method are not so great as commonly thought.

[20] *Davis* v. *Johnson* [1979] A.C. 264 at p. 350 (H.L.).

BOOK III

Wider Dimensions of the Law and Legal Method

Chapter 14

THE CHANGING LAW

Law students are constantly being asked not just what the law
is, but how it should be changed. The question is important.
Laws do not remain static for long. To understand the nature
of law, one needs to understand why and how it can change
and the role played by lawyers in the process of change.

THE NATURE OF LEGAL CHANGE

Discussion of legal change may raise two different types of
questions: first, how should the law be changed to meet
changing social goals and policies. Secondly, how should the
law be changed to give greater coherence and sense to the
existing framework of principles. In his book *Law and Society*,
Professor Sawer describes the first type of change as "policy
change" and suggests that this type of change will be most
clearly associated with what he terms "social administration
law," *e.g.* laws concerned with social welfare, regulation of the
economy and environment or promotion of social policies such
as good race relations. The second type of change he refers to
as "law reform" and suggests that it is most closely associated
with "lawyers' law," that is the technical law primarily
developed by lawyers such as tort, contract or equity.[1]

Obviously the distinction between the two types of law and
types of change is not always so clear. Professor Sawer

225

observes that particular aspects of lawyers' law may occasionally "become connected with questions of social administration." Thus, recent criticisms of the operation of tort law have led to suggestions that it should be replaced by a system of state compensation for all accident victims. This clearly raises an issue of social policy. Equally an area of social administration law, originally created in response to tsocial change, may subsequently be left to the lawyers to develop and may be subject to "law reform" changes to give greater coherence to its principles. Nevertheless, despite the overlap between the types of law and types of change, the distinction provides a useful basis for our discussion. We shall consider, first, legal change in response to policy and then law reform in its narrower sense.

LEGAL CHANGE AND LEGAL POLICY

There is a rough correspondence between the laws of a society and its policies, goals and attitudes. Thus to take a crude example, the laws of the United Kingdom and the U.S.A. tend to reflect the individualistic, libertarian nature of our society while those of the U.S.S.R. reflect the collectivist, corporate nature of their society. But the differences between the two types of legal system also reflect other historical traditions as to the role of law in society and, as we shall see in the next chapter, this is particularly the case with countries such as China and Japan. Law is not simply a passive embodiment of the goals of a particular society, it also has its own traditions, principles and concepts. To quote Professor Sawer again, the relationship of law and society is "a two-way process in which the relative roles of social behaviour and legal norms are both important."[2]

Seen in this light, it is not surprising to find that changes in social policy or behaviour are not always reflected in the law. It may be possible to adapt the concepts of the law to new circumstances without any dramatic outward change. Thus, the modern development of credit sales has been met by an adaptation of the old concepts of hire and option to purchase and the gradual development of a body of hire purchase law. Again, for a variety of reasons the law may remain totally unchanged, leaving new social conditions to be dealt with by other techniques. Thus collective bargaining which forms the basis of industrial relations is largely unregulated by the law. Until recently the concepts of employment law have remained rooted in the social conditions of an earlier age, in the notion of the "master-servant" relationship. Such gaps between legal theory and social reality are not uncommon and not necessarily a weakness in our system.[3] But for the most part law is gradually adjusted to reflect social changes. Indeed, it may be used to promote changes in social attitudes. Recent legislation designed to prevent discrimination against persons on the grounds of race or sex is a good example. It aims to transform public behaviour. That is its social goal. Evidently the relationship of legal change and social policy presents a complex pattern and much literature has been devoted to its study. Our primary concern here is with a somewhat narrower issue, that of the methods used to achieve such change.

LEGAL CHANGE AND LEGAL METHOD

Legal change of the kind we have just discussed is normally regarded as being a matter for the legislature and not for the judges. Lord Reid has put the point in the following terms[4]: "Matters which directly affect the lives and interests of large sections of the community and which raise issues which are the subject of public controversy, and on which laymen are as well able to decide as are lawyers. On such matters it is not for the courts to proceed on their view of public policy for that would be to encroach on the province of Parliament." It is the province of Parliament to deal with such issues for under our Constitution,[5] it is Parliament or rather the dominant House of Commons which is answerable to the people. The judges are not so answerable and for them to deal with such issues would appear undemocratic.[6]

The democratic ideal suggests that the proposal to make such legal changes should be part of a party's election mani-

festo and hence part of its mandate if elected and that the
details of the change should be determined by the elected
M.P.s. In reality the picture is not so simple. Only part of a
government's eventual legislative programme may appear in
its manifesto. Other proposals may arise during its period in
office in response to particular pressures both within and
outside Parliament.[7] Pressure groups representing particular
sections of the community such as the T.U.C. or C.B.I. or
representing particular causes, such as housing the homeless
in the case of Shelter, may play a significant role in persuading
the government to introduce legal change. The homeless
persons legislation discussed in chapter 10 is a good example of
the different pressures. Its origin in the 1970s owed much to
the work of the pressure group Shelter outside Parliament and
the existence of the Lib-Lab pact within Parliament. The details
of the legal change are usually incorporated in legislation
which is debated in Parliament but again the details are
perhaps as much influenced by pressure groups and above all,
by the civil service through its advice to government departments. The details can affect the whole tenor of the change. It
was the detailed amendments to the homeless persons legislation which led one commentator to describe it as a "perfect
example of a liberal ideal seized upon by a reactionary element
and converted to a form not insignificantly antipathetic to its
original intent."[8] The M.P.s, caught up in party politics,
following the instructions of a whip, may have little real say in
either the proposal or its details.

Legal changes on social issues are normally the product of
political pressures of the kind we have briefly described. For a
variety of reasons, governments may occasionally adopt a
different approach to problems of legal change; they may refer
the question to a Royal Commission, a body of a dozen or so
eminent individuals selected for their knowledge of the particular issue or the balance of their interests and views, *e.g.*
Northerners and Southerners, the "left" and the "right," male
and female, etc. The Commission will spend a considerable
amount of time (and money) investigating the problem and
finally make a recommendation. In the 15 years between 1964
and 1979, 19 such Commissions were established. Not all dealt
with major issues but some did. Perhaps the three best known

recent examples are those concerning accident compensation, legal services and criminal procedure. They are often referred to as the Pearson Commission, the Benson Commission and the Phillips Commission after their respective chairmen. As a method of introducing change, the Commissions have been subject to considerable criticism.[9] They have been seen by some as a tactical device to legitimate government inactivity—they give the government a breathing space of three or four years whilst they investigate, report and their report is considered. Not surprisingly their recommendations often reflect a compromise between the balanced factions making up the Commission, a compromise which may not attract much support from politicians with one eye on their own supporting faction. In the case of our three examples little has so far been done to implement their recommendations. No Royal Commissions have been established since 1979. Perhaps in reaction to the failures of compromise, the present government has preferred to take direct responsibility for formulating change, consulting as necessary to ease the introduction of new policies. Thus the 1989 proposals for reform of the legal profession and the N.H.S. were introduced respectively by Green Papers and White Papers. (Green Papers contain a statement of provisional views and invite full consultation whilst White Papers embody more of a commitment to a particular strategy.) Whether this more radical approach to reform will prove to be more successful than the consensus approach of the past only time will tell.

LAW REFORM AND LEGAL METHOD

The judges play a relatively minor role in promoting the kind of legal change we have just discussed. To an extent both they and the legal profession as a whole may function as a pressure group, particularly influential when their work is likely to be affected by any change—as was the case with the three Royal Commission topics we mentioned. The Law Lords may also exert a direct influence on the details of changes through their Parliamentary position in the legislative House of Lords. But by and large, the judges would adhere to the view of Lord Reid that such matters are not properly within their province. However, when it comes to "lawyers' law," to reform any legal rules and principles developed over many years largely through the case law decisions of the judges, there seems to be little constitutional objection to judges changing or reforming that law. In recent years the judges have displayed an increasing willingness to overturn old case law and develop new principles more appropriate to modern conditions. The rise and fall of liability for defective property which we traced in chapter 8 is an example of the new found freedom of judges to direct the development of the law. Nevertheless there are limitations to judicial decision-making as a method of law reform.

LIMITATIONS OF JUDICIAL LAW REFORM

Apart from the doctrines of precedent and *stare decisis* which we discussed in chapter 7, there are three further considerations which limit the potential of judicial law reform. First, any judicial change of the law will have a retrospective effect for the parties—this could only be avoided if English courts adopt the American practice of prospective overruling. As a consequence, judicial change may produce injustice for those who have organised their affairs, *e.g.* by effecting insurance policies or settling claims on the basis of the old law.[10] Secondly, the lack of information presented to the judge may inhibit change. It may be easy for the judge to realise that the present law is wrong, less easy on the basis of the limited information relating to the particular case before him to know what general principles applicable to all cases should replace the existing law.[11] A third related problem arises where the proposed reform requires not simply the replacement of one general principle with another but rather with more detailed provisions. The court can explain how a reform applies to the particular case before it and leave future cases to work out the details of the reform in other factual contexts[12] but the resulting uncertainty may produce more injustice than leaving the law unreformed. Where law reform demands a wide ranging investigation of available information and detailed reforming provisions with no retrospective effect, the courts are clearly not the most appropriate medium. Rather the task is better left to the permanent law reform agencies.

PERMANENT LAW REFORM AGENCIES

The main law reform agency in England and Wales is the Law Commission which was established in 1965. The Commission was given a responsibility to promote law reform on issues of its own choice and those referred to it by government. Its staff of expert lawyers prepare working papers containing provisional recommendations for reform. These are publicised and, following wide consultation with both the legal profession and other interested parties, the Commission will submit a final report on the reform proposal along with a draft bill containing the details. Not all types of reform issues are considered by the Commission. The more technical and less controversial issues of criminal or civil law are often referred to more specialist agencies, the Criminal Law Revision Committee and the Law Reform Committee respectively. At the other extreme issues which raise important political and policy considerations, *e.g.* labour law or constitutional law issues, may be withheld from the Law Commission—often being referred instead to a Royal Commission. Despite these limitations, the Law Commission has been highly successful. By the end of 1989 it had produced well over 100 reform proposals, over three quarters of which have been implemented by legislation. In the view of one of its past chairmen, Lord Justice Kerr, its only real problems have concerned its attempt at codification which we discussed earlier in chapter 11, and its difficulty in finding parliamentary time for consideration of its proposals.[13]

THE PATTERN OF LEGAL CHANGE

We have examined the main methods by which legal change is promoted. In practice particular changes do not fit as neatly under one or other head as our description might imply. For example, the question whether there should be a change in the law which gives a person accused of an offence a "right to silence" when being questioned has been considered by judges, the Criminal Law Revision Committee, a Royal Commission and the government. It could not be said that there was just one appropriate method for considering a change of law on this topic. Perhaps the best way to convey an impression of the varied pattern of legal change and its methods is to take a particular area of law. In the remaining part of this chapter we will consider some particular changes in the law of tort.

CHANGING TORT LAW

The law of tort has undergone considerable change in recent years. The judges have played an active role in developing new principles. The law reform agencies have produced a dozen or so reports recommending change and many of these have been implemented. A Royal Commission has spent several years considering the wider reform of tort law. To survey this whole changing scene is not possible within the confines of this book. Instead, we will concentrate on three particular issues; first, the relatively technical but nonetheless very important issue of compensation for loss of future earnings; secondly a broader issue of principle, whether there should be liability for defective premises; thirdly, a fundamental issue of social policy, whether a state benefit scheme should replace tort law as the method of compensating accident victims.

Compensation for Loss of Future Earnings—The Lost Years Rule

A person injured by the negligence of a defendant is able to claim from him compensation for his loss of future earnings caused by the injury. However, there was a clear rule stemming from the case of *Oliver* v. *Ashman*[14] to the effect that if his injury had reduced his life expectancy, his future earnings compensation would only cover the period of his reduced expectancy. It would not cover the years of life expectancy that he had lost. Thus a man injured at the age of 35 with his life expectancy reduced as a result to 40, would only be compensated for five years of future earnings loss—his actual life expectancy. He would receive nothing for his lost 25 years' earnings. The harshness of this rule was mitigated to some extent by the fact that on his death his dependants had a statutory right under the Fatal Accidents Acts to claim compensation for the loss of financial benefit that they would have expected to receive from the full period of his life. The dependants' compensation was not affected by the victim's lost years of life expectancy. However their statutory claim for compensation was only available after the victim's death and only if the victim had not obtained compensation himself during his reduced lifetime. Thus in our example of the 35 year old with life expectancy reduced to 40, he and his family would be faced by a cruel dilemma. Should he take compensation now, thus easing any financial problems in his last few years but in the knowledge that he and his family were forever foregoing compensation for his "lost years," earnings; or should he take no compensation, die in circumstances of financial hardship but with the knowledge that his family would have a full claim for compensation unaffected by his lost years? It was clear that the *Oliver* rule produced injustice and needed to be changed—but how and by whom?

Reform was considered first by the Law Commission. Assessment of damages was one of the items selected for its first programme of reform. In 1973 it recommended that the *Oliver* rule be abolished but that the compensation for the lost years be limited to the losses suffered by the dependants.[15] The Commission considered that this result could be achieved by three alternative means: first, the victim could be entitled to claim compensation for his lost years' earnings minus what he would have spent on himself in those years; secondly, the victim could be allowed to "join" his dependants in his legal action so that he would be compensated for earnings in his lost years to the extent of their dependancy; thirdly, the victim could claim compensation for earnings during his actual life expectancy and on his death his dependants could be allowed a further claim for the extent of their dependancy. All three proposals would produce roughly the same result and in particular they would have resulted in a victim without dependants getting no more than his actual life expectancy earnings as compensation. Of the three proposals the Commission favoured the first. To appreciate the reason for their choice one would have to read their detailed report but what should be clear from this discussion is that the reversal of the *Oliver* rule needed to be accompanied by detailed provisions to prevent over-compensation beyond the needs of dependants. The Commission's draft Bill detailing the reform did not reach Parliament, for just as the Commission was completing its work, the government established a Royal Commission to undertake a wider review of compensation principles. Obviously there was no point enacting the Law Commission's proposals if there was a possibility that they would be superseded. In fact the Royal Commission endorsed the Law Commission's proposals for reform of the *Oliver* rule but their report was not published until 1978 and by that time the rule had been considered by the House of Lords in the case of *Pickett* v. *British Rail*.[16]

The *Pickett* case was a classic illustration of the injustice caused by the *Oliver* rule. Pickett was a fit man of 50 when he developed lung disease due to the fact that his employer had negligently allowed him to be exposed to asbestos dust. He decided to claim compensation and at the time of his action his life expectancy had been reduced to one year by the disease. At the trial he was awarded future loss of earnings compensation for just that one year—£1,500. His wife and two children got nothing in respect of the further 15 or so years during which he would otherwise have been able to support them from his earnings. As he had chosen to sue, they would not be able to bring an action under the Fatal Accident Acts once he was dead. On appeal, the House of Lords overturned the *Oliver* rule and gave compensation for loss of earnings in the lost years. The Law Lords supported their decision by reference to the obvious injustice of the old rule and the reform recommendations of the Law Commission. They realised that reversing the rule could lead to over-compensation but as the facts of the particular case did not raise that particular problem, no solution was necessary. Lord Wilberforce said:

"If there is a choice between taking a view of the law which mitigates a clear and recognised injustice in cases of normal occurrence, at the cost of the possibility in fewer cases of excess payments being made, or leaving the law as it is, I think our duty is clear. We should carry the judicial process of seeking a just principle as far as we can, confident that a wise legislator will correct resultant anomalies."

Unfortunately, to the extent that the legislature was at all concerned, it was with the broader implications of the Royal Commission report and it was the House of Lords itself which was left to face the anomalies. In the words of Lord Denning,[17] the "chickens came home to roost" in the case of *Gammell* v. *Wilson*.[18] Gammell was a young man of 22 when he was killed in a motor accident caused by the negligence of the defendant. Obviously he could not sue. However, there is a general rule of law under which when a person dies his causes of action, *i.e.* the claims he could have brought, pass to his estate, *i.e.* usually his next of kin. Gammell's next of kin, his father, sued on behalf of the dead man. Before *Pickett*, he would have received no compensation for loss of future earnings as his son, being killed instantly, had no expectation of life; all his years were lost. However, following the logic of the *Pickett* decision, the Lords reluctantly awarded the father £6,500 compensation in respect of the lost years' earnings. Father Gammell had indeed suffered a great sadness in the loss of his son but he had suffered little financial loss as a dependant and he would have been entitled to far less under the Fatal Accidents Act than he actually received by suing on behalf of the estate. The compensation was, in this sense, a pure windfall. The Lords all regretted this result. The law, said Lord Diplock, had "reached a state for which I can see no social, moral or logical justification." But they recognised that it was their own fault and that only the legislature could extricate them from the "morass." Lord Scarman suggested that the legislature should solve the particular problem by providing the claims for loss of earnings for the lost years should not pass to the deceased's estate with the result that the next of kin could only claim if they were dependants and not simply because they were inheritors of the estate.

This proposal has now been implemented in the Administration of Justice Act 1982. This Act contains a number of fragmented reforms on different topics. When introducing it in Parliament, Lord Hailsham described it as "darning old socks." As one commentator has suggested,[19] buying new socks might have been preferable. The Law Commission's detailed proposals would have provided such a new sock. Without it, more darning may be necessary. Only the most blatant example of over-compensation has been dealt with. The other problems foreseen by the Law Commission remain.

Liability for Defective Premises

An owner of premises was for long regarded as owing no duty of care to anyone to whom he sold them. The owner might negligently have built a house or indeed a housing estate with the result that many years later the premises suffered from subsidence, but under the old rule he would not have been liable to the purchasers. However, if the builder was not also the owner/seller he would have been liable to the purchasers under the general *Donoghue* v. *Stevenson* principle. Thus a house purchaser's rights against a negligent builder depended entirely upon whether the builder was also the owner, a result which was capricious, unjust and, in the light of the steadily widening *Donoghue* duty principle, increasingly anomalous.

As with the assessment of damages, this problem was also included in the Law Commission's first programme of reform. The Commission reported in 1970 recommending that the owner's immunity from negligence liability should be abolished.[20] The Commission went further and recommended that all those who undertake work in connection with dwellings should owe a duty of care to anyone acquiring an interest in the property to see that their work was done in a proper manner. This duty would obviously be broken by a negligent builder but also by one who simply provided work of a defective quality. Finally, the Commission recommended that the limitation period for bringing a claim for breach of this proposed duty should be six years from the date of completion of the work. These recommendations were enacted in the Defective Premises Act 1972, section 1 of which established the new statutory duty and section 3 abolished the owners' immunity.

By an unfortunate coincidence, just after the Defective Premises Bill was introduced into Parliament in December 1971, the Court of Appeal itself decided upon reform in its decision in *Dutton* v. *Bognor Regis U.D.C.*[21] There the majority stated that the owner immunity principle was wrong and that a builder/owner owed a duty of care like anyone else. Subsequent cases have clearly established this to be the new common law. Thus with the decision in *Dutton*, section 3 of the Act became redundant. It is, in the words of one commentator,[22] "an unparalleled instance of legislation being otiose before it has even been passed."

Worse was to follow. In *Dutton*, Lord Denning had stated that the six year limitation period for common law claims against the builder should run from the date of his negligent work, as that and not the date when cracks appeared was the date of the damage and limitation periods for the tort of negligence run from the date of damage. At least on this basis, a plaintiff would not be disadvantaged by suing under the statute rather than under common law and section 1 would still offer the advantage of imposing a stricter duty on the builder. But in a case called *Sparham-Souter* v. *Town & Country Developments*[23] in 1976, Lord Denning and the Court of Appeal changed their view as to the date from which the common law limitation period should run. Now they decided that the period should run only from the date on which the damage might reasonably have been discovered by the plaintiff. Take the common case where the evidence of the builder's negligent work, the subsidence, etc., does not appear until more than six years from the completion of work: the plaintiff could not sue the builder under section 1 of the Act as the statutory limitation period has expired but he could sue at common law following the *Sparham-Souter* decision. The Court in *Sparham-Souter* recognised that their decision effectively out-reformed the reform legislation but they saw the problem in terms of a lack of co-ordination. Roskill L.J. said, "in the [early 1970s] law reform was being pursued through two different channels, the Law

Commission and Parliament on the one hand, and the court on the other . . . without either apparently appreciating what developments the other was seeking to make."

Sparham-Souter upset the neat pattern of law reform recommended by the Law Commission, but worse still was to follow. What it did was to open up the possibility of claims against the builder and others being brought many years after the completion of the work. In *Dennis* v. *Charnwood B.C.*[24] in 1982, the house owners brought a claim over 25 years after the house was completed. They succeeded because the damage that occurred could not reasonably have been discovered until 21 years from completion and they claimed within six years from that date. In fact the owners in this case sued the local authority for negligently approving the builder's poor foundations. They did not sue the building firm probably because they were no longer in existence. Many claims of this nature have been made against local authorities. The long periods between completion and claim puts them in a very difficult position. Many will not have any records relating to what they did thirty years ago. In his concluding remarks in *Dennis*, Lawton L.J. suggested that a compulsory insurance scheme for builders might solve the problem, but this type of reform is certainly beyond the scope of the judiciary and most likely the Law Commission as well.

The House of Lords then moved to provide at least a temporary half-solution. In late 1982 in the case of *Pirelli General Cable Works Ltd.* v. *(Oscar) Faber & Partners*,[25] they decided that both the views of limitation periods taken in *Sparham-Souter* and *Dutton* were wrong. The period should run from the date when the damage actually occurred. This might be years before it could have been reasonably discovered but equally it might be years after completion. However, the judges recognised that this solution was a stop-gap, pending comprehensive legislation. As Lord Scarman said:

"The reform needed is not the substitution of a new principle or rule of law for an existing one but a detailed set of provisions to replace existing statute law. The true way forward is not departure from precedent but by amending legislation."

This came with the Latent Damage Act 1986, which introduced a complex compromise under which there is a basic six year limitation period running from the date of damage, a further three year period running from the date of discoverability of the damage, and a final "cut off" period of 15 years from the date of negligence beyond which no action can be brought.

Compensating Accident Victims

Under the principles of tort law the victim of an accident can generally only claim compensation from the person causing the accident if he was at fault in being negligent. As we have seen from our discussion of the *Whitehouse* case in chapter 5, it may be very difficult to prove such negligence. There may be no witnesses to the accident. They may have disappeared or they may be unable to recall the events precisely at the trial many years later. In addition to this "fault" based compensation system of tort law, there is a "no-fault" state compensation system which applies to accidents at work. The victim of such an accident may be entitled to injury benefits paid by the state whether or not anyone was at fault in causing the accident. Other common law countries have gone further along this "no-fault" road. In Canada there have been "no-fault compensation" schemes for victims of road accidents for many years. In 1967 a Royal Commission in New Zealand recommended a much broader "no-fault" scheme for a wide range of accident victims and also recommended the abolition of the tort action for injuries covered by the scheme. These proposals were implemented in 1972.

Against this background, pressure developed in the 1960s to change the mainly fault based system operating in the United Kingdom but it was not until the "thalidomide" tragedy was brought fully to light by the media in 1972 that any official action to promote change was taken. In November 1972 the government requested the Law Commission to investigate the issue of civil liability for ante-natal injuries, *i.e.* injuries of the "thalidomide" type caused to the child before birth. The following month a Royal Commission was established to examine the broader question of civil liability for personal injuries. In 1974 the Law Commission recommended that, with some qualifications, a child should have the right to sue in respect of

injuries caused before birth through the negligence of the
defendant.[26] This recommendation was enacted in the Congeni-
tal Disabilities (Civil Liability) Act 1976. Although this legislation resolved previous doubts whether a child could sue for
such injuries, it did nothing to alter the "fault" principle.
Victims of a "thalidomide" type of tragedy would still have to
show that someone had acted negligently and this would still
present a major problem.[27] It was this in part which led the
Royal Commission to criticise the Law Commission's proposals. The Royal Commission chairman commented that the
legislation:

> "so far from dealing comprehensively with a highly distress-
> ing social problem, could result in compensation for no
> more than a minute proportion of the children concerned.
> The legislation therefore would raise many false hopes, not
> least by its very title."[28]

Unlike the Law Commission, the Royal Commission had the
advantage of undertaking a comprehensive review of the
compensation problem, but when it reported in 1978[29] it was
evident that it had not been able to agree upon a coherent
overall approach to the problem. For most types of injury it
recommended little change in the law but in the case of
severely damaged children it did recommend a new state social
security benefit payable whether or not their damage was
caused by negligence. But along with this "no-fault" system it
proposed to retain the "fault" based tort system as reformed by
the 1976 Disability Act. In the case of road accidents, its
recommendations followed a similar pattern—a "no-fault"
based benefit system similar to the industrial accident system
but the retention of "fault" based tort compensation. Where
was the money to come from to operate both "fault" and "no-
fault" compensation systems for damaged children and road
accident victims? In part the answer lay in a complex series of
recommendations by the Commission which would have had
the effect of reducing considerably the level of tort compensation in certain types of case. The savings in compensation on
the "fault" side could be seen as making way for greater
compensation on the "no-fault" side.

Some commentators have suggested[30] that the members of
the Commission split into three groups; those favouring the

abolition of tort and its replacement by a general "no-fault" system; those favouring the existing fault based system and thirdly those favouring a "wait and see" approach, *i.e.* try a "no-fault" system for just road accidents and damaged children, if it worked extend it and if that worked, abolish the tort action. The result was somewhat predictable. Lacking a clear principle behind which support could be galvanised, the Commission report was briefly debated by the politicians and then shelved. In 1982 a couple of its relatively minor recommendations including the abolition of the *Oliver* rule, where enacted in the Administration of Justice Act, but that is all. In the words of Lord Denning:

> "Nothing to remedy the injustice to the child or grown-up who is injured by another person's negligence but has no witness to prove it. Nothing to institute a system of no-fault liability. . . . Nothing done to reappraise the principles on which damages are to be assessed. . . . Five years in the lives of Lord Pearson and his colleagues have been spent in vain. Scurvy treatment by an ungrateful government."[31]

With major reform by the legislature unlikely, it may be left to the judiciary to introduce some element of reform by the back door. Some judges would like to see a "no-fault" system—see for example the comments of Lawton L.J., in the *Whitehouse* case, *ante* p. 71. This is beyond the scope of judicial law reform. Other judges have tried to make it easier for a plaintiff to prove that his injury was caused by the defendant's fault. Thus in a number of cases[32] the Court of Appeal took the view that the plaintiff need only prove that the defendant's fault had increased the chance of him suffering the injury in question, rather than having to prove that it had actually caused the injury. However, in 1988 in the case of *Wilsher* v. *Essex A.H.A.*[33] the House of Lords reasserted the orthodox principle that the plaintiff must actually prove that the fault caused the damage. Lord Bridge concluded his judgment thus:

> "Many may feel that such a result [the requirement of proving causation] serves only to highlight the shortcomings of a system in which the victim of some grievous misfortune will recover substantial compensation or none at all according to the unpredictable hazards of the forensic process. But,

The Changing Law

whether we like it or not, the law, which only Parliament can change, requires proof of fault causing damage as the basis of liability in tort."

Unfortunately Parliament, or rather the government, does not appear too interested in the problem.

CONCLUSION

The examples we have chosen do not illustrate a smooth progress of legal change by the most appropriate method. To an extent they may give an unfair impression for there are many areas of law where smooth change has been achieved, particularly through the activities of the Law Commission. But our examples do serve to counteract any impression created by the earlier section of the chapter, that legal change can be fitted into neat analytical compartments.

Our examples illustrate other problems too. They illustrate the difficulties of judicial law reform. In the case of the "lost years" problem, the courts were unable to produce a sufficiently comprehensive reform. Their step by step approach resulted in anomalies. In the case of defective premises, they produced a comprehensive change of principle but they failed to foresee all its consequences. Indeed, these were not simply confined to "lawyers' law" for they produced a situation in which local authorities were made widely responsible for defects in premises they had inspected many years ago. The examples also illustrate the problems facing law reform bodies. Where the bodies are asked to consider "lawyers' law," there is a risk that the judges will get there first and produce their own reforms. Where they are asked to consider broader policy matters, as was the case with accident compensation, there is a risk that the politicians who requested the investigation will not support its results.

Our conclusion is that although it is useful to analyse the different types of legal change and the different methods of achieving it, real life does not fit neatly into the categories. Reform of "lawyers' law" may indirectly raise issues of social policy and vice versa. Judges, reform agencies and politicians all have their own interest in promoting change. Rather than holding back to leave the matter to the most appropriate body, they may plunge in with the feeling that it is better to do something when the opportunity arises rather than to wait for the perfect time and approach. All this is part of the "internal dynamic" of the law. It is this dynamic—the ever changing nature of law—which makes its study both stimulating and challenging.

Notes

[1] Sawer, *Law in Society*, Chap. 8.
[2] Sawer, *Law in Society*, p. 171.
[3] The nature of such "gaps" is often studied in "Law & Society" courses and is discussed in such books as Roshier & Teff, *Law & Society*.
[4] *Pettit* v. *Pettit* [1970] A.C. 777 at p. 794.
[5] The position may be different under a constitution such as that of the United States which gives the judiciary a more active role.
[6] See the comments of Lord Simon in *Stock* v. *Frank Jones (Tipton) Ltd.* [1978] 1 All E.R. 948 at p. 953.
[7] See Farrar, *Law Reform and the Law Commission*, Chap. 6 and Roshier & Teff, *Law and Society*, Chap. 2.
[8] Arden (1977) 127 N.L.J. 1140.
[9] See particularly Thomas, "Royal Commissions," (1982) Stat.L.R. 40.
[10] See, *e.g.*, *Morgans* v. *Launchberry* [1973] A.C. 127 where the fear of upsetting insurance arrangements was one of the considerations which led the House of Lords to decide against making a change in the law which would have had retrospective effect.
[11] See the comments of Lord Simon in *Miliangos* v. *George Frank (Textiles) Ltd.* [1976] A.C. 477.
[12] This was the approach adopted by Megarry V.-C. in the case of *Ross* v. *Caunters* [1980] Ch. 297.
[13] Kerr (1980) 96 L.Q.R. 515.
[14] [1961] 1 Q.B. 337.
[15] Law Com. Report No. 56.
[16] [1980] A.C. 136.
[17] Denning, *What Next in the Law?*, p. 147.
[18] [1981] 2 W.L.R. 248.
[19] (1983) 46 M.L.R. 191.
[20] Law Com. Rep. No. 40.
[21] [1972] 1 Q.B. 373.
[22] Winfield & Jolowicz, *Tort* (11th ed.), p. 227.
[23] [1976] Q.B. 858.
[24] [1982] 3 W.L.R. 1064.
[25] [1983] 2 W.L.R. 6.
[26] Law Com. Rep. No. 60.

[27] See further Teff & Munro, *Thalidomide: The Legal Aftermath.*
[28] Letter of Lord Pearson to *The Times*, January 28, 1976.
[29] Royal Commission Report, Cmnd. 7054.
[30] See Atiyah's *Accidents, Compensation and the Law* (4th ed.).
[31] Denning, *What Next in the Law?*, p. 157.
[32] *Wilsher* v. *Essex A.H.A.* [1987] Q.B. 730; *Fitzgerald* v. *Lane* [1987] Q.B. 781.
[33] [1987] A.C. 750.

Chapter 15

COMPARATIVE LEGAL CULTURES AND METHOD

There are two tendencies which are often found amongst common lawyers which must be resisted at all costs. The first is the erroneous belief that the common law tradition is the most important legal tradition in the world and the second is a related belief that it is in every respect the best system in the world. The fact that these beliefs are common demonstrates the narrowness and bigotry of conventional legal education. In this chapter we shall attempt a preliminary study of some other legal traditions and cultures and their method. A principal reason for doing this will be, to paraphrase the Scots poet Robert Burns, to see ourselves as others see us.

THE CONCEPT OF LEGAL CULTURE

You may have noticed that we started off by talking about legal tradition, then we introduced the term culture. Both tradition and culture possess rather sponge-like qualities[1] but tradition can perhaps be regarded as a species of culture which has been handed down over a period of time.[2] Culture can include some more recent practices. Tradition has been described as a set of deeply rooted, historically conditioned attitudes about the nature of law, about the role of law in society and the political

245

system, about the proper organisation and operation of a legal
system, and about the way law is or should be made, applied,
studied and taught.[3] The legal tradition relates the legal system
to the culture of which it is a partial expression.

In the past it has been common amongst anthropologists to
analyse culture in terms of either patterns or social structure. In
so far as studies have been made of comparative legal cultures
they have generally been in terms of cultural patterns rather
than social structure. The literature has tended to adopt a
pluralist approach rather than a universalist one,[4] although
some sociologists of law adopting a Marxian analysis have
attempted a return to universalism through the identification of
dominant paradigms.[5] In this chapter we take a more relativist
approach. We recognise that, as Alan Watson has argued,[6] law
is more an expression of the culture of the lawmaking elite
rather than that of society at large, and that the variety of
interests and attitudes possessed by such elites may thwart
attempts to generalise.

TYPES OF LEGAL CULTURE

The common law tradition is not the oldest surviving legal
tradition in the world. The Civilian system which is the system
which prevails in Western Europe and Latin America as well as
Quebec and Louisiana is older.[7] It dates back to Roman law
although the law is now mostly contained in codes which are
the product of the nineteenth century.

Another major cultural grouping is what might be described
as the Communist system.[8] All the European countries which
are still under Communist domination were formerly countries
of the Civilian tradition. After revolution or in the case of some
of them invasion, they adopted Communist regimes, yet
within the Communist tradition traces of the old Civilian
background remain. One Communist country which stands
entirely outside this tradition is China and we shall have more
to say on this later.

There are a number of countries in the world which can be
subsumed under the heading of Islamic tradition as far as their

private law is concerned, but most of these countries were colonies of European powers and now have mixed systems. These countries are usually grouped for economic and political purposes under the heading of the Third World where they accompany the less developed members of the British Commonwealth, almost all of which inherited the common law tradition. Although these jurisdictions have received diverse laws they have problems of source and method which make it useful to group them together for comparison with the others.

The Civilian Tradition

This is the oldest of the surviving traditions and can perhaps be traced to 450 B.C., the date of the XII Tables in Rome which were a priestly codification of early Roman law.[9]

It is the tradition of the original six member states of the E.E.C. and Spain and Portugal together with their former colonies. It is the background to much of the early development of the E.E.C. and indeed it has had a strong influence on the development of both public and private international law.[10]

Roman law developed from a priestly system to a highly developed secular system through the influence of jurists (jurisconsults) who did not actually perform the function of a modern lawyer but wrote systematic treatises on particular branches of law. The law itself consisted of the *jus civile*, which only applied to citizens of the Roman empire, and the more flexible *jus gentium* which applied to non citizens. Both systems underwent considerable modification over centuries. In the sixth century A.D. the emperor Justinian arranged for the production of a Digest and codification of the law which assimilated the laws and doctrinal writings, eliminating conflict. Institutes were also prepared as a primer for law students. This mammoth work of rationalisation enabled Roman law to survive the decline and ultimate destruction of the Roman Empire.[11] The Roman law tradition survived the Dark Ages and was studied in the medieval universities as the basis of rational principles of law.

However, it not only survived as a scholarly tradition, but also as a source of common law of nations at a time when

Europe was subject to a multiplicity of local customs and laws.[12] Voltaire reckoned that one changed one's laws as often as one changed one's horse in riding through eighteenth century France. In arriving at a just solution of mercantile disputes Roman law was often resorted to on the Continent. It also influenced the development of the canon law of the Christian Church and the movement towards the early conceptions of international law.

So, therefore, an important ingredient in the civilian tradition is the common inheritance of Roman law. However, a combination of the enlightenment of the eighteenth century and revolution created an impetus to modern codification. This was achieved in the Napoleonic period in France at the beginning of the nineteenth century, although Frederick the Great had attempted a less successful codification of parts of Prussian law in the eighteenth century. The Code Napoléon was a masterly codification of French customary law and Roman law as it stood at 1804. Directly and indirectly it was the blueprint for much European codification.[13] Its basis was simple clear statements of law which left much unsaid. A different approach was adopted in the German codification measures of the end of the nineteenth century. Here the emphasis was on detail and a self contained code—every answer was to be found in the code itself. Most modern Civilian systems opt for one of these two models of codification although each system has areas of law which are not completely codified.

A further characteristic of Civilian systems is the high status accorded to doctrinal writings. While not a source of law as such they rank as high as or of higher status than judicial precedent as a guide to the interpretation of the codes.[14] Where the law is codified the code is the definitive source. The status of judicial precedent is naturally less than in common law systems. It is not that precedent is unimportant in practice but that in theory its validity derives from the words of the code itself. Individual precedents are not binding. A body of precedent is regarded as good evidence of the true meaning of the code.[15]

The Civilian tradition employs different terminology from English law with regard to interpretation, but as we have seen, the substance of the Civilian approaches does not differ too greatly from those of the Common Law. The basic approaches of both systems consist of a literal approach, a more liberal approach and a reluctance to admit extrinsic materials as aids to interpretation.[16]

Last, the Civilian tradition tends to employ more inquisitorial procedures with regard to fact finding than the common law and the whole of its procedure is administered by a career judiciary.[17]

The Common Law Tradition

Much of the common law tradition has been discussed already in earlier chapters. Here we shall mainly focus on the differences between it and the civilian tradition.

First, the common law, while slightly influenced by the form, did not receive the substance of the Roman law inheritance.[18] It steadfastly resisted it for reasons which were partly political and partly professional. Roman law was linked with Catholicism and later with Stuart autocracy. England, unlike Scotland, developed its own professional structure and tradition from an early date. This was until remarkably recently outside the university framework. English law was not taught at the universities until the eighteenth century, but was the province of the Inns of Court and the profession. The history of legal education in the seventeenth and eighteenth century is rather appalling.[19] Small parts of Roman law did influence some aspects of the common law, but this is mainly as a result of nineteenth century rationalisation.

Secondly, in spite of Bentham and the codification movement in the nineteenth century, the only area of codification has been in commercial law,—the Bills of Exchange Act 1882, the Partnership Act 1890, the Sale of Goods Act 1893 (now 1979) and the Marine Insurance Act 1906. These owe something to commercial pressures, but much to individual initiative.[20] The Law Commissions, although mandated to consider codification, have been unsuccessful and give the impression of being full of doubts as to its necessity.[21]

Thirdly, as we have seen, although text books by living authors are now cited there still is less status accorded to doctrinal writing in the common law tradition. The status seems to depend *ad hominem* to a greater extent than in the civilian system and reflects perhaps the closed social world of the English judiciary.[22]

Fourthly, the status of judicial precedent is much higher and it is an actual source of law. The standard of the judiciary in the common law world has been high and the process of ratiocination is more obvious in a common law judgment than in the bleak arrested style of a French judgment. As a continuing source, however, with the multiplication of reports the form of the law remains irrational and almost uncontrollable.

Fifthly, the terminology, but not necessarily the practice of interpretation, differs from the civilian tradition as we have seen.

Last, the common law tradition shows a marked preference for adversarial procedure before judges with forensic experience.[23] The emphasis is perhaps more on justice than on truth.[24]

Socialist Legal Culture

The Bolshevik revolution of 1917 was supposed to result in a victory of communism over the bourgeois state. Law as part of the bourgeois state was to wither away. In Russia, however, the legal tradition had never been strong, but at the time of the revolution Russia had at least in form a civilian system. This did not survive the revolution. It was replaced by party rule by means of administrative decrees. Law was to be replaced by economic and political regulation and administration. The result was chaos.

In 1921, however, there was a return to something approximating to law with the emphasis on contract. This was later swept away and a police state developed with greater resort to legal procedures as a means of control. Law nevertheless was and remains subordinate to party rule. In the last 20 years or so there has been an increase in laws and codes of law and recognition of limited rights of private property.[25] In other European communist countries established civilian systems have been replaced in whole or in part by communist legal culture.

Comparing these countries with the civilian and common law legal traditions the following points emerge. First, the Roman law inheritance is a thing of the past. It was replaced by Marxist Leninism which devalued traditional Western conceptions of law. Legal rights were subordinated to economic realities. The rule of law was superseded by the concept of Socialist legality. However, there are currently drastic changes in the Eastern bloc countries, and many are returning to the Rule of Law. The comments made here probably only relate to the USSR and even this is undergoing change.

Secondly, although codes of law are produced their status is problematic. Socialist legality means that legal rights, even fundamental rights, cannot ultimately be relied on in the face of party opposition. Nevertheless there is a recognised hierarchy of sources of law.[26] There is usually a constitution which is regarded as basic. From this the legislature derives its powers. Communist constitutions generally reject the doctrine of separation of powers and the constitution is capable of yielding on occasion to the expedience of the day expressed as subordinate legislation, decree or party directive of the highest level.

Thirdly, the laws themselves and the courts are regarded as secondary organs of society. The communist systems nevertheless seem to make greater use of education through adjudication both in local courts and larger show trials. The theory and practice of judical precedent seems to be closer to the Civilian tradition than that of the common law. Cases are not official sources but are often reported and referred to.[27]

Fourthly, the lower courts tend to follow a literal approach to interpretation of laws, but the ultimate purpose is to be derived from Party explanations of the Marxist Leninist context of the legislation. Soviet writers distinguish between authentic, judicial and doctrinal interpretation. Authentic interpretation is by the legislature, the Praesidium of the Supreme Soviet, which is given the power to give definitive interpretations under the Soviet Constitution. Judicial interpretations though binding in the particular case are not generally binding precedents for the future. However, the Supreme Court of the U.S.S.R. is empowered to give binding directives.[28] This perhaps represents a compromise between the Civilian and common law traditions[29] and is not unlike the relevant jurisdiction of the European Court of Justice. Russian courts make use of the analogy of the statute in civil matters. This is distinguished from extensive interpretation since it covers a *casus omissus*. Formerly, this was used in criminal law but this has now been abandoned in the higher courts.[30]

Last, the Communist approach uses both accusatorial and inquisitorial methods although there is perhaps a greater tendency to use the latter.

The Cultures Compared

Some writers suggest that each of these three cultures has its own internal logic, locking together its parts like a jigsaw.[31] Thus the logic of the common law system is centered around the role of law as a means of resolving disputes in courts. That of civil law is based upon the notion of law as a set of rules of conduct and that of socialist systems upon the educational and ideological role of law. It is further argued that an element from one culture cannot be transplanted into another because it will not fit into the jigsaw, the internal logic of the other system. Thus, it is said that codes will never fit properly within the common law system. We have reservations about this kind of argument. In the first place, it underestimates the variations of approach to be found within the same broad cultural heritage. In their approach to lawmaking for example, English judges behave more like their cautious continental cousins than their dynamic American brethren. Secondly, it underestimates the capacity for change within the lawmaking elite and the effect of outside pressures on that elite. Thus the pressures resulting from the government's reforms of profession and procedure in the 1980s and those resulting from the European market in legal services opening in 1992 may alter the picture of English legal culture and the shape of the jigsaw pieces that fit into it.

The Legal Cultures and Problems of the Third World

Most of the countries in the Third World were colonies of European countries. As such they inherited either the civilian or common law traditions. Where there was an established religion such as Islam or Hinduism with a developed system of private law the colonial regimes often left that part intact, although they eventually tended to take control of the administration of the court systems. In some countries such as those of the Middle East the position is further complicated by virtue of earlier colonisation by a foreign power and by developments after independence. The Moghul and Ottoman empires imposed their own systems and parts of the law were codified. Later, many of the countries fell under Western influence. After independence some countries fell under the influence of another similar country which in its turn was influenced by a former colonial power. A classic case is Jordan where a traditional Islamic system was replaced in part by Ottoman law which was partly codified in the nineteenth century. Jordan after independence fell under English influence. Later it was influenced by Egypt which in its turn had been influenced by French legal culture. Jordan then returned to English law for some aspects of its commercial law.

Another striking example is Japan which is not regarded as a member of the Third World. Japan had a traditional system for centuries but then since 1868 adopted a policy of thoroughgoing westernisation of its laws. In carrying out this policy it borrowed from both the Civilian and common law traditions. However, it has been asserted that in the actual process of adjudication and settling of disputes traditional attitudes often prevail.[32] China is perhaps now undergoing the same kind of transition in legal culture. Ancient China had a traditional system of Mandarin adjudication and had merely taken a few fitful steps towards a Western legal system at the time of the Communist revolution. One result of this which cannot be over emphasised is the lack of a legal language in the sense of specialised terminology.[33] Mao for a time favoured the abolition of law and legal procedures but now, with the increasing emphasis on the importance of commerce, the government has been developing commercial law, *e.g.* on patents, along western lines. In other areas the position of law has never been and is never likely to be high.

India represents an even more complicated story. A Hindu tradition was subjected to Moslem domination and then the introduction of much of the substance of the English common law mainly through the medium of codes, a Civilian technique. While India is now generally regarded as falling within the common law world much social life particularly in rural areas is influenced more by traditional Hindu practice. The result is a complex mixture. The common law postulates equality before the law, which contradicts the caste system. The common law method has a narrower approach to a case and what is considered relevant and admissible in argument and evidence. It also makes a final decision which is enforced. Whereas justice is blind, lawyers are partisan. These latter factors ran counter to traditional methods of settling disputes. The recording of customary law in a body of precedents tended to fossilise it. The result of the adoption of the common law method has been control and chaos. The courts have been much used but respect for the law has diminished. The imposition of the courts had damaged the traditional methods of solving disputes. The common law has thus some of the characteristics of an external law, centrally imposed. This has continued after independence because of the continuation of central control. At times attempts have been made to seek internal model alternatives in the form of panchayats or local village councils, but with no great success.[34] Law through the medium of legislation is increasingly used to unify, modernise and to secularise Indian society.

The legal cultural problems of such countries are many and acute. A basic problem is one of establishing an independent legal identity suited to the needs of that country given its history, demography, resources and present affiliations. The adoption of a Western system particularly in the area of family law may prove superficial. The form might be observed but older traditional practices continued. This gives rise to complex questions of legal validity. Thus, when Turkey adopted a westernised system based on Swiss models in 1926, there were many such problems.[35] It is interesting in such a context to see the recent resurgence of fundamentalism which has swept the Moslem world in the wake of the Islamic revolution in Iran. This is raising difficult questions concerning both the rule and role of law in those countries.

Furthermore, the inheritance of a Western legal tradition as a result of colonisation creates a situation of dependence which survives political independence. One cannot overestimate the cultural significance of this in even a developed society such as Canada or New Zealand. For less developed countries the problems are much more difficult. There is a need to use law to unify diverse groups in society where the removal of colonial administration has resulted in the creation of new and often artificial nation states.[36] There is a need to use law as a means of planning development to increase production, relieve poverty and achieve a fairer distribution of resources.[37] Yet at the same time the number of languages and lack of resources and trained professionals hinder the process. The assimilation of Western legal traditions with a socialised economy and often one party rule given these natural disadvantages, presents, a formidable challenge. In many developing countries there are the practical problems of ensuring adequate promulgation of legislation, the production of reliable law reports kept up to date and the absence of local textbooks and periodical literature. These practical problems are, however, common to all small jurisdictions irrespective of the state of economic and political development.

It is little wonder then that developing countries faced with these problems sometimes show perhaps a greater enthusiasm than Western countries for an international harmonisation measure to be promoted by the United Nations. Whereas such countries have little or no influence on the development of modern civil law or common law which they are obliged passively to receive, they are at least represented on the relevant United Nations committees and their voices can be heard. The specialist organisations of the United Nations have been extremely productive in the area of international trade and maritime law. It is to be hoped that out of this develops a uniform approach to basic questions of legal method which will draw on the strengths of all the major systems and yet meet the legal needs of the Third World.

Notes

[1] See C. Wright Mills, *The Sociological Imagination*, p. 177.
[2] *cf.* Henry W. Ehrmann, *Comparative Legal Cultures*, p. 8.
[3] J. H. Merryman, *The Civil Law Tradition*, p. 2.
[4] See Encyclopedia of the Social Sciences, "Culture."
[5] *Cf.* P. Beirne and Richard Quinney (ed.), *Marxism and Law.*
[6] A. Watson, *Failures of the legal Imagination*, p. 146.
[7] See Ehrmann, *op. cit.*, p. 13.
[8] *Ibid.*, p. 16.
[9] Merryman, *op. cit.*, pp. 2–3.
[10] J. Mackintosh, *Roman Law in Modern Practice*, pp. 94 *et seq.*
[11] For more details see B. Nicholas, *An Introduction to Roman Law*, Chap. 1.
[12] See Lord Macmillan, *Law and Other Things*, pp. 76 *et seq.*
[13] R. David & J. Brierley, *Major Legal Systems of the World* (3rd ed.).
[14] See chap. 12, *ante.*
[15] Merryman, *op. cit.*, p. 35; H. C. Gutteridge *Comparative Law*, Chap. VII.
[16] See Chap. 9, *ante; cf.* Merryman, *op. cit.*, Chap. VII; Gutteridge, *op. cit.*, Chap. VIII.
[17] Merryman, *op. cit.*, pp. 126–128; *cf.* chap. 5, *ante.*
[18] See Buckland and McNair, *Roman Law and Common Law* (2nd ed. by F. H. Lawson).
[19] See the Ormrod Report on Legal Education, Cmnd. 4595.
[20] See R. B. Ferguson, "Legal Ideology and Commercial Interests," (1977) 4 B.J.L.S. 18.
[21] See J. H. Farrar, "Law Reform Now—A Comparative View" (1976) 25 I.C.L.Q. 214.
[22] See Chap. 12, *ante.*
[23] See Chap. 5, *ante.*
[24] Lord Scarman, *Truth in the Legal Process.*
[25] See D. Lloyd, *An Introduction to Jurisprudence* (3rd ed.).
[26] See E. L. Johnson, *An Introduction to the Soviet Legal System*, p. 77.
[27] *Ibid.*, p. 85.
[28] *Ibid.*, p. 84. See, further, the dated but nevertheless interesting explanation in A. Y. Vyshinsky, *The Law of the Soviet State*, pp. 336 *et seq.*
[29] Johnson, *op. cit.*, p. 84.
[30] F. J. M. Feldbrugge, *Encyclopedia of Soviet Law*, Vol. 1, p. 45.
[31] See Örücü, "An exercise on the internal logic of legal systems," (1987) 7 L.S. 310.
[32] Ehrmann, *op. cit.*, p. 18.
[33] See *Contemporary Chinese Law: Research Problems and Perspectives* by J. A. Cohen (ed.), and especially the essay by S. Lubman, "Methodological Problems in Studying Chinese Communist Civil Law," at p. 230.
[34] For a very interesting account see Robert L. Kidder, "Western Law in India, External Law and Local Response," in Harry M. Johnson (ed.), *Social System and Legal Process*, pp. 155 *et seq.*
[35] See M. B. Hooker, *Legal Pluralism*, pp. 364 *et seq.*
[36] *Op. cit., passim.*
[37] See Robert B. Seidman, *The State, Law and Development*, Part Four.

Chapter 16

LAW, JUSTICE AND POLICY

QUESTIONS OF VALUE IN THE LAW

Courts of law are often described as courts of justice. This is of course a euphemism. Law is not necessarily synonymous with justice and some laws may be regarded as unjust. Justice is an ideal to which law aspires. It is a branch of morality. Nevertheless, as we saw in chapter 1, there is a close relationship and partial overlap between law and morality. There is a strong value element in law—in its language, structure and method. There are some moral values which feature in the form of laws in such phrases as "just and equitable," "fair and reasonable." To this extent they seem to be internalised. Then there are values which characterise good law. These are often regarded as the standards of good legal craftsmanship or good legal process. There are also some substantive values which represent operative goals of the legal system. All of these seem to be internal to the legal order to some extent. Yet some of them at least represent general values accepted by society at large. This confusion arises because of the essentially open character of the common law. It is not a closed system of categories or values. The boundaries between law and not-law are not clearly and inexorably drawn. A system based on analogy necessarily has these characteristics. It is a source of both strength and weakness. It avoids the danger of remoteness from every day life and thinking. On the other hand it results in uncertainties and gaps. These strengths and weaknesses can, however, be exaggerated.

One of the hardest things for a person turning to law for the first time is to cope with the value elements in law. This is harder than learning the basics about precedent and interpretation of statutes. Yet without it the law seems more mechanical than it is. With it one appreciates something of the dynamism of law in action.

STANDARDS OF GOOD LEGAL CRAFTSMANSHIP AND PROCESS

There are some values such as the rules of natural justice—"no man shall be judge in his own cause" and "hear the other side"—which are hallmarks of good laws in their formulation, adjudication and administration. Some of these have been referred to by one American writer, Professor Lon Fuller[1], as the inner morality of law. Another American writer, Professor Robert Summers[2], refers to them as process values—standards of value by which a legal process may be judged good as a process, apart from any good results it may produce. Fuller included such matters as generality, adequate promulgation, avoidance of retroactivity, clarity, avoidance of contradiction and consistency between rule and administrative action. Summers refers to such matters as public participation, legitimacy, rationality and fairness. These are possibly better regarded not as inner morality but as the standards of good legal craftsmanship or process[3] whereby the products of a lawyer's handiwork are judged and appreciated. In the past some of them have been subsumed under the concept of the Rule of Law. This is a vague concept but was interpreted by Dicey[4] to comprehend the supremacy of law and equality before the law. Although Dicey's formulation has been criticised, the Rule of Law still survives as a supra-national concept in the western world and there is an increasing tendency to define it in terms of recognition of certain basic human rights.[5] There is also a further tendency of seeking to crystallise such rights into operative legal principles. In some countries this is done through a Bill of Rights in the Constitution.[6] In the case of the United Kingdom this is taking place through our membership of the United Nations and our adoption of the European Convention on Human Rights. Also some basic jurisprudence of human rights is beginning to emanate from the Court of Justice of the European Communities influenced by the Convention and the constitutional rules of member states.[7]

IDENTIFYING SUBSTANTIVE LEGAL VALUES

There are some substantive values which have been absorbed into the law as goals or ideals although their identity and scope are not well settled.

The Roman jurist, Ulpian, summed up the basic precepts of the law as being *"honeste vivere, alterum non laedere, suum cuique tribuere"* which being roughly translated means that the law should cause one to live honestly, not to harm another and to give to each person his or her due. Clearly, these values are rather general and vague. Nevertheless, they were adopted by Justinian's Institutes[8] which were produced as a primer for Roman law students and to a certain extent they are reflected in the content of modern writings.

As regards the basic values recognised within a more modern legal system, Roscoe Pound[9] identified in 1910 what he called the "jural postulates" of American society. These comprised security of the person from intentional aggression; security of possession of property under the existing social order; good faith in transactions; due care not to cause unreasonable risk of injury upon others; and control of dangerous things. Pound intended these as the basic underlying assumptions of the law. In 1942, he updated the list to include job security and the absorption by society of risk of misfortune to individuals. The actual list has been attacked for being outdated and for omitting important matters such as the sanctity of family life and the Rule of Law. Also, there is no attempt at ranking the postulates into any kind of hierarchy.

More recently, R. W. M. Dias has attempted to extract contemporary legal values from English case law. Like Pound, he has listed the sanctity of the person and property but he has also included the safety of the state, social welfare and equality (under which he subsumes justice). Last, he has included a miscellaneous quartet of fidelity to tradition, morality, convenience and international comity. It is obvious that there is a measure of overlap between some of them, for example between morality and justice. His overall conclusion based on a study of the English cases seems a reasonable one applicable to the whole of the United Kingdom, namely, that "national and social safety override all other considerations and sanctity of the person is superior to sanctity of property, but beyond this the pattern is kaleidoscopic, not hierarchical."[10]

More recently still, Professor Peter Stein and John Shand in their book *Legal Values in Western Society*, have identified what appear to them to be the three master values of a western democratic legal system—law and order, justice and freedom of the individual. It is not altogether clear on what basis the choice has been made and indeed whether "law and order" is a value at all, rather than a state of affairs. It appears, however, to be a reference to the Rule of Law. The other values which they identify are the values of life, privacy, property and certain other more particular values which they perceive in commercial transactions. They also mention briefly utility but do not rate it highly.

There is a danger in isolating values from their context in particular disputes and talking about hierarchies of values in the abstract. It is not how judges work and for good reason. They have no special insight into ethics and, in spite of claims sometimes made, into what is public opinion—if one regards that as the ultimate arbiter of public values.

In the past, much discussion of values was centered around the concept of justice as some kind of matrix but recently there has been a tendency to shift to the more fluid concept of policy. Both concepts are interesting in their own right and in their relationship to each other and for those reasons we shall devote the remainder of this chapter to them.

THE CONCEPT OF JUSTICE

Justice, like many concepts in legal and political philosophy, is capable of being used in many different ways.[11] It can refer to simple reciprocity or proportionality in vengeance as for instance in the Old Testament rule of an eye for an eye and a tooth for a tooth which was the first step towards social order and civilisation. At the other end of the spectrum it has been equated with virtue in general in ancient Greece or brotherly love in Christian doctrine. This elasticity has led a distinguished Scandinavian jurist, Professor Alf Ross,[12] to say:

"To invoke justice is the same thing as banging on the table: an emotional expression which turns one's demand into an absolute postulate. That is no proper way to mutual understanding. It is impossible to have a rational discussion with a man who mobilises justice because he says nothing that can be argued for or against. His words are persuasions, not arguments. The ideology of justice leads to implacability and conflict, since on the one hand it incites to the belief that one's demand is not merely the expression of a certain interest in conflict with opposing interests, but that it possesses a higher, absolute validity; and on the other it precludes all rational argument and discussion of a settlement. The ideology of justice is a militant attitude of a biological-emotional kind, to which one incites oneself for the implacable and blind defence of certain interests."

However, this goes too far. There are aspects of the concept of justice which are relatively uncontroversial. The most systematic and enduring analysis of justice is that of Aristotle in his *Ethics*, Book V.[13] Aristotle divided justice into the following divisions:

legal justice and equity,
distributive and corrective justice,
social or political justice and non political justice,
natural and conventional justice.

Legal justice is the impartial application of general legal rules. It is strict compliance with the Rule of Law.

Equity is a supplement to the law and goes beyond it. Aristotle in his *Ethics*, Book V, Chapter 10, explains the differences between legal justice and equity in the following way[14]:

"Equity, though a higher thing than one form of justice, is itself just and is not generically different from justice. Thus, so far as both are good, they coincide, though equity is to be preferred. What puzzles people is the fact that equity, though just, is not the justice of the law courts but a method of restoring the balance of justice when it has been tilted by the law. The need for such a rectification arises from the circumstances that law can do more than generalize, and there are cases which cannot be settled by a general statement. So in matters where it is necessary to make a general statement, and yet that statement cannot exclude the possibility of error, the law takes no account of particular cases, though well aware that this is not a strictly correct proceeding. Yet that does not make it a bad law, the error lying not in the law or the lawgiver but in the nature of the case; the data of human behaviour simply will not be reduced to uniformity. So when a case arises where the law states a general rule, but there is an exception to the rule, it is then right, when the lawgiver owing to the generality of his language left a loophole for error to creep in, to fill the gap by such a modified statement as the lawgiver himself would make, if he was present at the time, and such an enactment as he would have made, if he had known the special circumstances. So, while it is true that equity is just and in some circumstances better than justice, it is not better than absolute justice. All we can say is that it is better than the error which is generated by the unqualified language in which absolute justice must be stated. And equity essentially is just this rectification of the law, where the law has to be amplified because of the general terms in which it has to be couched."

As we have seen, this classification has influenced the development of the common law/equity distinction as well as the equity of the statute idea in English law.[15]

Distributive justice as its name suggests is concerned with distribution of goods in society. Given a certain good to be distributed between A and B it is to be distributed according to their respective merits. Merit is assessed differently in different states—in a democracy freedom is the standard and all free men are deemed equal; in an oligarchy the standard is wealth or noble birth. Distributive justice is conceived in geometric terms—A: B=C: D—as a mean between giving more to A than his share and more to B than his.

Corrective justice is not concerned with the parties but with transactions which are divided into voluntary and involuntary.

The first include sale and loans, the second theft and assault. The correction arises because of breach of contract in the first category. Here law operates on the basis of equality and looks to the nature of the injury. The result is not geometric but arithmetic—

Where   A + C
               B − C

The judge achieves corrective justice thus:

$$A + C - C = B - C + C.$$

Social or political justice is that which exists between citizens of a free state and is characterised by equality.

It can be seen that whereas legal justice, equity and corrective justice are relatively uncontroversial, distributive and social justice are not. The identification and recognition of merits and equality are not only controversial but also potentially antagonistic. Recognition of one man's merit may result in another man's inequality. Aristotle had a further classification of political justice into natural and conventional justice. The latter differed from state to state. However, he recognised that natural justice also was capable of change.

There has been a tendency amongst modern writers to emphasise the conventional character of justice. This was emphasised by the eighteenth century Scots philosopher, David Hume,[16] and has recently been taken up by Marxist critiques of justice. Modern Marxists[17] regard justice in its outward form as the highest expression of the rationality of social facts from a bourgeois juridical point of view but in its reality, the measure by which a capitalist system judges itself. Insofar as there is underlying economic unfairness implicit in such a system it will be absorbed into the concept of justice. Because of perceptions of these and other similar criticisms some Western political and legal philosophers have sought to formulate alternative models of justice which give priority to the otherwise least advantaged members of society. The most famous of these theories is that of Professor John Rawls[18] who has produced a model which attempts to combine the notion of social justice with that of individual freedom. This rests on the hypothesis of a social contract entered into by men from whom are concealed by a veil of ignorance certain facts of life which motivate men away from equality.

The theory is built on the foundations laid by the classical social contract philosophers; Kant, for example, used the contract hypothesis as a justification of the rationality of the principles which are eventually chosen. In some ways, it is simplified abstract reconstruction of the type of situation which led to the adoption of the American Constitution. Starting from this hypothesis it arrives at two basic principles which are (in order of priority), first, each person is to have an equal right to the most extensive system of basic liberties compatible with a similar system of liberty for all and, secondly, social and economic inequalities are to be arranged so that they are attached to positions open to all, under conditions of equality of opportunity and are to the greatest benefit of the least privileged. It then proceeds to design the basic structure of institutions and practices in accordance with these principles.

The theory is complex and has many aspects. Numerous criticisms have been made of it which range from the basic intellectual techniques adopted to the minutiae of particular propositions. The most important criticisms for our purposes at this stage are centred on Rawls' notion of the veil of ignorance, which is a vast and crucial assumption to make, even in the postulation of a theory of this kind. A detailed analysis of the theory and the criticisms of it, however, must be postponed until later in your course of academic studies. It is sufficient to note at this stage that it represents the most elaborate analysis of the concept of justice that has been attempted in recent times and is the most coherent expression of a set of values for rational evaluation of law in a Western democratic society.

Questions of distributive and social justice tend more and more to be subsumed under the broader heading of policy to which we must now turn but before we do so we would hazard the opinion that the reason for this development which many regard as the result of socialism has its roots in Victorian utilitarianism. This propounded a single master value of utility which was measurable in the sense of being equated with the greatest happiness of the greatest number.[19] It bore an ill defined relationship with justice which has never been adequately resolved.[20] The first phase of utilitarianism was individualism and was characterised by Victorian liberalism. The second phase was collectivism. Policy is a concept which has become fashionable in this second phase.

THE CONCEPT OF POLICY

Like justice the concept of policy is fluid and accommodates a number of ideas. The following are some definitions which have been put forward by political scientists[21]:

"the structure or confluence of values and behaviour involving a governmental prescription;
decisions giving direction, coherence and continuity to the courses of action for which the decision-making body is responsible;
decisions about the goals of the system and the share of the costs that each member, or group of members, is expected to pay; general directives on the main lines of action to be followed;
changing directives as to how tasks should be interpreted and performed."

The key ideas here are goals, values and sharing costs. Probably a more comprehensive definition of policy for legal purposes is the interaction of internal values with competing interests in the legal institutional setting. Litigants in court are pursuing competing interests in a forum which in English law is basically adversarial. The law to be applied encapsulates certain values in a non hierarchic and pluralistic fashion and is applied in an institutional setting. This institutional setting takes into account practical factors such as cost, consistency and convenience[22] as well as being influenced to some degree by the attitudes of the judiciary and officials of the system. The resulting mixture is potentially quite complex and one must resist the temptation to concentrate on one set of variables to the exclusion of others.[23] However, at the end of the day policy is not just the mere interaction of such variables but is about positive choice.[24]

Any concept of legal policy must also overlap with public policy at large since a large part of modern law is legislation and legislation is the product of politicians and the legislature.[25] Here the input is broader and more heterogeneous.

In recent years an attempt has been made by Professor Ronald Dworkin[26] to restore confidence in the ideal of objective justice by distinguishing between legal principle and legal policy. The first is about some ethical standard recognised by the law; the second about some economic, social or political goal at which the law is aimed. The former and not the latter is regarded as the proper domain of the judiciary who operate in what is at least in theory a gapless legal universe in which there is a right answer to "hard cases." In *McLoughlin* v. *O'Brian*[27], Lord Scarman appeared to accept this approach when he said:

> "The common law, which in a constitutional context includes judicially developed equity, covers everything which is not covered by statute. It knows no gaps: there can be no *casus omissus*. The function of the court is to decide the case before it, even though the decision may require the extension or adaptation of a principle or in some cases the creation of new law to meet the justice of the case. But, whatever the court decides to do, it starts from a baseline of existing principle and seeks a solution consistent with or analogous to a principle or principles already recognised.
>
> The distinguishing feature of the common law is the judicial development and formulation of principle. Policy considerations will have to be weighed; but the objective of the judges is the formulation of principle. And, if principle inexorably requires a decision which entails a degree of policy risk, the court's function is to adjudicate according to principle, leaving policy curtailment to the judgment of Parliament. Here lies the true role of the two law-making institutions in our constitution. By concentrating on principle the judges can keep the common law alive, flexible and consistent, and can keep the legal system clear of policy problems which neither they, nor the forensic process which it is their duty to operate, are equipped to resolve. If principle leads to results which are thought to be socially unacceptable, Parliament can legislate to draw a line or map out a new path."

This met with a forceful response from Lord Edmund-Davies to whom policy was justiciable. It seems oversimple to separate principle and policy. Legal principle is not a clearcut concept to be reduced in this way and policy in the sense of broader based practical considerations of the kind we have mentioned seems to have an integral part in case law reasoning.

Law and economics.

Law is the product of centuries of experiment with social control and regulation. Economics in its modern garb is a recent social science although economic ideas have been debated since the Ancient Greeks. Economics is principally concerned with the problems of rational choice and the allocation of scarce resources. Thus both law and economics are imperialistic in the sense that they attempt to cover all areas of social life. Both are concerned with social policy so it is inevitable that they overlap. They are not, however, identical.

The common law contains a number of doctrines in contract, tort and property law which have been described as "economically sensible but not economically subtle."[28] Judges are not usually trained economists and their views of economic issues are often commonsensical and intuitive. Many modern legal doctrines were developed in the nineteenth century in an age of laissez-faire and economic growth. The growth, however, was not consistent and there were periods of "boom and bust". Lawyers and judges, while not trained economists, were influenced by the spirit of the age and the popular economic ideas of the time, particularly the writings of Jeremy Bentham and John Stuart Mill. The principles of utilitarianism—"the greatest happiness of the greatest number"—sought to reduce questions of policy and value to measurable units in a calculus of felicity. This, in spite of its grotesqueness, provided useful foundations for both legal and economic policy although Mill himself found it difficult to reconcile utility and justice. With much in common in subject matter and something in common in technique, law and economics pull ultimately in different directions since they pursue different ends—justice and efficiency. Added to this is the tendency of much modern economics to employ mathematical and complex logical reasoning. Economics is more strictly logical but often in consequence its propositions seem elaborate tautologies to lawyers who are impatient with what they perceive to be their impracticality. This is based on a failure to understand the nature of the enquiry which is usually some allocational question of wealth maximisation. Economic reasoning is about relativities—"is X more efficient that Y"? To this end economics use a number of different techniques—analysis, prediction, evaluation and model building. To economists law often seems primitive in the sense of less logical, less mathematical and more concerned with elaborate discussions of the meaning of words and *ad hoc* evaluations. Law is concerned with distributive and corrective questions. In many areas law adopts a winner takes all solution. For instance a person either has or has not a legal title to land. It is only in certain areas of tort such as contributory negligence that a relativist approach is adopted in principle although in practice adjustments are sometimes made through the courts' discretion in awarding legal costs.

Integrity and the right answer.

Within the legal order there are conceptions of orthodoxy and unorthodoxy. Lord Denning was always capable of unorthodox reasoning to cater for the equity of a particular case. Professor Ronald Dworkin has argued for integrity in legal reasoning.[29] In his view it is not to be found in the economic approach which lacks any defensible philosophical foundation. Rather, it is to be found in the judge testing "his interpretation of any part of the great network of political structures and decisions of his community by asking whether it could form part of a coherent theory justifying the network as a whole." This is potentially a complex exercise requiring a mixture of institutional fit and normative evaluation. Hence he postulates by way of model a superhuman judge whom he calls Hercules.[30] Possibly because Dworkin postulates an heroic and yet essentially conservative role for Hercules his writings are beginning to find support from some of the judges while driving more radical thinkers into a frenzy. As a result, legal philosophy, after a long time in the doldrums, is beginning to be interesting and bear some relationship to reality.

JUSTICE, POLICY AND PRACTICAL REASONING

Law, justice and policy all involve decision—making. Decision—making is a process which can be judged as such by the
tenets of rationality. Rationality, however, like justice can, as
we have seen, mean different things. It can mean, logical, in
the stricter sense of the syllogism or in the looser sense of
induction. It can mean, tested by the empirical observation of
cause and effect. It can also simply mean supported by
reasons. Law, justice and policy are largely about practical
reasoning in supporting conclusions or courses of action by
reasons. In the past we have lacked a theory of reasons and
particularly the adequacy of value reasons. This was partly
because legal philosophers got bogged down in what is known
as the is/ought distinction that one cannot logically derive a fact
from a social standard or vice versa.[31] However, we are now
beginning to realise that practical reasoning in the sense of
reason giving is not operating in this logical vacuum and that
what one is concerned with is the weight and adequacy of both
factual and value reasons, judged in the aggregate.[32] Another
reason for lack of a theory of reasons was the trend towards
relativism in beliefs. As Professor J. A. Passmore[33] wrote:

"We have lost confidence, I have already suggested, in our
capacity to distinguish. We have lost confidence that Mozart
is a better composer than the creator of the latest pop-song,
lost confidence that it is better to think rationally and
critically than to succumb to occultism, lost confidence that
public life is anything more than a display room for egoistic
opportunities."

Yet this is a culture of defeat and we are now beginning to
see an attempt to produce criteria of rational justification not
just as ends in themselves but as means. First, philosophers
are attempting to classify types of reasons and some seek to
construct a meta language to enable us to analyse value
conflicts without resort to value—laden language. Secondly,
complex reasons are tending to be broken down into constitu-
tent parts so that the value dimension can be clearly identified.
Thirdly, many value questions are being measured in terms of
practical consequences of acceptance. Fourthly, some reasons

are being assessed by reference to practical standards which are adjusted in the light of changing conditions, *e.g.* U.G.C. norms for university rooms which seem to get smaller and smaller.[34]

A useful start in the taxonomy of reasons in common law justification has been made by Professor Robert Summers.[35] His overall classification of reasons is into substantive, authority, factual, interpretational and critical reasons. He concentrates on substantive reasons which he divides into goal reasons and rightness reasons. Goal reasons are future—regarding and causal. Rightness reasons are essentially evaluative and non—causal. Summers lists as examples of goal reasons generally safety, public health and family harmony, and as examples of rightness reasons conscionability, due care, justified reliance. It is to be noted that the former are rather abstract social goals and the latter are very much internalised values of the legal system of a relatively specific kind. Indeed due care is almost a legal standard in itself. It is submitted that Professor Summers has made a useful start and that this general classification more than his actual examples are helpful.

Another interesting classification of reasons has been put forward by J. R. Lucas. He distinguishes between first-personal reasons and omni-personal reasons. The fallacy of Alf Ross according to Lucas is that he seems to equate justice with selfish reasons.[36] Omni-personal reasons are those which lay claim on anyone and everyone. They are intended to be cogent, and to compel assent from every reasonable man. As John Stuart Mill wrote, "When we think a person is bound in justice to do a thing it is an ordinary form of language to say that he ought to be compelled to do it."[37] Omni-personal reasons are universals, but their adequacy as reasons is not simply because of their form but because of the measure of weight or support which they carry and give to the other reasons for a particular decision.

When we characterise a particular law or decision as just or politic it is normally because on balance the reasons for it exceed the force of the reasons against. The process is dialectic. Law is about authority, but it is also about justification through such reasoning. Justice involves reasoning about decisions in such a way that we would accept them even though they went against us. Policy involves such justification in the larger context of the public good. The three concepts overlap and employ the same methods. They involve consideration of factual situations, weighing of evidence, selection of principles and ordering of preferences. But they are not, however, identical and each can learn from the others. While lawyers and judges are not experts about justice and policy they have collectively a wealth of experience of practical reasoning and judgment. It is for this reason that the distinguished Belgian philosopher, Chaim Perelman, who has written much on justice and rhetoric, wrote:

" . . . in studying with attention and analysing with care the techniques of legal procedure and interpretation which permit men to live under the Rule of Law, the philosopher, instead of dreaming of the Utopia of an ideal society, can derive inspiration . . . from what secular experience has taught men, charged with the task of organising a reasonable society on earth."[38]

Notes

[1] *The Morality of Law*, Chap. II.
[2] "Evaluating and Improving Legal Process—A Plea for Process Values," 60 Cornell L.R. 1 (1974).
[3] See H. L. A. Hart's book review in 78 Harv.L.R. 1281 (1965) and R. S. Summers, "Professor Fuller on Morality and Law" (1965) 18 *Journal of Legal Education* 1, 24–27.
[4] A. V. Dicey, *Law of the Constitution*, Chap. IV.
[5] See *The Rule of Law and Human Rights, Principles and Definitions* (International Commission of Jurists), and Norman Marsh, "The Rule of Law as a Supra-National Concept" in *Oxford Essays in Jurisprudence* (1st series), ed. by A. G. Guest, Chap. IX.
[6] See *Legislation in Human Rights*—a Discussion Document issued by the Home Office; Sir Leslie Scarman, *English Law—The New Dimension*, Part II; Michael Zander, "A Bill of Rights?" and Lord Lloyd of Hampstead, "Do We Need A Bill of Rights" (1976) 39 M.L.R. 121.
[7] See T. C. Hartley, *The Foundations of European Community Law*, pp. 122 *et seq.*
[8] *The Institutes of Justinian*, Book I, tit. I, 3–4 (translated by J. B. Moyle), p. 3.
[9] See *Social Control Through Law*, pp. 112–116.
[10] See R. W. M. Dias, *Jurisprudence* (5th ed.), p. 260.
[11] For useful discussions see, *e.g.*, F. E. Dowrick, *Justice According to the English Common Lawyers*; J. R. Lucas, *On Justice*; *Justice*, ed. by E. Kamenka and Alice Erh-Soon Tay.

[12] *On Law and Justice*, p. 274.
[13] See the Penguin translation, *The Ethics of Aristotle*, by J. A. K. Thomson and Sir W. D. Ross, *Aristotle*, on which this is based.
[14] *The Ethics of Aristotle*, pp. 166–167.
[15] See Chaps. 3 and 9 above.
[16] *A Treatise of Human Nature*, Part II.
[17] See the valuable discussions in Wieslaw Lang, "Marxism, Liberalism and Justice" in Kamenka and Tay, *Justice*, pp. 116 *et seq.* and Allen W. Wood, "The Marxian Critique of Justice" (1971–1972) in *Philosophy and Public Affairs*, 244 *et seq.*
[18] In his *Theory of Justice*.
[19] See J. Plamenatz, *The English Utilitarians*.
[20] See J. S. Mill's *Utilitarianism*, in Plamenatz, *op. cit.*, p. 205 for a noble attempt to reconcile the two.
[21] See Brian Smith, *Policy Making in British Government*, p. 12.
[22] The first named author of this book foolishly attempted to reduce this to diagrammatic form in the first edition of this book. *cf.* the even more complex diagram in Glendon Schubert, *Judicial Policy Making* (revised ed.), p. 140.
[23] See for instance the chapter on American Realism in D. Lloyd, "*Introduction to Jurisprudence*" (5th ed.), Chap. 8 and *cf.* J. A. G. Griffith, "*The Politics of the Judiciary.*"
[24] See Smith, *op. cit.*, p. 13.
[25] See Lord Radcliffe, *The Law and its Compass*, pp. 37 *et seq.*
[26] *Taking Rights Seriously*, *passim* esp. pp. 22, 82.
[27] *McLoughlin* v. *O'Brian* [1982] 2 W.L.R. 982 at p. 997.
[28] See R. Posner, *Economic Analysis of Law*, 3rd ed.
[29] See his *Law's Empire*, Chap. 6, where he restates his arguments and answers critics. For a recent critique see J. W. Harris "Unger's Critique of Formalism in Legal Reasoning: Hero, Hercules, and Humdrum," (1989) 52 M.L.R. 42.
[30] See "Hard Cases" (1975) 88 Harv. L. Rev. 1057. Hercules is described with humour and erudition by Dr. Harris, *op. cit.*, pp. 48–55.
[31] See D. Lloyd, *Introduction to Jurisprudence* (5th ed.), Chap. 1.
[32] *Ibid.*, 920, quoting J. Wisdom. *cf.* J. Raz, *Practical Reason and Norms*, for an advanced study of this subject.
[33] "Civil Justice and its Rivals" in Kamenka and Tay, *Justice*, p. 48.
[34] For an excellent discussion see Z. Najder, *Values and Evaluations*, Chap. IV.
[35] "Two Types of Substantive Reasons: The Core of Common Law Justification," 63 Cornell L.R. 707 (1978).
[36] See J. R. Lucas, *On Justice*, pp. 37 *et seq.*
[37] *Utilitarianism*, Chap. 5.
[38] C. Perelman, *Justice et Raison*, p. 255 (John Farrar's translation).

APPENDICES

1. *The Law Library, Legal Materials and Their Use*

2. *Specimen Sources*

Appendix 1

THE LAW LIBRARY, LEGAL MATERIALS AND THEIR USE

You will spend a lot of your time working in the law library if you are at all conscientious as a law student. It is often said that a good lawyer is one who knows where to look for the law. At first it all seems a bit bewildering. You may have a library tour organised by a member of staff or librarian. If so what follows may duplicate what they say to some extent. A more detailed guide is given in P. A. Thomas and J. Dane, *How to use a Law Library*.

UNITED KINGDOM AND IRELAND

We will deal first with United Kingdom and Irish materials. These can be usefully classified into primary and secondary sources. Primary sources are those which actually make law—statutes, delegated legislation and reports of cases. Secondary sources are texts of various sorts which summarise and sometimes discuss the law—things like textbooks, legal encyclopedias, digests and legal periodicals.

Primary Sources

1. Statutes

Although people often talk of the "Statute Book" there is no such thing. Early statutes as we saw in Chapter 9 were decrees issued by the King or more usually the King in Council in a variety of forms. Later they became a tripartite enactment by the King, the Lords and the Commons in Parliament assembled.

Hawkins and Ruffhead made a useful unofficial collection in the eighteenth century of statutes then in force. There were other unofficial collections but in the period 1810 to 1822 Commissioners appointed by the House of Commons produced nine volumes known as *Statutes of the Realm* which covered the period 1235 to 1713 but excluding the interregnum. The interregnum is covered by Firth and Rait, *Acts and Ordinances of the Interregnum*.

In 1868 the Statute Law Committee was set up and produced *Statutes Revised* covering the period 1235 to 1948. From 1947 to 1965 there was a specialist branch of the Office of Parliamentary Counsel dealing with consolidation. In 1965 the Law Commissions took over responsibility for comprehensive consolidation and statute law revision. As a result of this work a new series has been produced entitled *Statutes in Force*. In the foreword to this Lord Hailsham explained the nature of purpose of the new series in the following way:

"The Third Edition of *Statutes Revised* was published in 1950 under the supervision of the Statute Law Committee as part of the programme of statute law reform inaugurated soon after the end of the last war. At that time, it was recognised that a further edition would be needed when the projected work on consolidation and statute law revision had borne some fruit. The time has now been reached when a large amount of consolidation and revision has been done. The combined effect of this work and of the ordinary legislation passed since 1950 has been to repeal or amend a large part of the Acts contained in the Third Edition. The Committee has therefore decided to undertake the publication of a new official revised edition of the statutes.

The three editions of *Statutes Revised* published between 1885 and 1950 were bound collections of the Public General Acts as amended. The Third Edition and the succeeding annual volumes were supplemented by an annual noter-up service which provided details of subsequent amendments and repeals. This was a useful service, but noting up is a laborious process and can easily be a source of error.

The new edition is renamed *Statutes in Force*. It is designed as a self-renewing, self-expanding and thus permanent edition. The Acts will be printed as separate booklets and assembled in loose-leaf binders. In this way it will be possible to keep the new edition up to date without disfiguring the text.
It is to be an official edition of the statutes currently in force and is published by authority. An Editorial Board is responsible for developing the work until it includes all Public General Acts in force, and for keeping it continuously up to date.
The new edition offers an arrangement by subject-matter. Those who require all the statutes currently in force will be served by the complete edition so arranged. But those whose interest is limited and who require part only of the statute law do not have to buy the whole work. They will be able to make their own selection.
Statutes in Force is designed to meet the obligation of the State to provide an accurate and up-to-date text of all statutes currently in force, edited in a helpful and comprehensive way, but without commentary."

Copies of individual Acts can usually be obtained from the Government Bookshops which are branches of Her Majesty's Stationery Office. A copy of the Human Organ Transplants Act 1989 with annotations is set out in Appendix 1 to this book.

Each year H.M.S.O. publishes volumes containing Public General Acts (with which you will usually be concerned) and Local and Private Acts. It also publishes a Chronological Table of Statutes. This covers *Statutes of the Realm* and all Public General Acts from 1714. Together with this is the *Index to Statutes in Force* which is arranged alphabetically. These are quite useful tools for historical research together with the annotated Halsbury's *Statutes* to which we shall refer below.

The Incorporated Council of Law Reporting publish statutes under the rather silly title *Law Reports—Statutes*. These cover the period 1866 onwards.

The old practice was to cite statutes by regnal year and chapter. The regnal year is the year of the reign of the particular monarch and the chapter refers to the place in the records of a particular session of Parliament. Thus the Sale of Goods Act 1893 was 56 & 57 Vict. c. 71. It is still sometimes used but statutes nowadays are generally cited by their short title which is usually set out for some odd reason at the end of an English statute. It gives a brief description of the subject-matter of the Act and the calendar year in which it was passed.

There is a series of Northern Ireland statutes, the name of which has differed from time to time.

Statutes of the Republic of Ireland are contained in the series knows as *The Acts of the Oireachtas* which is in English and Gaelic. There is an index volume covering 1922 to 1968.

2. Delegated legislation

The most important pieces of delegated legislation are usually referred to as statutory instruments because this term is used as a generic term in the Statutory Instruments Act 1946. It covers such things as Orders in Council and ministerial orders, rules and regulations. Like statutes they are sold separately by H.M.S.O. They are also collected annually and there is a collection called *Statutory Instruments* which is published by H.M.S.O. and kept up to date with annual volumes and an index. A *Table of Government Orders* records the effect of instruments made after 1949 on earlier instruments.

3. Law reports

As you can see from the report of *Gold* v. *Haringey Health Authority* [1988] Q.B. 481 set out in Appendix 1, a modern law report gives the name of the case, its date, the court and the judges who sat in it, a headnote, an outline of the facts and pleadings, the name of counsel, sometimes a summary of their argument and always a detailed report of the judgment. This particular format became reasonably settled after 1765. It is useful to know a little of the history of law reporting since there have been significant changes in the system over the years. A list of authorised abbreviations for modern reports is set out on page 281.

The Year Books 1282–1537. As a beginning it is unlikely that you will be referred to the Year Books which are the oldest species of report. They are not complete reports but are thought to have been notes taken by students and practitioners, for educational or professional purposes. Originally the proceedings reported were in Norman French and the reports continued to be in what became known as "Law French" long after English has begun to be used in the courts.

Named reporters 1537–1865. Eventually the form of reports began to change to include summaries of counsel's arguments and the judgments. These eventually appeared under the reporter's name. Some of them were made for the reporter's own use; gradually however, they became mainly commercial ventures. They differ greatly in style and quality.

In the early period the most famous are those of *Coke* and *Plowden* in the common law courts. Both were distinguished lawyers who added notes to their reports. Coke's reports were often very discursive and sometimes positively long-winded. The include much by way of commentary as well as actual reports. They are nevertheless an invaluable source of early law. *Burrow's Reports* in the eighteenth century are probably the first of the modern reports although even he often reported the sense rather than the words verbatim.

In Chancery the early reports known as *Cases in Chancery* are often very terse. The first good reports were those of *Piere Williams* from 1695 to 1736. *Vesey Senior* and *Junior, Hare* and *Beavan* were the other major reporters.

The English reports full reprint. Most libraries do not hold the nominate reports but most of the reports can be found in convenient form in the English Reports which reprint about 100,000 earlier reports verbatim, with citations and editorial notes. The reports are arranged by courts and there are useful index volumes and a conversion wall chart which enables you to convert from a citation in the nominate report to the appropriate citation in the *English Reports*.

There is another series knows as *Revised Reports*, which covers some of the same ground and has cases which do not appear in the *English Reports*, but many libraries do not stock it.

Law Reports 1865 to date. The legal profession formed the Incorporated Council of Law Reporting in 1865 which superseded the nominate reporters and publishes a "semi-official" series of reports which are now known as the *Law Reports*. The judges revise them and it is the custom of the courts to require citation of them if a case is reported in them.

The first series covers the period from 1865 to the Judicature Acts' reorganisation of the courts. A proper citation is to refer to the court thus, *e.g.* L.R. 8 Ex. 132 although it is now common to add the year as well.

The second series covers 1875 to 1890 and refers to the particular division. Thus *Heaven* v. *Pender* decided in 1883 is 11 Q.B.D. 503. Again it is now common to add the date.

The third series which is still current dates from 1891. Here the date appears in square brackets and the "D" disappears. Thus, *Le Lievre* v. *Gould* is reported in [1893] 1 Q.B. 491.

The present reports are:

Appeal Cases covering the House of Lords and Judicial Committee of the Privy Council cited as A.C.; reports of the divisions: *Queen's Bench Division*—Q.B.; *Chancery Division*—Ch. and formerly the *Probate, Divorce and Admiralty Division*—P. but now the *Family Division*—Fam. Court of Appeal cases go not in Appeal Cases but in the reports of the Division from which the case came.

In addition there are specialist reports such as the *Reports of Restrictive Practices Cases* (R.P.) and the *Industrial Court Reports* (I.C.R.).

From 1866 to 1952 the Council Published *Weekly Notes* (W.N.) which contained summary reports of recent cases before they appeared in the main reports. From January 1, 1953, these were replaced by the *Weekly Law Reports* (W.L.R.).

Other Series. The best known commercial series is the *All England Law Reports* still using the tedious abbreviation "All E.R." despite the attempt of some learned writers to convert it to "A.E.R." These reports began in 1936 and aim to be quicker than other series although there is now little to choose between them and the *Weekly Law Reports*. They incorporate the *Law Times Reports* (L.T.) from 1948 and the *Law Journal Reports*, (*e.g.*

L.J. 9 Q.B. 126) from 1950. There is a useful reprint of selected old cases which now covers the period 1558–1935.

The *Times Law Reports* (T.L.R.) cover the period 1884 to 1952. *The Times* newspaper has reports which are cited by reference to the date of the particular issue. Since 1981, Commercial Law Reports have been appearing in the *Financial Times*. More recently *The Guardian* and *The Independent* have started publishing law reports.

Other reports are contained in *The Solicitors' Journal* (S.J.), the *Justice of the Peace* (J.P.) both of which date back to the nineteenth century.

Commercial firms also produce specialist reports such as *Lloyd's List Law Reports* cited now as Lloyd's Rep.; and *Criminal Appeal Reports*—Cr.App.R.

Scotland. Scotland had nominate reports until the end of the nineteenth century. Now the principal cases are reported in *Session Cases*—S.C. and *Scots Law Times*—S.L.T.

Ireland. A number of Irish cases appear in nominate reports but the main series is now *Irish Reports*—I.R. since 1894. Northern Irish cases are reported in *Northern Ireland Law Reports*—cited N.I.

Authorised Abbreviations for Modern Law Reports

A.C.	Appeals Cases, 1891–
A.C.L.R.	Australian Company Law Reports
A.D.I.L.	Annual Digest of Public International Law Cases, 1919–49
A.L.J.R.	Australian Law Journal Reports, 1958–
A.L.R.	American Law Reports, First series, 1918–1948
A.L.R.2d.	American Law Reports, Second series, 1948–1965
A.L.R.3d.	American Law Reports, Third series, 1965–1980

A.L.R.4th	American Law Reports, Fourth series, 1980–
A.L.R.Fed.	American Law Reports, Federal 1969–
A.T.C.	Accountant Tax Cases, 1922–26. Continued as Annotated Tax Cases, 1927–
Acct. L. Rep.	Accountant Law Reports, 1922–37
ACTR	Australian Capital Territory Reports, 1973–
All E.R.	All England Reports, 1936–
All E.R. Rep.	All England Reports, Reprints, 1558–1935
All N.L.R.	All Nigeria Law Reports, 1967–71
ALR	Australian Law Reports
Ann. Tax Cas.	Annotated Tax Cases, 1927–1975
App. Cas.	Appeals Cases, 1875–90
B.C.L.	British Company Law Cases, 1983–
B.C.L.C.	Butterworths Company Law Cases, 1983–
B.I.L.C.	British International Law Cases
B.W.C.C.	Butterworths' Workmens' Compensation Cases, 1908–1950
C.L.R.	Commonwealth Law Reports, 1903–
C.M.L.R.	Common Market Law Reports, 1962–
C.P.D.	Common Pleas Division, 1875–1880
Ch.	Chancery, 1891–
Ch.D.	Chancery Division, 1875–1890
Col. L.J.	Colonial Law Journal (New Zealand) 1865–1875
Com. Cas.	Commercial Cases, 1895–1941
Con. L.R.	Construction Law Reports, 1985–
Cox C.C.	Cox's Criminal Law Cases, 1843–1941
Cr. App.R.	Criminal Appeal Reports, 1908–
Cr. App.R.(S)	Criminal Appeal Reports (Sentencing), 1980–
Ct. App. N.Z.	Court of Appeals Reports (New Zealand), 1867–1877
D.L.R.	Dominion Law Reports, 1912-
E.C.C.	European Commercial Cases
E.C.R.	European Court Reports, 1954–
E.G.L.R.	Estates Gazette Law Reports, 1985–
	Estates Gazette Planning Law Reports, 1988–

E.P.O.R.	European Patent Office Reports, 1986–
E.R.	English Reports, 1220–1865
Eur. Court H.R. Series A or Series B	Publications of the European Court of Human Rights, series A or B
Ex.D.	Exchequer Division, 1875–1880
F.L.R.	Family Law Reports, 1980–
F.L.R.	Federal Law Reports (Australia), 1956/61–
F.S.R.	Fleet Street Reports
Fam.	Family Division, 1972–
Gaz.L.R., G.L.R.	Gazette Law Reports, (New Zealand 1893–1953)
H.L.R.	Housing Law Reports, 1982–
I.C.J.Rep.	International Court of Justice Reports
I.C.R.	Industrial Court Reports, 1972–1974, continued as Industrial Cases Reports, 1975–
I.L.R.	International Law Reports, 1950–
I.L.R.	Insurance Law Reports, 1982–84
Imm. A.R.	Immigration Appeal Reports, 1976–
I.R. or Ir.R.	Irish Reports, 1838–
I.R.L.R.	Industrial Relations Law Reports, 1972-
I.T.R.	Industrial Tribunal Reports, 1966–1978
J.C.	Justiciary Cases (Scotland), 1916–[in Session Cases]
J.P.	Justice of the Peace Reports, 1837–
K.I.R.	Knights' Industrial Reports, 1966–1974
Knox.	Knox's Reports, New South Wales, 1877
L.E.	United States Supreme Court Reports, Lawyer's Edition 1882–1955
L.E.2d.	United States Supreme Court Reports, Lawyer's Edition, 1956–
L.G.R.	Local Government Reports, 1903–1943
L.J. or L.J.R.	Law Journal Reports, 1831–1949
L.J.C.C.A.	Law Journal Newspaper County Court Appeals, 1935

L.J.N.C.C.R.	Law Journal Newspaper County Court Reports, 1934–1947
L.J.O.S.	Law Journal Reports, Old Series, 1822–1831
L.R.A. & E.	Admiralty and Ecclesiastical, 1865–1875
L.R.A.C.	Appeal Cases, 1891
L.R. App.Cas.	Appeal Cases, 1875–1890
L.R.C.C.R.	Crown Cases Reserved, 1865–1875
L.R.C.P.	Common Pleas, 1865–1875
L.R.C.P.D.	Common Pleas Division, 1875–1880
L.R. Ch.	Chancery Cases, 1891–
L.R. Ch.App.	Chancery Appeal, 1865–1875
L.R. Ch.D.	Chancery Division, 1875–1890
L.R. Eq.	Equity Cases, 1865–1875
L.R. Ex.	Exchequer, 1865–1875
L.R.Ex.D.	Exchequer Division, 1875–1880
L.R.H.L.	English and irish Appeals to the House of Lords, 1865–1875
L.R.H.L.	English and Irish Appeals to the House of lords, 1865–1875
L.R.P.	Probate, 1891–1971
L.R.P.C.	Privy Council Appeals, 1865–1875
L.R.P. & D.	Probate and Divorce, 1865–1875
L.R.P.D.	Probate, 1875–1890
L.R.Q.B.	Queen's Bench, 1865–1875
L.R.Q.B.D.	Queen's Bench Division, 1875–1890
L.R.Sc. & Div.	Scottish and Divorce Appeals, 1865–1875
L.T.	Law Times Reports, 1859–1962
Legge	Legge's Supreme Court Cases, New South Wales, 1825–1962
Ll.L.R.	Lloyd's List Law Reports, 1919–1950
Lloyd's Rep.	Lloyd's List Law Reports, 1925–
Macas.	Macassey's Reports (New Zealand) 1861–1872
Man.Law	Managerial Law, 1975–
N.I.	Northern Ireland Law Reports, 1925–
N.S.W.S.C.R.	New South Wales Supreme Court Reports, 1862–1879
N.S.W.L.R.	New South Wales Law Reports, 1880–1900

N.S.W.L.R.	New South Wales law Reports, 1971–
N.Z.Jur.	New Zealand Jurist. 1873–1878
N.Z.L.R.	New Zealand Law Reports, 1883–
N.Z.P.C.C.	New Zealand Privy Council Cases, 1840–1932
O.R.	Ontario Reports, 1931–
Oll.B. & F.	Olliver, Bell & Fitzgerald's Reports (New Zealand), 1878–1880
P.	Probate, 1891–1971
P.C.L.	Palmer's Company Cases, 1985–
P. & C.R.	Planning and Compensation Reports, 1949–1967. Continued as Property and Compensation Reports, 1968–
P.D.	Probate, Divorce and Admiralty Division, 1875–1890
Pelham	Pelham's Reports, South Australia, 1865–1866
Q.B. or K.B.	Queen's (or King's) Bench, 1891–
Q.B.D. or K.B.D.	Queen's (or King's) Bench, 1875–1890
Q.L.J.	Queensland Law Journal Reports, 1881–1901
Q.L.R.	Queensland Law Reports, 1876–1878
Q.S.C.R.	Queensland Supreme Court Reports, 1860–1881
Q.S.R.	State Reports (Queensland), 1902–1957
Qd.R.	Queensland Reports, 1958–
R.Int'L.Arb.	Awards Reports of International Arbitral Awards, 1965–
R.P.	Restrictive Practices, 1958–1972
R.P.C.	Reports of Patent, Design and Trade Mark Case 1884–
Rep.Com.Cas.	Reports of Commercial Cases, 1895–1941
RTR	Road Traffic Reports, 1976–
Rec.	Recueil de la Jurisprudence de la Cour, 1954/55–
S.A.	South African Law Reports, 1947–

S.A.L.R.	South Australian Law Reports, 1865–1920
S.A.S.R.	South Australian State Reports, 1921–
S.C. or Sess.Cas.	Sessions Cases, 1906–
S.L.T.	Scottish Law Times (Reports) 1893–
S.R. (N.S.W.)	State Reports of New South Wales, 1901–1970
S.T.C.	Simon's Tax Cases, 1973
St.R.QD.	State Reports, Queensland, 1902–1957
St.Tr.	State Trials, 1163–1820
T.C.	Tax Cases, 1875–
T.L.R.	Times Law Reports, 1884–1952
Tas.S.R.	Tasmanian State Reports, 1941–
U.S. Sup.Ct.(L.Ed).	U.S. Supreme Court Reports (Lawyer's edition), 1882–
V.A.T.T.R.	Value Added Tax Tribunal Reports, 1973–
V.L.R.	Victorian Law Reports, 1875–1956
V.R.	Victorian Reports, 1870–1872
V.R.	Victorian Reports, 1957–
Vict. L.R.	Victorian Law Reports, 1875–1956
W.A.L.R.	Western Australian Law Reports, 1899–1959
W.A.R.	Western Australian Reports, 1960–
W.L.R.	Weekly Law Reports, 1953–
W.N.	Weekly Notes (Reports), 1866–1952
W.W.R.	Western Weekly Reporter
Wyatt, W & A'B	Wyatt, Webb & A'Beckett's Reports, Victoria, 1864–1869

Law Reports, 1st, 2nd and 3rd series
1st 1865–1875   2nd 1875–1890   3rd 1891–

Appeals Cases and Predecessors, i.e.:

L.R.H.L.	1865–75 English & Irish Appeals to the House of Lords
L.R.P.C.	1865–75 Privy Council Appeals
L.R.Sc. & Div.	1865–75 Scottish and Divorce Appeals
App. Cas.	1875–90 Appeals Cases
A.C.	1891– Appeals Cases

Chancery and Predecessors, i.e.:

L.R.ChApp.	1865–75 Chancery Appeals
L.R.Eq.	1865–75 Equity Cases
Ch.D.	1875–90 Chancery Division
Ch.	1991– Chancery

Queen's (or King's) Bench and Predecessors, i.e.:

L.R.C.P.	1865–75 Common Pleas
L.R.C.G.R.	1865–75 Crown Cases Reserved
L.R.Ex.	1865–75 Exchequer
L.R.Q.B.	1865–75 Queen's Bench
C.P.D.	1875–80 Common Pleas Division

Ex.D.   1875–80 Exchequer Division
Q.B.D.   1875–90 Queen's Bench Division
Q.B.   1891–   Queen's (or King's) Bench

Probate and Predecessors, i.e.:

L.R.A. & E.   1865–75 Admiralty and Ecclesiastical
L.R.P. & D.   1865–75 Probate and Divorce
P.D.   1875–90 Probate, Divorce and Admiralty
                         Division
P.   1891–1971 Probate
Fam.   1972–   Family

Restrictive Practices

R.P.   1958–72 Restrictive Practices

Industrial Court Reports

I.C.R.   1972–   Industrial Court Reports

Computer Retrieval of Primary Source Material

Over the coming years many law libraries are likely to be
equipped with computer based systems for retrieving legal
information. Solicitors' offices and Barristers' chambers are also
likely to acquire such systems. At some stage, it is quite likely
that you will use the systems or rely on others to do so. Either
way, you will need some knowledge of how the systems work.
A full understanding can only be acquired from special training
courses and plenty of practice. We can merely give the briefest
explanation of their nature and use.

The most widely used system in the U.K. is LEXIS. The full
text of cases and statutes are stored on the computer's *database*.
The user sits at a terminal which resembles a home computer—
a keyboard with a display screen. The terminal is linked to the

computer's database by telephone line. By using the keyboard the user can instruct the computer to search the database and display the results of the search. The search takes the form of requesting the computer to look for the use of particular words in the texts contained in the database. Perhaps an example can most clearly illustrate the process. In Chapter 10 we noted that by spring 1989 there had been some seventy or so cases before the higher courts concerned with the interpretation of section 60 of the Housing Act 1985 and its predecessor, section 17 of the Homeless Persons Act 1977. We discovered this by using LEXIS. Our search request for section 17 was *Homeless W/10 1977* and *Intention! W/20 17*. This means we asked the computer to find all the cases in which both the word Homeless had appeared within ten words of the number 1977 and a word beginning with Intention (! means that any ending is caught, *e.g.* intentional, or intentionally) had appeared within twenty words of the numbers 17. We chose this search because all cases on section 17 would be likely to contain in their text this combination of words and numbers and cases not dealing with section 17 would be very unlikely to contain this combination. After a couple of minutes our LEXIS terminal displayed the fifty or so cases. A search instruction "*Homeless w/10 1985* and *Intention! w/20 60*" produced another 20 cases. If we had then wanted to see the full text of any of those cases, we could have instructed the computer accordingly.

Many of the cases that were displayed were not reported in any of the Law Reports mentioned earlier in this appendix. This is because the texts on the database are drawn not only from the Law Reports but also from the transcripts of otherwise unreported judgments. Access to unreported decisions is just one of the facilities afforded by some of these systems— although whether the judges will welcome the citation of such decisions in court is a different matter—see the adverse comments of the House of Lords in *Roberts Petroleum* v. *Bernard Kenney Ltd.* [1983] A.C. 192. The systems provide many other benefits. For example, they enable a user to ascertain swiftly whether a particular statutory provision is in force, whether any statutory instruments have been issued under it, whether they have been applied in any case. But it should not be thought that the system will do away with the need for lawyers—a lawyers skill, experience and judgment is called for to formulate the most appropriate search request. The systems are rather a powerful research tool and, in the U.S.A. at least, their use is widespread.

Secondary Materials

Encyclopedias of English Law

With the exception of Halsbury's *Laws of England*, "all general encyclopedias of English Law became casualties of the First or the Second World War."[1]

In 1866, a Commission was appointed to inquire into the exposition of a digest of law. After publishing a first report, it died out but fortunately commercial publishers undertook the execution in its main outlines of the scheme recommended by the Commission. The basic aim was "to furnish a complete statement of English law in the convenient and accessible form of a series of connected treatises on every branch of the law, each written by experts in the particular subject."[2] The first edition was published under the General Editorship of Lord Halsbury who was then Lord Chancellor.

The work is now in its fourth edition. The contributors are judges, practising lawyers and academics whose names are disclosed. The structure is analytical. The law is divided into units which are sometimes smaller than the orthodox divisions of the law adopted by academic professional writers. The work is set out in alphabetical order and contains cross-references to the companion work, Halsbury's *Statutes of England* and also to *The Digest* (formerly in *English and Empire Digest*) which we will mention below.

Each volume is indexed with a table of cases and statutes and there is a useful general index for the whole series.

There are cumulative supplements published annually, a loose-leaf current service and an annual abridgment. The latter is a survey of the legal developments in the particular year.

There are special editions for some Commonwealth countries for which supplementary volumes are added. Thus there is an

Australian Pilot and a *Canadian Converter* which set out the Australian and Canadian authorities respectively.

Halsbury's *Statutes* are now in their fourth edition. The first edition was published in 1930. The primary purpose is to render easily available the correct and amended text of enactments together with explanatory notes. It contains almost all public Acts relating to England and Wales and London by-laws. For reasons which are not obvious, Acts or parts of Acts affecting Scotland only are not included but annotations are included concerning the application of Acts to Northern Ireland. The work is kept up to day by annual cumulative supplements and loose-leaf current service.

Digests

Similar but less ambitious in scope to Halsbury are various digests and abridgments of the law. The best of the early abridgments and digests are those of *Rolle, Comyn* and *Bacon*. *Viner's* abridgment in the eighteenth century is more comprehensive but does not enjoy quite the same reputation as the others.

In modern times, Butterworths have produced *The Digest* which is a digest of cases. It gives useful summaries of the cases and their subsequent history and is kept reasonably up to date by cumulative volumes. We have found its main use to research in legal history. It is certainly not an easy source of the modern law although it now has a three volume case index making it easier to use.

Much more useful are *Current Law, Scottish Current Law* and the *Current Law Yearbooks* published by Sweet and Maxwell/ Stevens and W. Green and Son. These began in 1947 and are the nearest approach to a complete and convenient index of recent law in one place. The separate Scots edition is even more useful, covering Scots material as well. The yearbooks provide a digest and index on an annual basis.

Textbooks

The question of doctrine has already been discussed in Chapter 12. Included under this head are the "classics" such as

Bracton, Coke, Hale and *Blackstone* and as we have seen greater weight is accorded them than more modern writings. Later writers such as *Pollock, Anson* and *Dicey* are held in high repute. For a detailed list of authors, see Sweet & Maxwell's *Legal Bibliography* and consult the catalogue of your law library.

The Scottish Institutional Writers

Reference has already been made to the Scottish approach to doctrine in Chapter 12.

The principal writers are Viscount Stair, *The Institutions of the Law of Scotland*, 1681; John Erksine, *An Institute of the Laws of Scotland*, 1773; and George Bell, *Commentaries on the Law of Scotland*, 1804, and *Principles of the Law of Scotland*, 1829. Butterworths have now produced the *Laws of Scotland* (Stair Memorial Encyclopedia) which is similar to Halsbury's Laws.

Legal Dictionaries

The three best dictionaries are Stroud's *Judicial Dictionary,* Jowitt's *Dictionary of English Law* and *Words and Phrases Legally Defined*. Bouvier's *Law Dictionary* is a useful American legal dictionary. There are also dictionaries of legal abbreviations— the latest and fullest being Raistrick's, *Index to Legal Citations and Abbreviations.*

Smaller and inexpensive dictionaries which you might find useful are Osborn's *Concise Law Dictionary* (7th ed., 1983) and Mozley and Whiteley's *Law Dictionary* (10th ed., 1988).

On the whole, legal dictionaries are not of so much use except to check the meaning of a technical term when you begin your studies or to get research ideas later on. A word of caution even then must be uttered. Legal words and concepts are often chameleon-like. They change their meaning with their context. It is much better, therefore, to check their meaning if possible in the textbook in the particular area where the word crops up or in the particular part of Halsbury's *Laws*. It is easy to get misled by the meaning given in a different context by the dictionary.

Periodicals

These occupy roughly the same status as textbooks.

The main academic journals are the *Law Quarterly Review*, the *Cambridge Law Journal*, the *Modern Law Review*, *Legal Studies*, the *Oxford Journal of Legal Studies*, the *Juridical Review*, the *Northern Ireland Law Quarterly*, the *Irish Jurist*, *Current Legal Problems*, the *Cambrian Law Review* and the *Anglo-American Law Review*. These are general publications.

In addition, there are specialist journals such as the *Criminal Law Review*, the *Journal of Business Law*, *The Conveyancer*, the *Civil Justice Quarterly*, the *International and Comparative Law Quarterly*, *Public Law*, *Family Law*, the *Industrial Law Journal*, the *Journal of Law and Society*, the *British Journal of Criminology*, the *British Tax Review*, the *European Law Review*, and the *Journal of Planning and Environment Law*.

Useful practitioners' journals are the *New Law Journal*, the *Solicitors' Journal*, *Law Society Gazette*, the *Scots Law Times* and the *Journal of the Law Society of Scotland*.

Legal Journals Index is a very useful index to articles in journals published in the United Kingdom. The American publication, *Index to Legal Periodicals*, is also a valuable source of reference to learned articles.

Law reform materials

You will often be referred to law proposals. Before 1965, the Law Revision Committee (later reconstituted as the Law Reform Committee), the Private International Law Committee, the Criminal Law Revision Committee and the Law Reform Committee for Scotland all produced reports. Since 1965, the English and Scottish Law Commissions have been set up and the practice is to issue programmes and working papers and only later to issue reports. Often draft legislation is appended. The Law Reform Committee and the Criminal Law Revision Committee still exist and produce reports.

Other sources of law reform proposals are the Reports of Royal Commissions and Departmental Committees.

All of these are obtainable from H.M.S.O., unless they are out of print.

The reports of *Justice*—the British branch of the International Commission of Jurists—are also useful materials and you will no doubt be referred to them.

AUSTRALIA

You will find a useful introduction to Australian law in the volume on Australia in the *British Commonwealth, Its Laws and Constitutions* series; *An Introduction to Law* by Derham, Maher and Waller; and *The Australian and the Law* by Geoffrey Sawer.

Primary Materials

Statutes

Australia is a federal jurisdiction. There are *Commonwealth Statutes* covering federal laws, and statutes for each state nearly all of which have been consolidated.

Law reports

Cases in the High Court and Privy Council are found in *Commonwealth Law Reports*, the *Australian Argus Law Reports* and the *Australian Law Journal Reports*. Privy Council cases also usually appear in the English Appeal Cases, *All England Reports* and the *Weekly Law Reports*.

There are various state reports. New South Wales had three sets—*State Reports* (N.S.W), *Weekly Notes* (N.S.W.) and *New South Wales Reports*, for a time.

Secondary Materials

Encyclopedias

Reference has been made to the *Australian Pilot* to Halsbury's *Laws*.

There is an *Australian Digest* which digests case law and Butterworths produce *Australian and New Zealand Annotations to the All England Reports*.

Textbooks

There are Australian editions of some English textbooks but there are many excellent textbooks of Australian law.

Periodicals

Most Australian universities produce their own law review although not all of these appear regularly.

The *Australian Law Journal* also has many useful articles.

Law reform materials

Each state has its own law reform committee which produces reports. There is also a federal law commission. Details of law reform activities in Australia and New Zealand are collated by the Law Reform Commission of Australia which produces a regular bulletin called *Reform*.

CANADA

You will find a useful survey of Canadian law and the legal system in Bora Laskin, *The British Tradition in Canadian Law*.

Primary Materials

Statutes

Canada, like Australia, is a federal jurisdiction. Federal statutes are set out topic by topic in *Revised Statutes of Canada*. This kept up to date by *Statutes of Canada*.

Each province produces its own set of statutes, *e.g. Revised Statutes of Ontario* which is kept up to date by *Statutes of Ontario*.

Law reports

Canada Law Reports report cases from the federal courts in Canada.

Dominion Law Reports is a very useful set of reports covering both federal and provincial cases.

There are various sets of reports for cases from particular provinces, *e.g.* the *Ontario Reports* and *Rapports Judiciaries Officiels* of Quebec and regional reports, *e.g. Western Weekly Reports* which cover Alberta, British Columbia, Manitoba and Saskatchewan.

Secondary Materials

Encyclopedias

The *Canadian Abridgement* is a digest of cases from federal and provincial courts.

The *Canadian Encyclopedia Digest* is a law encyclopedia rather like the *Corpus Juris Secundum* in the U.S.A.

Textbooks

There are an increasing number of specialists works by Canadian authors.

Periodicals

The most likely periodicals which you will consult are the *Canadian Bar Review* and the various university law journals. Unlike England, the law schools tend to produce their own journals.

Law reform materials

Each province has its law reform body and there is a federal law reform commission. The latter has so far mainly operated in the areas of criminal and family law. Its reports show a fresh, popular style which is uncharacteristic of most commonwealth law reform reports.

NEW ZEALAND

There is a useful general survey of New Zealand law in the relevant volume in *The British Commonwealth Series* (edited by Dr. J. L. Robson, formerly Secretary of Justice) which is now in its second edition.

Primary Materials

Statutes

These are contained in a series known as *Statutes of New Zealand* which is gradually being replaced by the *Reprinted Statutes of New Zealand*. Prior to the earlier series, which dates back to 1854, there are ordinances.

Law reports

The principal reports are the *New Zealand Law Reports*. Occasionally, you may get a case in a series known as the *Gazette Law Reports* which date from 1899–1953.

Secondary Materials

Encyclopedias

There is a *New Zealand Commentary* to Halsbury's *Laws*. In addition, there were numerous digests of the case law in the nineteenth century. The present case law digest is the Abridgement of New Zealand case law.

Textbooks

Although English textbooks are often used, there is an increasing number of New Zealand specialist texts.

Periodicals

Auckland, Wellington, Canterbury and Otago law schools produce their own journals. In addition, there is the *New Zealand Universities' Law Review*.

The *New Zealand Law Journal* is a practitioners' journal which sometimes contains articles useful to a student.

Law reform materials

There is a Law Reform Commission which has satellite committees. Although part time these are productive.

THE UNITED STATES OF AMERICA

Primary Materials

Statutes

The United States is a federal jurisdiction with a written constitution. Federal legislation is contained in *Statutes at Large* but you are most likely to find it in your library in the form of the *United States Code Annotated* and the *Federal Code Annotated*.

There are separate sets of statutes of each state which are often called codes. These are broken down into subjects like the Canadian legislation.

Law reports

The American system of reports is complicated. Supreme Court cases are reported in *United States Supreme Court Reports*. Federal cases are covered in *United States Reports* and the *Federal Reporter*. Prior to these, there were nominate reports.

Each state has its own set of reports but you are most likely to find in your library some or all of the *National Reporter System* which divides the United State up into seven groups—Pacific, North-Western, South-Western, North-Eastern, Atlantic, South-Eastern and Southern. There is a very useful map showing the states covered by each group facing p. 70 of *How to Find the Law* (6th ed.) by William R. Roalfe.

Another set of reports which you may come across is *American Law Reports Annotated*.

Secondary Materials

Encyclopedias

There are two excellent encyclopedias of American law—the *American Jurisprudence* and the *Corpus Juris Secundum* which both resemble Halsbury's *Laws of England* in their coverage. There are some encyclopedias of state laws also but your library is unlikely to stock them.

The main digest is the *American Digest System* which follows the scheme of the *National Reporter System*.

Textbooks

The United States is rich in practitioners' texts but the tendency in academic law nowadays is towards cases and materials books with brief interlocking texts.

Periodicals

The United States produces an abundance of university law journals. The articles to which you will be referred will tend to appear in magazines such as the *Harvard Law Review*, the *Yale Law Journal*, the *Columbia Law Review* and the *Chicago Law Review* although there are many other excellent journals.

It is unlikely that you will be referred to practitioners' journals but there are specialist journals such as the *Business Lawyer* to which occasional reference might be made.

Law reform materials

Each state has its own law reform body which produces reports. There are often ad hoc committees. In addition, you are likely to be referred to the *American Restatements* which emanates from the American Law Institute. It is drafted like law but has doctrinal influence rather than direct legal application.

FRANCE

Two very useful introductory books are Amos & Walton *Introduction to French Law* (3rd ed.), ed. by Lawson, Anton and Brown; and *A Source-book on French Law* by Kahn-Freund, Levy and Rudden. Rene David's *French Law—Its Structure, Sources and Methodology* is also useful.

Most of French law is codified. The Codes can be obtained in pocket editions in the series *Petits Codes Dalloz*. These have some annotations.

The major encyclopedia is the *Encyclopedie Dalloz*.

GERMANY

A useful introduction is Dr. E. J. Cohn's two volume *Manual of German Law* (2nd ed.).

German law, like French law, is largely codified. Pocket editions of the codes are produced by C. H. Beck'sche Ver-lagsbuchhand-lung of Munich.

There is no German equivalent of *Halsbury* or the *Encyclopedie Dalloz*. Reifferscheidt's *Erganzbares Lexikon des Rechts* is a large law dictionary.

EUROPEAN COMMUNITY

The basic law, as we saw, is contained in the treaties. There is a useful edition of these produced by Sweet & Maxwell, now in its fourth edition. E.C. legislation can be found in the legislation volumes of the *Official Journal of the European Communities*. There are official law reports of the European Court but the main English series is *Common Market Law Reports*.

Sweet & Maxwell produce an *Encyclopedia of European Community Law*.

There are a number of introductory texts, the simplest of which is Mathijsen's *Guide to European Community Law*.

Specialist journals include the *Common Market Law Review* and the *European Law Review*. Each Member State tends to produce its own literature to which the specialist must refer.

---

[1] Miles O. Price and Harry Bitner, *Effective Legal Research* (3rd ed.), p. 331.
[2] Viscount Hailsham in his Introduction to the second edition.

SPECIMEN SOURCES

Human Organ Transplants Act 1989

1

1989 CHAPTER 31

2

An Act to prohibit commercial dealings in human organs intended for transplanting; to restrict the transplanting of such organs between persons who are not genetically related; and for supplementary purposes connected with those matters.

3
4

[27th July 1989]

5

B E IT ENACTED by the Queen's most Excellent Majesty, by and with the advice and consent of the Lords Spiritual and Temporal, and Commons, in this present Parliament assembled, and by the authority of the same, as follows:—

6

7

1.—(1) A person is guilty of an offence if in Great Britain he—

  (a) makes or receives any payment for the supply of, or for an offer to supply, an organ which has been or is to be removed from a dead or living person and is intended to be transplanted into another person whether in Great Britain or elsewhere;

  (b) seeks to find a person willing to supply for payment such an organ as is mentioned in paragraph (a) above or offers to supply such an organ for payment;

  (c) initiates or negotiates any arrangement involving the making of any payment for the supply of, or for an offer to supply, such an organ; or

  (d) takes part in the management or control of a body of persons corporate or unincorporate whose activities consist of or include the initiation or negotiation of such arrangements.

Prohibition of commercial dealings in human organs.

8

(2) Without prejudice to paragraph (b) of subsection (1) above, a person is guilty of an offence if he causes to be published or distributed, or knowingly publishes or distributes, in Great Britain an advertisement—

  (a) inviting persons to supply for payment any such organs as are mentioned in paragraph (a) of that subsection or offering to supply any such organs for payment; or

9

---

1. Short Title. **2.** Number. **3.** Long Title.
4. Note absence of Preamble. **5.** Date of Act. **6.** Enacting Words.
7. Section. **8.** Marginal note. **9.** Subsection.

     (b) indicating that the advertiser is willing to initiate or negotiate any such arrangement as is mentioned in paragraph (c) of that subsection.

(3) In this section "payment" means payment in money or money's worth but does not include any payment for defraying or reimbursing—

     (a) the cost of removing, transporting or preserving the organ to be supplied; or

     (b) any expenses or loss of earnings incurred by a person so far as reasonably and directly attributable to his supplying an organ from his body.

(4) In this section "advertisement" includes any form of advertising whether to the public generally, to any section of the public or individually to selected persons.

(5) A person guilty of an offence under subsection (1) above is liable on summary conviction to imprisonment for a term not exceeding three months or a fine not exceeding level 5 on the standard scale or both; and a person guilty of an offence under subsection (2) above is liable on summary conviction to a fine not exceeding level 5 on that scale.

Restriction on transplants between persons not genetically related.

2.—(1) Subject to subsection (3) below, a person is guilty of an offence if in Great Britain he—

     (a) removes from a living person an organ intended to be transplanted into another person; or

     (b) transplants an organ removed from a living person into another person,

unless the person into whom the organ is to be or, as the case may be, is transplanted is genetically related to the person from whom the organ is removed.

(2) For the purposes of this section a person is genetically related to—

     (a) his natural parents and children;

     (b) his brothers and sisters of the whole or half blood;

     (c) the brothers and sisters of the whole or half blood of either of his natural parents; and

     (d) the natural children of his brothers and sisters of the whole or half blood or of the brothers and sisters of the whole or half blood of either of his natural parents;

but persons shall not in any particular case be treated as related in any of those ways unless the fact of the relationship has been established by such means as are specified by regulations made by the Secretary of State.

(3) The Secretary of State may by regulations provide that the prohibition in subsection (1) above shall not apply in cases where—

     (a) such authority as is specified in or constituted by the regulations is satisfied—

          (i) that no payment has been or is to be made in contravention of section 1 above; and

          (ii) that such other conditions as are specified in the regulations are satisfied; and

(b) such other requirements as may be specified in the regulations are complied with.

(4) The expenses of any such authority shall be defrayed by the Secretary of State out of money provided by Parliament.

(5) A person guilty of an offence under this section is liable on summary conviction to imprisonment for a term not exceeding three months or a fine not exceeding level 5 on the standard scale or both.

(6) The power to make regulations under this section shall be exercisable by statutory instrument.

(7) Regulations under subsection (2) above shall be subject to annulment in pursuance of a resolution of either House of Parliament; and no regulations shall be made under subsection (3) above unless a draft of them has been laid before and approved by a resolution of each House of Parliament.

3.—(1) The Secretary of State may make regulations requiring such persons as are specified in the regulations to supply to such authority as is so specified such information as may be so specified with respect to transplants that have been or are proposed to be carried out in Great Britain using organs removed from dead or living persons. *Information about transplant operations.*

(2) Any such authority shall keep a record of information supplied to it in pursuance of the regulations made under this section.

(3) Any person who without reasonable excuse fails to comply with those regulations is guilty of an offence and liable on summary conviction to a fine not exceeding level 3 on the standard scale; and any person who, in purported compliance with those regulations, knowingly or recklessly supplies information which is false or misleading in a material respect is guilty of an offence and liable on summary conviction to a fine not exceeding level 5 on the standard scale.

(4) The power to make regulations under this section shall be exercisable by statutory instrument subject to annulment in pursuance of a resolution of either House of Parliament.

4.—(1) Where an offence under this Act committed by a body corporate is proved to have been committed with the consent or connivance of, or to be attributable to any neglect on the part of, any director, manager, secretary or other similar officer of the body corporate or any person who was purporting to act in any such capacity, he as well as the body corporate is guilty of the offence and is liable to be proceeded against and punished accordingly. *Offences by bodies corporate.*

(2) Where the affairs of a body corporate are managed by its members, subsection (1) above shall apply to the acts and defaults of a member in connection with his functions of management as if he were a director of the body corporate.

5. No proceedings for an offence under section 1 or 2 above shall be instituted in England and Wales except by or with the consent of the Director of Public Prosecutions. *Prosecutions.*

Northern
Ireland.
1974 c. 28.

6. An Order in Council under paragraph 1(1)(b) of Schedule 1 to the Northern Ireland Act 1974 (legislation for Northern Ireland in the interim period) which contains a statement that it is made only for purposes corresponding to the purposes of this Act—

(a) shall not be subject to paragraph 1(4) and (5) of that Schedule (affirmative resolution of both Houses of Parliament); but

(b) shall be subject to annulment in pursuance of a resolution of either House of Parliament.

10

Short title,
interpretation.
commencement
and extent.

7.—(1) This Act may be cited as the Human Organ Transplants Act 1989.

(2) In this Act "organ" means any part of a human body consisting of a structured arrangement of tissues which, if wholly removed, cannot be replicated by the body.

(3) Section 1 above shall not come into force until the day after that on which this Act is passed and section 2(1) above shall not come into force until such day as the Secretary of State may appoint by an order made by statutory instrument.

(4) Except for section 6 this Act does not extend to Northern Ireland.

11

---

10. Amendment Provision.
11. Area of Operation.

1

1974 No. 654

WAGES COUNCILS

2

The Boot and Floor Polish Wages Council (Great Britain) (Abolition) Order 1974

Made - - - -	1*st April* 1974
Laid before Parliament	10*th April* 1974
Coming into Operation	13*th May* 1974

3

Whereas the Secretary of State in accordance with section 4 of and Schedule 1 to the Wages Councils Act 1959(**a**) published notice of his intention to make an order abolishing the Boot and Floor Polish Wages Council (Great Britain):

And whereas no objection has been made with respect to the draft order referred to in the said notice:

Now, therefore, the Secretary of State in exercise of powers conferred by section 4(1)(*b*) of, and paragraph 4 of Schedule 1 to, the said Act and now vested in him (**b**), and of all other powers enabling him in that behalf, hereby makes the following Order:—

4

1. The Boot and Floor Polish Wages Council (Great Britain) is hereby abolished.

2.—(1) This Order may be cited as the Boot and Floor Polish Wages Council (Great Britain) (Abolition) Order 1974 and shall come into operation on 13th May 1974.

(2) The Interpretation Act 1889(**c**) shall apply to the interpretation of this Order as it applies to the interpretation of an Act of Parliament.

Signed by order of the Secretary of State.

5

1st April 1974.

6

Harold Walker,
Joint Parliamentary Under Secretary of State,
Department of Employment.

(**a**) 1959 c. 69.
(**b**) S.I.1959/1769, 1968/729 (1959 I, p. 1795; 1968 II, p. 2108).
(**c**) 1889 c. 63.

---

1. Number. **2.** Title. **3.** Preamble **4.** Paragraph
5. Date. **6.** Signature.

EXPLANATORY NOTE
(This Note is not part of the Order.)

This Order abolishes the Boot and Floor Polish Wages Council (Great Britain), which was established as a Trade Board under the Trade Boards Acts 1909 and 1918 (c. 22 and c. 32), and became a Wages Council by virtue of the Wages Councils Act 1945 (c. 17).

The abolition of the Council was recommended by the Commission on Industrial Relations on the grounds that the Council is no longer necessary in order to maintain adequate pay and conditions for the workers in the boot and floor polish industry.

1 AUDITEUR DU TRAVAIL AT THE TRIBUNAL DE
MONS *v.* CAGNON AND TAQUET (Case 69/74)

BEFORE THE COURT OF JUSTICE OF THE EUROPEAN COMMUNITIES

(*The President,* Judge R. Lecourt; Judges J. Mertens de Wilmars,
Lord Mackenzie Stuart, A. M. Donner, R. Monaco, P. Pescatore,
H. Kutscher, M. Sørensen and A. O'Keeffe.) Herr Gerhard Reischl,
Advocate General.   18 February 1975

Reference by the Tribunal de Police de Mons under **Article 177** EEC.

Road transport. Driving conditions. Daily rest periods. In
Article 11 (2) of the Road Transport (Driving Conditions)
Regulation (543/69), the phrase 'every crew member... shall
have had ... a ... rest period' of at least 10 consecutive hours
means that the provisions on daily rest must be observed both
by the crew members (*e.g.,* drivers) themselves, who are required
to stop all activities referred to in Article 14 of the Regulation
for the minimum period laid down, and also by the employer
running a road transport undertaking, who is required to take
the necessary measures to permit the crew members to have the
daily rest laid down. [10]

The Court interpreted Article 11 (2) of Regulation 543/69 (the Road
Transport (Driving Conditions) Regulation 1969) to the effect that its
provisions relating to a daily rest period are binding not only on the
employer but also on the drivers of road transport vehicles.

> *Marc Sohier,* legal adviser to the E.C. Commission, for the
> Commission as *amicus curiae.*
> *Maître Detaeye* for the defendants.

No cases were referred to.

Facts

Article 11 (2), first paragraph, of Council Regulation 543/69 of
25 March 1969 on the harmonisation of certain social legislation
relating to road transport provides:

---

1. Case name.   2. Court.   3. Headnote.   4. Summary of facts.

1975

*Auditeur
du Travail
(Mons)* v.
Cagnon

European
Court
of Justice

' Every crew member engaged in the carriage of passengers shall have had, during the twenty-four-hour period preceding any time when he is performing any activity covered by Article 14 (2) (c) or (d):

—a daily rest period of not less than ten consecutive hours, which shall not be reduced during the week, or

. . .'

Article 14 (2) (c) of the same regulation refers to ' driving periods '.

The present proceedings result from an action pending before the Tribunal de Police de Mons in which the Auditeur du Travail (at the Tribunal du Travail de Mons) is prosecuting Jean-Pierre Cagnon, coach driver, as the defendant and Jean-Paul Taquet, his employer who is civilly and jointly liable. In the summons the defendant is charged with not having complied with the provisions of the first paragraph of Article 11 (2) of the aforementioned Council Regulation 543/69 of 25 March 1969 and of section 2 of the Belgian Royal Decree of 23 March 1970 implementing the said regulation by reason of the fact that during a trip to Germany,

' being a member of a crew engaged in the carriage of passengers, not having had, during the twenty-four-hour period preceding any time when he is perfoming an activity covered by Article 14 (2) (c) of Regulation 543/69, a daily rest period of not less than ten consecutive hours.'

During the main proceedings the defendant did not dispute the facts with which he was charged, but objected that the Community provision in question did not involve any obligation on his part in that it was only employers who were bound to respect the daily rest period and not crew members of road vehicles.

The Tribunal de Police de Mons found first of all that since the defence raised by the employer, according to which Mr. Cagnon had been instructed to spend the night at Dortmund, the destination of the vehicle driven by the defendant, had not been challenged, there was no misconduct on the part of Mr. Taquet. It then stated that the defence related to the interpretation of the first paragraph of Article 11 (2) of Regulation 543/69 since it was a question of whether ' the driver must have had the possibility of taking the rest laid down by the legislation or whether, on the other hand, he is required to respect the regulation, that is to say, to have in fact rested '.

Following a suggestion by the prosecutor to request the Court of Justice to give a ruling on the question of interpretation thus raised, the Tribunal de Police de Mons by judgment of 6 September 1974 stayed the proceedings and referred to the Court of Justice under **Article 177** of the EEC Treaty the question:

' What is the meaning of the words " shall have had . . . a . . . rest period " in the first paragraph of Article 11 (2) of Regulation 543/69.'

1975

Submissions of the Advocate General (Herr Gerhard Reischl)

Auditeur du Travail (Mons) v. *Cagnon*

European Court of Justice

Submissions (Reischl A.G.)

5

In connection with a case pending before it, the Tribunal de Police de Mons has requested the Court's interpretation of a provision of Council Regulation 543/69 on the harmonisation of certain legislation relating to road transport.

That regulation, which *inter alia* was made to implement a common transport policy on the basis of **Article 75** of the EEC Treaty, provides—in so far as we are concerned here—in Article 11 (2) that every crew member engaged in the carriage of passengers shall have had, during the 24-hour period preceding any time when he is performing any activity covered by Article 14 (2) (c) or (d) (that is driving or attending at work) a daily rest period of not less than 10 consecutive hours, which shall not be reduced during the week. Article 14 (2) of the regulation further provides that members of the crew shall enter in the daily sheets of the individual control book details *inter alia* of breaks from work of not less than 15 minutes. It is the task of the member-States under Article 18 of the regulation to adopt such laws, regulations or administrative provisions as may be necessary for the implementation of the regulation and such measures have to cover, *inter alia*, penalties to be imposed in case of breach.

A Royal Decree was accordingly issued on 23 March 1970 in Belgium. Section 3 thereof refers to section 2 of the Transport Treaties Implementation Act of 18 February 1969 (*Loi relative aux mesures d'exécution des traités et actes internationaux en matière de transport par route, par chemin de fer ou par voie navigable*) and declares that infringements of the said Council regulation are punishable in a certain manner.

Criminal proceedings were brought against Jean-Pierre Cagnon, coach driver, and his employer, Jean-Paul Taquet, transport contractor, under those provisions. Apart from failure to enter breaks from work of not less than 15 minutes under Article 14 (2) of the Council regulation, an infringement which does not concern us further here, the former is charged with being engaged in the carriage of passengers in Germany and not having had, during the 24-hour period preceding the time when he was performing his activity, a daily rest period of not less than 10 consecutive hours. The employer, who stated that the driver had been directed to spend the night in question at the destination in Germany, was, in view of his evidence, not criminally liable. Should the driver indeed have committed an infringement in performing the work entrusted to him by the employer, the latter would, however, be jointly liable under section 2 (4) of the Act of 18 February 1969 for all the fines imposed on the driver, and the costs of the proceedings. This is the reason that he was not dismissed from the case.

The accused driver's main defence to the proceedings was the argument that Article 11 (2) of the regulation gave rise to obligations

---

5. Submissions of Advocate General.

only on the part of the employer and not the crew members. He alleged that it was sufficient under this provision for the employer to see that the possibility existed of taking the daily rest period and that it was not necessary for crew members in fact to rest. If this interpretation were correct, it would obviously not be possible after the statements made in the main proceedings to impose penalties on the accused driver.

In view of these facts, which require an interpretation of Regulation 543/69, the Tribunal de Police de Mons considered it proper to stay the proceedings by the order of 6 September 1974 and to refer for a preliminary ruling under **Article 177** of the EEC Treaty the question of how the words ' shall have had . . . a . . . rest period ' in Article 11 (2) of Regulation 543/69 are to be understood.

Only the Commission of the European Communities has made observations on this question. It has recommended an interpretation according to which Article 11 of the regulation also imposes an obligation on crew members actually to observe the daily rest periods, that is breaks from the activities referred to in Article 14 (2) (c) or (d).

I find this view and reasons convincing and propose that the Court should adopt them.

First it is important to maintain that the provision requiring interpretation is part of a regulation, that is a document which under **Article 189** of the EEC Treaty has general application, is binding in its entirety and directly applicable in all member-States.

The Commission is also right in stating that the wording of Article 11 (2) makes it clear that there is an obligation not only on the transport contractor to provide the possibility of having daily rest periods but also on the crew members actually to observe the provisions on daily rest periods. In fact it is stated in Article 11 (2) —so far as it concerns us here: ' every crew member engaged in the carriage of passengers shall have had, during the twenty-four hours preceding any time when he is performing any activity covered by Article 14 (2) (c) or (d): a daily rest period of not less than ten consecutive hours, which shall not be reduced during the week. . . . ' This provision would certainly have been differently worded if it had been the intention of the draftsman of the regulation simply to require the transport contractors to give their drivers the possibility of daily rest periods. Daily rest periods within the meaning of Article 11 of the regulation—as the Commission likewise rightly stresses—must be contrasted with the driving periods and other periods of attendance at work mentioned in Article 11 by reference to Article 14. This means that crew members doubtless have a certain freedom in how they use their rest periods; what however is ruled out, in any event, is driving activity and attendance at work.

The correctness of this interpretation does not appear from Article 11 (2) alone. Support is obtained from a glance at Articles 7 and 8

1975
——
Auditeur du Travail (Mons) v. *Cagnon*
——
European Court of Justice
——
Submissions (Reischl A.G.)

1975

*Auditeur
du Travail
(Mons)* v.
Cagnon
—
European
Court
of Justice
—
Judgment
(Monaco J.)

of the regulation, in which the limitation on driving periods is related to the daily rest periods. This accords with the interpretation that there is a direct and clear obligation on crew members to respect not only the driving periods but also the rest periods.

Finally, the objectives of the regulation as expressed in its pre-amble must not be forgotten. The objective is the harmonisation of certain provisions affecting competition in transport by rail, road and inland waterway, as is shown by the reference to the Council Decision of 13 May 1965.[1] Reference is made to the promotion of ' social progress ' and, not least, to the improvement of road safety. It appears to me quite obvious that these objectives could not be achieved if Article 11, as the accused in the main proceedings thinks, were limited to providing the possibility of observing the rest periods. In such circumstances nothing would be done for the harmonisation of the provisions affecting competition and certainly no improve-ment in road safety would be achieved, nor could there be any promotion of social progress but rather regression in comparison with the previous legal situation obtaining in the member-States.

For all these reasons the question from the Tribunal de Police de Mons should be answered as follows:

Article 11 (2) of Regulation 543/69 is to be interpreted as meaning that it also gives rise to an obligation on the part of crew members to observe the provisions on rest periods, so that during the periods provided for, the activities mentioned in Article 14 (2) (c) or (d) are not pursued.

JUDGMENT (drafting judge, Monaco J.)

6

[1] By judgment dated 6 September 1974, filed at the Registry of the Court on 18 September 1974, the Tribunal de Police de Mons requested a preliminary ruling under **Article 177** of the EEC Treaty on the interpretation of the first paragraph of Article 11 (2) of Council Regulation 543/69 of 25 March 1969 on the harmonisation of certain social legislation relating to road transport.

[2] The question arose in police proceedings in which a coach driver was charged with not having taken, as a crew member engaged in the carriage of passengers, the daily rest referred to in the aforementioned first paragraph of Article 11 (2).

[3] The defendant challenged the validity of the proceedings on the ground that only employers had to observe the requirement for daily rest and not crew members of road vehicles.

[4] The Court is requested for this purpose to rule as to the meaning which must be given to the words ' shall have had . . . a . . . rest period '.

[5] The first paragraph of Article 11 (2) of Regulation 543/69

---

[1] J.O. 1500/65.

---

6. Judgment. Note formality and brevity.

1975

Auditeur du Travail (Mons) v. *Cagnon*

European Court of Justice

Judgment (Monaco J.)

provides ' every crew member engaged in the carriage of passengers shall have had, during the twenty-four-hour period preceding any time he is performing any activity covered by Article 14 (2) (c) or (d): a daily rest period of not less than ten consecutive hours, which shall not be reduced during the week . . .'.

[6] Article 14 (2) (c) and (d) refers to ' driving periods ' and ' other periods of attendance at work '.

[7] The third and tenth recitals of Regulation 543/69 show that the regulation has among other objectives ' to improve road safety ' for which purpose it is desirable ' to lay down the minimum duration of and other conditions governing the daily and weekly rest periods of crew members '.

[8] Such an objective would not be achieved if the provisions enacted in relation to daily and weekly rest applied only to the employer running the road transport service, and did not likewise apply to crew members by requiring them to have in fact rested for the prescribed minimum period.

[9] For the precise purpose of ensuring that this requirement is observed, Article 14 of the said regulation provides that crew members shall carry an individual control book.

[10] As a result the phrase ' shall have had . . . a . . . rest period ' in the first paragraph of Article 11 (2) of Regulation 543/69 of 25 March 1969 must be interpreted as meaning that the provisions on daily rest must be observed both by crew members themselves, who are required to stop all activities referred to in Article 14 of the regulation for the minimum period laid down, and by the employer running a road transport undertaking, who is required to take the necessary measures to permit the crew members to have the daily rest period laid down.

Costs

[11] The costs incurred by the Commission of the European Communities, which has submitted observations to the Court, are not recoverable.

[12] Since the proceedings are, in so far as the parties to the main action are concerned, a step in the action before the national court, costs are a matter for that court.

On those grounds, THE COURT, in answer to the question referred to it by the Tribunal de Police de Mons by judgment of 6 September 1974,

HEREBY RULES:

> The phrase ' shall have had . . . a . . . rest period ' in the first paragraph of Article 11 (2) of Regulation 543/69 of 25 March 1969 must be interpreted as meaning that the provisions on daily rest must be observed both by crew

7. Reasons.   8. Ruling.

1975

*Auditeur
du Travail
(Mons)* v.
Cagnon

European
Court
of Justice

Arrêt
(Monaco J.)

members themselves, who are required to stop all activities
referred to in Article 14 of the regulation for the minimum
period laid down, and by the employer running a road
transport undertaking, who is required to take the necessary
measures to permit the crew members to have the daily rest
period laid down.

ARRET

[1] Attendu que, par jugement du 6 septembre 1974, parvenu au
greffe de la Cour le 18 septembre 1974, le Tribunal de Police de
Mons a posé, en vertu de l'**article 177** du traité C.E.E., une question
concernant l'interprétation de l'article 11, § 2, al. 1ᵉʳ du règlement
n° 543/69 du Conseil du 25 mars 1969, relatif à l'harmonisation de
certaines dispositions en matière sociale dans le domaine des transports par route;

[2] que la question a été soulevée à l'occasion d'une procédure de
police, au cours de laquelle il est notamment reproché au conducteur
d'un car de ne pas avoir pris, en qualité de membre d'un équipage
affecté au transport de voyageurs, le repos journalier visé à l'article
11, § 2, al. 1ᵉʳ précité;

[3] que le prévenu a contesté le bien-fondé de cette procédure,
en soutenant que le respect de l'obligation du repos journalier ne
s'imposerait qu'aux employeurs et non aux membres des équipages
des véhicules routiers;

[4] qu'à ces fins il est demandé à la Cour de dire dans quel sens
doit être comprise l'expression ' avoir bénéficié d'un repos ';

[5] Attendu qu'aux termes de l'article 11, § 2, al. 1ᵉʳ du règlement
n° 543/69, 'tout membre d'un équipage affecté aux transports de
voyageurs doit avoir bénéficié, au cours de la période de 24 heures
précédant tout moment où il exerce une des activités indiquées à
l'article 14, § 2 sous (c) et (d), d'un repos journalier de 10 heures
consécutives au moins, sans possibilité de réduction au cours de la
semaine . . .';

[6] que l'article 14, § 2 se réfère, sous (c) et (d), à des ' periodes
de conduite ' et aux ' autres périodes de présence au travail ';

[7] qu'il ressort des troisième et dixième considérants que le règlement n° 543/69 a, parmi d'autres objets, notamment celui d'
' améliorer la sécurité routière ' aux fins de laquelle il est apparu
nécessaire de ' fixer les durées minimales et les autres conditions
auxquelles les repos journalier et hebdomadaire des membres
d'équipages sont soumis ';

[8] qu'un tel objectif ne serait pas atteint si les dispositions
arrêtées en matière de repos journalier et hebdomadaire ne devaient
s'imposer qu'au seul employeur, exploitant d'un service de transport
routier, et ne devaient également s'appliquer aux membres d'équipages, en les obligeant à prendre effectivement le repos minimal
prescrit;

[9] qu'en vue précisément d'assurer le respect de cette obligation, ledit règlement prévoit, à son article 14, l'institution d'un livret individuel de contrôle obligatoire pour les membres d'équipages;

[10] qu'en conséquence, l'expression ' avoir bénéficié d'un repos,' figurant à l'article 11, § 2, al. 1er du règlement (CEE) n° 543/69 du 25 mars 1969, doit être interprétée comme imposant le respect des dispositions relatives au repos journalier tant aux membres d'équipages eux-mêmes, auxquels il est fait obligation de suspendre effectivement, pendant la durée minimale prescrite, tout exercise des activités indiquées à l'article 14, § 2, sous (c) et (d) du même règlement, qu'à l'employeur exploitant d'un service de transport routier, tenu de prendre les mesures nécessaires afin de permettre aux membres d'équipages de bénéficier du repos journalier prescrit;

1975
—
*Auditeur
du Travail
(Mons)* v.
Cagnon
—
European
Court
of Justice
—
Arrêt
(Monaco J.)

Sur les dépens

[11] Attendu que les frais exposés par la Commission des C.E., qui a soumis des observations à la Cour, ne peuvent faire l'objet de remboursement;

[12] que la procédure revêtant, à l'égard des parties au principal, le caractère d'un incident soulevé devant la juridiction nationale, il appartient à celle-ci de statuer sur les dépens;

par ces motifs, LA COUR, statuant sur la question à elle soumise par le Tribunal de Police de Mons par jugement du 6 septembre 1974,

DIT POUR DROIT:

L'expression ' avoir bénéficié d'un repos,' figurant à l'article 11, § 2, al. 1er du règlement (CEE) n° 543/69 du 25 mars 1969, doit être interprétée comme imposant le respect des dispositions relatives au repos journalier tant aux membres d'équipages eux-mêmes, auxquels il est fait obligation de suspendre effectivement, pendant la durée minimale prescrite, tout exercise des activités indiquées à l'article 14, § 2, sous (c) et (d) du même règlement, qu'à l'employeur exploitant d'un service de transport routier, tenu de prendre les mesures nécessaires afin de permettre aux membres d'équipages de bénéficier du repos journalier prescrit.

A

1

2

GOLD v. HARINGEY HEALTH AUTHORITY

1987   March 10, 11, 12;   Watkins, Stephen Brown and Lloyd L.JJ.
       April 14

B
*Medical   Practitioner—Negligence—Duty   to   inform—Sterilisation
operation—Failure to give warning of possibility of fertility being
restored—Subsequent pregnancy—Claim in negligence for non-
disclosure of risk—Body of medical opinion against giving warning
as to risk of pregnancy—Whether accepted professional standard test
applicable to non-therapeutic advice*

    During the course of her third pregnancy in 1979, the plaintiff,
after indicating that she did not wish to have any more children,
C   was advised to undergo a sterilisation operation at the defendants'   **3**
hospital after the birth of her child. The operation was duly
carried out but the plaintiff later became pregnant and gave birth
to a fourth child. She brought an action for damages for negligence
against the defendants alleging, inter alia, that she had not been
warned of the failure rate of female sterilisation operations and
that if she had been warned her husband would have undergone a
vasectomy instead. Medical evidence was adduced at the trial that
D   there was a substantial body of responsible doctors who would not
have given any such warning in 1979. The judge however held that
the test whether there existed a substantial body of medical
opinion who would have acted as the defendants had done applied
only to advice given in a therapeutic context and did not apply to
advice given in a contraceptive context. Applying his own view as
to what information should have been given, he found that the
E   defendants had been negligent in not warning the plaintiff that the
operation might not succeed.
    On the defendants' appeal:—
    Held, allowing the appeal, that for the purposes of ascertaining
the test as to the duty of care owed by a doctor to a patient there
was no distinction to be made between advice given in a therapeutic
context and advice given in a non-therapeutic context; that,
accordingly, the judge erred in holding that advice given in a
F   contraceptive context was not to be judged by the contemporary
standards of a responsible body of medical opinion; and that, on
the evidence, there was a substantial body of responsible doctors
who would not in 1979 have warned the plaintiff of the failure rate
of female sterilisation operations (post, pp. 489F—490c, 491B–D,
492c–E).
    Bolam v. Friern Hospital Management Committee [1957] 1
G   W.L.R. 582 and *Sidaway v. Board of Governors of the Bethlem
Royal Hospital and the Maudsley Hospital* [1985] A.C. 871,
H.L.(E.) applied.
    Decision of Schiemann J. reversed.

The following cases are referred to in the judgments:

Bolam v. Friern Hospital Management Committee [1957] 1 W.L.R. 582; [1957]   **4**
H   2 All E.R. 118
Emeh v. Kensington and Chelsea and Westminster Area Health Authority [1985]
    Q.B. 1012; [1985] 2 W.L.R. 233; [1984] 3 All E.R. 1044, C.A.
Eyre v. Measday [1986] 1 All E.R. 488, C.A.
Jones v. Berkshire Area Health Authority (unreported), 2 July 1986, Ognall J.

---

1. The Court.   **2.** Date.   **3.** Headnote.   **4.** Cases cited.

Maynard v. West Midlands Regional Health Authority [1984] 1 W.L.R. 634; A
[1985] 1 All E.R. 635, H.L.(E.)
Saif Ali v. Sydney Mitchell & Co. [1980] A.C. 198; [1978] 3 W.L.R. 849;
[1978] 3 All E.R. 1033, H.L.(E.)
*Sidaway v. Board of Governors of the Bethlem Royal Hospital and the
Maudsley Hospital* [1985] A.C. 871; [1985] 2 W.L.R. 480; [1985] 1 All
E.R. 643, H.L.(E.)
Thake v. Maurice [1986] Q.B. 644; [1986] 2 W.L.R. 337; [1986] 1 All E.R. B
497, C.A.

The following additional cases were cited in argument:

Clarke v. Adams (1950) 94 S.J. 599
Hucks v. Cole (unreported), 8 May 1968; Court of Appeal (Civil Division)
Transcript No. 181 of 1968, C.A.

C

5

APPEAL from Schiemann J.

By a writ dated 10 October 1984 the plaintiff, Phyllis Gold, claimed
damages against the defendants, the Haringey Health Authority, for
negligence and breach of contract in the carrying out of a sterilisation
operation on her on 20 August 1979. In 1982 she gave birth to a child. It
was alleged that the defendants were negligent in failing to disclose to the D
plaintiff that the operation had a failure rate and was not guaranteed of

6

success and, further (during the trial, by leave of the judge), in failing to
discuss vasectomy with the plaintiff and/or the relative rates of failure of
that and sterilisation. It was further alleged that the defendants were in
breach of contract in that they undertook and guaranteed, alternatively
were reasonably understood by the plaintiff to have undertaken or
guaranteed, to make her permanently sterile.   E

The defendants denied liability, contending that the plaintiff had been
told that there was a failure rate with any sterilisation procedure and that,
in any event, in 1979 a failure to warn in such circumstances would not
have been negligent.

On 16 June 1986 the judge upheld the plaintiff's claim finding the
defendants negligent in not warning of a failure rate and in not mentioning F
vasectomy, and also finding the allegation of negligent misrepresentation
proved. He gave judgment for the plaintiff for £19,000.

By their notice of appeal, the defendants appealed on the grounds,
inter alia, that the judge misdirected himself in holding that there was a
distinction between advice given in a therapeutic context and advice given
in connection with contraceptive counselling which meant that the latter
was not to be judged by the contemporary reasonable standards of the G
medical profession; that he failed to attach any or sufficient weight to the
fact that the undisputed evidence on both sides was to the effect that in
1979 approximately half the medical profession would not have warned of
the risk of failure of an operation for sterilisation, nor, by implication,
would they have counselled as to other appropriate methods of sterilisation
or contraception; that he misdirected himself, or there was no evidence on
which he could have made a finding, that there was no responsible body of H
medical opinion which would have failed to warn or mention vasectomy as
an option in the context of someone seeking contraceptive advice; that he
misdirected himself in holding that the questions as to warning of the

---

5. Nature of Appeal   **6.** Summary of earlier proceeding.

A failure rates and the relative risks of vasectomy and sterilisation were to be determined by the court's view as to whether or not the person giving advice acted negligently; and that the judge misdirected himself in holding that the defendants had negligently misrepresented to the plaintiff that the operation for sterilisation would render her permanently sterile.

The facts are set out in the judgment of Lloyd L.J.

B *Stephen Miller* for the defendants. In directing himself on law in accordance with the test propounded in *Bolam v. Friern Hospital Management Committee* [1957] 1 W.L.R. 582 and the speeches of the majority of the House of Lords in *Sidaway v. Board of Governors of the Bethlem Royal Hospital and the Maudsley Hospital* [1985] A.C. 871, the judge failed to attach any or sufficient weight to the fact that the C undisputed evidence on both sides was to the effect that in 1979 approximately half the medical profession would not have warned of the risk of failure of an operation for sterilisation. Where, as here, there was clear evidence of a large number of responsible doctors not giving warning at that time, the judge ought not to have found negligence unless the practice was so wrong that no responsible doctor could subscribe to that view. Applying the *Sidaway* case, no distinction can be drawn between D advice given in a "therapeutic" context and advice given in connection with "contraceptive counselling" by which the latter is not to be judged by the contemporary reasonable standards of the medical profession. Accordingly the *Bolam* test should have been applied. The failure to advise the plaintiff of the possibility of failure of the operation did not amount to negligent misrepresentation: see *Eyre v. Measday* [1986] 1 All E.R. 488, 494.

E *Charles Lewis* for the plaintiff. The *Bolam* principle does not apply in the context of non-therapeutic situations. It is limited to the medical profession as it effectively takes away from the court the final decision as to whether the conduct complained of is negligent or not. If a doctor defendant produces evidence to the effect that there existed a body of competent medical opinion which would support the defendant's actions or decisions as reasonable, the matter is effectively out of the court's hands. F That is why the *Sidaway* case is confined to strictly therapeutic situations. On that basis *Bolam* should be distinguished. [Reference was made to *Eyre v. Measday* [1986] 1 All E.R. 488; *Jones v. Berkshire Area Health Authority* (unreported), 2 July 1986, *Thake v. Maurice* [1986] Q.B. 644; *Emeh v. Kensington and Chelsea and Westminster Area Health Authority* [1985] Q.B. 1012; *Clark v. Adams* (1950) 94 S.J. 599 and *Hucks v. Cole* G (unreported), 8 May 1968; Court of Appeal (Civil Division) Transcript No. 181 of 1968.]

Cur. adv. vult.

14 April. The following judgments were handed down.

H LLOYD L.J. On 20 August 1979 the plaintiff, Mrs. Phyllis Gold, underwent an operation for sterilisation at the North Middlesex Hospital. It was on the day after the birth of her third child. The operation did not succeed, for in October 1982 she gave birth to her fourth child, Darren. In

---

October 1984 she commenced these proceedings against Haringey Health A
Authority, despite the fact that she and her husband are delighted with
Darren, their first boy, and indeed have gone on to have a fifth child, born
in November 1984.

In her writ, as amended, she claims damages for negligence in carrying
out the operation. But that claim was rejected by the judge. He found that
the plaintiff had failed to prove that Dr. Arzanghi, who carried out the
operation, had been negligent. There is no appeal against that finding. B

But the judge went on to hold the defendants liable on another ground.
He held that they ought to have warned the plaintiff that the operation
might not succeed, and ought, in the circumstances, to have mentioned the
alternative of vasectomy. If they had, then, according to the judge's
findings, the plaintiff would not have consented to the operation, and Mr.
Gold would have been vasectomised instead. By inference, he has found C
that the vasectomy would have been effective to prevent the birth of the
fourth and fifth children. The failure rate for vasectomy was accepted as
being about five per ten thousand, compared with a failure rate for female
sterilisation of between two and six per thousand. The judge held that the
defendants were negligent in not informing the plaintiff of the failure rate
for female sterilisation, and that they are liable in damages accordingly,
which he assessed at £19,000. D

Before relating the history of the matter, I desire to make one point
clear. We are not in this case called on to decide whether it is desirable or
not that a plaintiff should be able to claim damages for the birth of a
healthy child, and a child which, in this particular case, the plaintiff and
her husband are now delighted to have. In *Jones v. Berkshire Area Health
Authority* (unreported), 2 July 1986, another unwanted pregnancy case, E
Ognall J. said:

> "I pause only to observe that, speaking purely personally, it remains a
> matter of surprise to me that the law acknowledges an entitlement in a
> mother to claim damages for the blessing of a healthy child. Certain it
> is that those who are afflicted with a handicapped child or who long
> desperately to have a child at all and are denied that good fortune F
> would regard an award for this sort of contingency with a measure of
> astonishment. But there it is: that is the law."

Many would no doubt agree with that observation. But the
desirability of permitting such a claim does not concern us here. At
one time there was a conflict of decisions at first instance as to
whether it was against public policy to allow a plaintiff to recover G
damages for the birth of a healthy child. But that conflict has been
resolved, so far as this court is concerned, by the unanimous decision
of this court in *Emeh v. Kensington and Chelsea and Westminster Area
Health Authority* [1985] Q.B. 1012. So in the present appeal we are
concerned solely with the question whether the plaintiff has established
negligence against the defendants by reason of their failure to warn
the plaintiff that the operation might not succeed. H

10 The history of the matter, very briefly, is as follows. The plaintiff's
first and second children, both girls, were born in December 1969 and
November 1972. There was then a long gap before she conceived her

---

10. Judgment Summarizes facts.

A   third child. In the course of her third pregnancy, she discussed with her husband the possibility of him having a vasectomy. According to Mr. Gold's evidence, they knew about vasectomy because two of his friends had had a vasectomy, including the plaintiff's brother-in-law. On 9 January 1982 the plaintiff went to see her general practitioner, Dr. Gomez. He confirmed she was pregnant. She told him that she and her husband were thinking of vasectomy. Dr. Gomez suggested sterilisation

B   instead. According to the plaintiff's evidence, Dr. Gomez was not against vasectomy, but said that sterilisation would be "handier" as the plaintiff would be in hospital in any event having her third child.

On 24 July 1982 the plaintiff saw Miss Witt, the consultant to whom she had been referred at the commencement of her pregnancy. The plaintiff told Miss Witt that she did not want any more children. Miss

C   Witt suggested sterilisation. She did not mention vasectomy as an alternative; but then neither did the plaintiff, although it had been discussed between her and her husband the previous January.

Soon after 24 July the plaintiff must have returned to see Dr. Gomez, her general practitioner. Regrettably Dr. Gomez was not called as a witness, so we do not know what took place on that occasion. All we know is that on 31 July he wrote to Miss Witt:

D
"Many thanks for considering this patient for sterilisation. She has two children aged 10 and 7 years and she is due for her confinement on 20 August 1979. The patient is aware that this is an irreversible operation."

It may be that there was some discussion about vasectomy, and that

E   Dr. Gomez repeated his earlier advice that sterilisation would be "handier;" but we do not know, since Dr. Gomez was not called, and the plaintiff was not asked.

On 14 August the plaintiff saw Dr. Plummer, the house surgeon. She told her that she wanted to be sterilised, and signed a written consent in the form then current. On 19 August she gave birth to Nicola. On 20 August the operation was performed. The judge has

F   found on the balance of probabilities that neither Miss Witt nor Dr. Plummer nor Dr. Arzanghi ever clearly explained that there was a risk of the operation failing. Mr. Miller, who appears for the defendants, does not seek to go behind that finding.

In her case as originally pleaded the plaintiff relied exclusively on the absence of any warning as to the failure rate of the operation, which, as

G   I have said, was accepted as being about two per thousand, or about six per thousand if carried out immediately after childbirth. But on the third day of the evidence, when one of the plaintiff's experts was being re-examined, the judge raised the question whether it might be the defendants' duty, not only to warn the plaintiff of the failure rate for sterilisation, but also to compare the failure rate for female sterilisation with the failure rate for male vasectomy. The point was taken up later

H   the same day with the first of the defendants' experts. On the following morning Mr. Lewis, for the plaintiff, applied to re-amend the statement of claim in accordance with the judge's indication, so as to allege that the defendants were negligent in failing to discuss vasectomy with the

[320]

plaintiff, and to mention the relative failure rates of the two operations.   A
Despite this amendment, Mr. Lewis made clear to us that his main case
rested, and had always rested, on the simple failure to warn that
sterilisation might not succeed.

I now turn to the evidence. The doctors were unanimous in their
view that though they themselves would have warned of the risk of
failure, nevertheless a substantial body of responsible doctors would not
have given any such warning in 1979. One of the witnesses put the   B
proportion of doctors who would not have given any such warning in
1979 as high as 50 per cent. How then did it come about that the judge
convicted the defendants of negligence?

11   In directing the jury in *Bolam v. Friern Hospital Management
Committee* [1957] 1 W.L.R. 582, 587, McNair J. said:

> "[A medical man] is not guilty of negligence if he has acted in   C
> accordance with a practice accepted as proper by a responsible body
> of medical men skilled in that particular art. . . . merely because
> there is a body of opinion who would take a contrary view."

In *Maynard v. West Midlands Regional Health Authority* [1984] 1
W.L.R. 634, the House of Lords applied the *Bolam* test to a case of
wrongful diagnosis. Lord Scarman said, at p. 638:   D

> "It is not enough to show that there is a body of competent
> professional opinion which considers that there was a wrong
> decision, if there also exists a body of professional opinion, equally
> competent, which supports the decision as reasonable in the
> circumstances. It is not enough to show that subsequent events
> show that the operation need never have been performed, if at the   E
> time the decision to operate was taken it was reasonable in the
> sense that a responsible body of medical opinion would have
> accepted it as proper."

In *Sidaway v. Board of Governors of the Bethlem Royal Hospital and
the Maudsley Hospital* [1985] A.C. 871, the House of Lords applied the
same test to a case in which a doctor, before carrying out an operation,   F
failed to warn his patient of a very small risk of very serious injury. It
would have been open to the House of Lords to hold that the *Bolam*
test applied to negligent diagnosis and negligent treatment, but not
negligent advice. In other words, the House of Lords could have
adopted the doctrine of "informed consent" favoured in the United
States of America and Canada. But the House of Lords declined to   G
follow that path. Lord Diplock said, at pp. 893–895:

> "In English jurisprudence the doctor's relationship with his patient
> which gives rise to the normal duty of care to exercise his skill and
> judgment to improve the patient's health in any particular respect in
> which the patient has sought his aid, has hitherto been treated as
> single comprehensive duty covering all the ways in which a doctor is
> called upon to exercise his skill and judgment in the improvement   H
> of the physical or mental condition of the patient for which his
> services either as a general practitioner or specialist have been
> engaged. This general duty is not subject to dissection into a

---

11. Judgment Summarizes law.

number of component parts to which different criteria of what satisfy the duty of care apply, such as diagnosis, treatment, advice (including warning of any risks of something going wrong however skilfully the treatment advised is carried out.) The *Bolam* case itself embraced failure to advise the patient of the risk involved in the electric shock treatment as one of the allegations of negligence against the surgeon as well as negligence in the actual carrying out of treatment in which that risk did result in injury to the patient. The same criteria were applied to both these aspects of the surgeon's duty of care. In modern medicine and surgery such dissection of the various things a doctor had to do in the exercise of his whole duty of care owed to his patient is neither legally meaningful nor medically practicable. Diagnosis itself may involve exploratory surgery, the insertion of drugs by injection (or vaccination) involves intrusion upon the body of the patient and oral treatment by drugs although it involves no physical intrusion by the doctor on the patient's body may in the case of particular patients involve serious and unforeseen risks. . . . My Lords. I venture to think that in making this separation between that part of the doctor's duty of care that he owes to each individual patient, which can be described as a duty to advise upon treatment and warn of its risks, the courts have misconceived their functions as the finders of fact in cases depending upon the negligent exercise of professional skill and judgment. In matters of diagnosis and the carrying out of treatment the court is not tempted to put itself in the surgeon's shoes; it has to rely upon and evaluate expert evidence, remembering that it is no part of its task of evaluation to give effect to any preference it may have for one responsible body of professional opinion over another, provided it is satisfied by the expert evidence that both qualify as responsible bodies of medical opinion. But when it comes to warning about risks, the kind of training and experience that a judge will have undergone at the Bar makes it natural for him to say (correctly) it is my right to decide whether any particular thing is done to my body, and I want to be fully informed of any risks there may be involved of which I am not already aware from my general knowledge as a highly educated man of experience, so that I may form my own judgment as to whether to refuse the advised treatment or not.

"No doubt if the patient in fact manifested this attitude by means of questioning, the doctor would tell him whatever it was the patient wanted to know; but we are concerned here with volunteering unsought information about risks of the proposed treatment failing to achieve the result sought or making the patient's physical or mental condition worse rather than better. The only effect that mention of risks can have on the patient's mind, if it has any at all, can be in the direction of deterring the patient from undergoing the treatment which in the expert opinion of the doctor it is in the patient's interest to undergo. To decide what risks the existence of which a patient should be voluntarily warned and the terms in which such warning, if any, should be given, having regard to the

12

effect that the warning may have, is as much an exercise of professional skill and judgment as any other part of the doctor's comprehensive duty of care to the individual patient, and expert medical evidence on this matter should be treated in just the same way. The *Bolam* test should be applied."

How then, I ask again, did it come about that the judge found the defendants guilty of negligence, when he accepted that there was a substantial body of responsible medical opinion in 1979 who would not have given any warning? The answer is that he drew a distinction between advice or warning in a therapeutic context and advice or warning in a contraceptive context. In a therapeutic context there was a body of responsible medical opinion which would not have warned of the failure rate. But in a contraceptive context there was no such body of responsible medical opinion. Even if there had been, he would still have found the defendants negligent, since in his view the *Bolam* test does not apply at all to advice given in a non-therapeutic context. He said:

"I accept that it was the view of the majority of the House of Lords that in the therapeutic context of that case the duty to give advice was subject to the same test as the duty to diagnose and treat, and that this test, known as the *Bolam* test after an earlier case, was that a doctor is not negligent if he acts in accordance with a practice accepted as proper by a responsible body of medical opinion even though other doctors adopt a different practice. This test is different from the one generally applied in actions in respect of negligent advice. I see nothing in the reasons given for adopting the *Bolam* test in the sort of circumstances under consideration in *Sidaway* which compels me to widen the application of this exceptional rule so as to cause it to apply to contraceptive counselling."

So the judge decided against the defendants on two grounds. First, he held that the *Bolam* test did not apply at all in a contraceptive context. Instead he applied his own judgment as to what should have been mentioned in that context. Secondly, if the *Bolam* test did apply, then he found as a fact that there was nobody of responsible medical opinion which would not, in a contraceptive context, have warned of the risk of failure. I have reversed these two grounds, since the first ground raises a question of considerable general importance.

Was the judge right when he held that the *Bolam* test is an exception to the ordinary rule in actions for negligence? If by an "exceptional rule" the judge meant that the *Bolam* test is confined to actions against doctors, then I would respectfully disagree. I have already quoted a passage from McNair J.'s summing up in *Bolam's* case. In an earlier passage he had said [1957] 1 W.L.R. 582, 586:

"where you get a situation which involves the use of some special skill or competence, then the test as to whether there has been negligence or not is not the test of the man on the top of a Clapham omnibus, because he has not got this special skill. The test is the standard of the ordinary skilled man exercising and professing to have that special skill."

---

12. Judgment analyses decision of trial judge.

A   So far as I know that passage has always been treated as being of general application whenever a defendant professes any special skill. It is so treated in *Charlesworth & Percy on Negligence*, 7th ed. (1983), p. 388 para. 6–17. The *Bolam* test is not confined to a defendant exercising or professing the particular skill of medicine. If there had been any doubt on the question, which I do not think there was, it was removed by the speech of Lord Diplock in the *Sidaway* case [1985] A.C.

B   871, 892. Lord Diplock made it clear that the *Bolam* test is rooted in an ancient rule of common law applicable to all artificers. In *Saif Ali v. Sydney Mitchell & Co.* [1980] A.C. 198, Lord Diplock treated the same test as applicable to barristers, although he did not mention the *Bolam* case by name. The question in that case was whether a barrister is immune from an action in negligence in relation to advice given out of

C   court. It was held that he is not. Lord Diplock said, at p. 220:

   "No matter what profession it may be, the common law does not impose on those who practise it any liability for damage resulting from what in the result turn out to have been errors of judgment, unless the error was such as no reasonably well-informed and competent member of that profession could have made."

D   Mr. Lewis did his best to argue that the *Bolam* test is confined to doctors. For the reasons I have given, I cannot accept that argument. I can see no possible ground for distinguishing between doctors and any other profession or calling which requires special skill, knowledge or experience. To be fair to the judge, it was not, I think, on this ground that he regarded the *Bolam* test as exceptional.

13

E   In passing, I should mention that the *Bolam* test is often thought of as limiting the duty of care. So in one sense it does. But it also extends the duty of care, as the second of the two passages I have quoted from McNair J.'s summing up in the *Bolam* case makes clear. The standard is not that of the man on the top of the Clapham omnibus, as in other fields of negligence, but the higher standard of the man skilled in the particular profession or calling.

F   Why then did the judge think that it would be an extension of the *Bolam* test to apply it in the present case? The reason can only have been that which I have already mentioned, namely, the distinction between therapeutic and non-therapeutic advice. Mr. Lewis took us through the *Sidaway* case [1985] A.C. 871 speech by speech, and paragraph by paragraph, in order to point the distinction. But I remain

G   unconvinced. In the first place the line between therapeutic and non-therapeutic medicine is elusive. A plastic surgeon carrying out a skin graft is presumably engaged in therapeutic surgery; but what if he is carrying out a face-lift, or some other cosmetic operation? Mr. Lewis found it hard to say.

   In the second place, a distinction between advice given in a therapeutic context and advice given in a non-therapeutic context would

H   be a departure from the principle on which the *Bolam* test is itself grounded. The principle does not depend on the context in which any act is performed, or any advice given. It depends on a man professing skill or competence in a field beyond that possessed by the man on the

---

13. Judgment discusses Counsel's arguments.

Clapham omnibus. If the giving of contraceptive advice required no A
special skill, then I could see an argument that the *Bolam* test should
not apply. But that was not, and could not have been, suggested. The
fact (if it be the fact) that giving contraceptive advice involves a different
sort of skill and competence from carrying out a surgical operation does
not mean that the *Bolam* test ceases to be applicable. It is clear from
Lord Diplock's speech in *Sidaway* that a doctor's duty of care in relation
to diagnosis, treatment and advice, whether the doctor be a specialist or B
general practitioner, is not to be dissected into its component parts. To
dissect a doctor's advice into that given in a therapeutic context and that
given in a contraceptive context would be to go against the whole thrust
of the decision of the majority of the House of Lords in that case. So I
would reject Mr. Lewis's argument under this head, and hold that the
judge was not free, as he thought, to form his own view of what warning C
and information ought to have been given, irrespective of any body of
responsible medical opinion to the contrary.

So I turn to the second question, which assumes, as I have held, that
the *Bolam* test applies. Here Mr. Lewis acknowledges that he is in some
difficulty. For in the course of the defence evidence the judge observed
to Mr. Lewis:

> "You are in the happy position of being able to say, as I understand D
> it, that all of the defence team, as it were, are all saying that they
> personally would have advised, and in one case they claim they did
> advise. You are in that happy position. You are in the unhappy
> position that they will say, as you have to accept, that there were
> squads of people who did not."

To which Mr. Lewis replied: "Yes, if we apply the *Bolam* test, I have E
had it on this limb certainly."

Indeed as late as Mr. Miller's closing submission the judge observed
that the defendants were "home and dry" if *Sidaway* applied, as I have
held it does. Yet when he came to give judgment, the judge had
changed his mind. For the sake of convenience I repeat here verbatim
the three relevant findings: F

> "[1] That in a non-contraceptive context, for instance if there had
> been a therapeutic reason for sterilising [the plaintiff], there was a
> responsible body of medical opinion which would not, unasked,
> have mentioned the fact that the operation involved an element of
> risk. [2] That in the context of someone seeking contraceptive
> advice there was such a body of medical opinion which would not, G
> unasked, have mentioned that the failure rate of a post partum
> sterilisation operation was several times as high as the ultimate
> failure rate of a vasectomy. [3] That in the context of someone
> seeking contraceptive advice there was no such body of medical
> opinion which would have failed to mention that there was a risk of
> failure of the post partum sterilisation or that vasectomy was an
> option or to make inquiries of the domestic situation of the party H
> seeking advice."

I can find nothing in the evidence which justifies the last of these
findings. Mr. Lewis relies on the documentary evidence, some of which

A   is set out in the judge's judgment. I need not refer to it in detail. As was to be expected, it emphasises the importance of counselling before deciding on an operation, whether for male or female sterilisation. In addition, the documents published by the medical defence bodies—again as was only to be expected—discourage the giving of any sort of guarantee of success. But this evidence does not meet the point made by Mr. Miller and by all the witnesses, including those called by the
B   plaintiff, who said that though they would themselves have warned the plaintiff of the risk of failure, there was a body of responsible doctors in 1979 who would not have done so. The judge accepted in his judgment that the distinction between advising in a contraceptive and non-contraceptive context was not "crystal clear" on the evidence. With respect, that is an understatement. The witnesses were never asked to
C   distinguish between the two cases. There was therefore only one finding open on the evidence, namely, that there was a body of responsible medical opinion which would not have given any warning as to the failure of female sterilisation, and the possible alternatives, in the circumstances in which the defendants actually found themselves. So I would not accept the second of the two grounds on which the judge decided against the defendants.

D   That makes it unnecessary to consider whether, if the defendants had been under a duty to warn, they were entitled to assume that an adequate warning had been given by Dr. Gomez, the general practitioner. We know from his letter of 31 July 1979 that he warned the plaintiff that the operation was irreversible. But since he was not called, we do not know what other warning, if any, he may have given.

E   Mr. Lewis referred us in passing to *Thake* v. *Maurice* [1986] Q.B. 644, where it was held to have been negligent on the part of a surgeon undertaking a vasectomy not to warn of the risk of failure in accordance with his usual practice. But in that case, as Kerr L.J. pointed out at p. 680, there was no independent medical evidence called by either side. So, as Mr. Lewis sensibly agreed, it does not help him in the present case. Nor does he get any help from *Jones* v. *Berkshire Area Health*
F   *Authority* (unreported), 2 July 1986 for in that case the duty to warn was admitted.

        Finally, I should mention the plaintiff's claim for negligent misrepresentation. In the statement of claim it is pleaded by amendment:

        "By reason of the matters pleaded in paragraphs 2–5 above the defendants negligently misrepresented to the plaintiff that the operation
G   would render her permanently sterile and/or that sterilisation was her only contraceptive option and in reliance upon such representation the plaintiff agreed to undergo the said operation."

        The judge deals with that allegation at the end of his judgment, and does so in a very few words for the sake, as he puts it, of completeness. He makes no finding as to the terms of the representation, or whether it
H   was express or implied. All he says is: "I find that allegation proved."
        The only possible justification for the judge's finding on the evidence is that it is to be inferred from the fact that the plaintiff was told that the operation was irreversible. But to draw that inference from the use

14

---

14. *Thake* v. *Maurice* distinguished.

of the word "irreversible" would be inconsistent with the decision of this A
court in *Eyre v. Measday* [1986] 1 All E.R. 488, where a similar
argument was advanced. Slade L.J. said, at p. 494:

"There has been some discussion in the course of argument on the
meaning of the phrase 'irreversible' and as to the relevance of the
statement, undoubtedly made by the defendant to the plaintiff, that
the proposed operation must be regarded as being irreversible.
However, I take the reference to irreversibility as simply meaning B
that the operative procedure in question is incapable of being
reversed, that what is about to be done cannot be undone. I do not
think it can reasonably be construed as a representation that the
operation is bound to achieve its acknowledged object, which is a
different matter altogether."

So I would reject the plaintiff's claim for negligent misrepresentation. C
For the reasons I have given the plaintiff has failed to make good her
claim for negligence. Accordingly, I would allow this appeal.

WATKINS L.J. I agree.

STEPHEN BROWN L.J. I agree that this appeal should be allowed. In
my judgment the test laid down in *Bolam v. Friern Hospital Management* D
Committee [1957] 1 W.L.R. 582, 587 as further considered and explained
by Lord Diplock in *Sidaway v. Board of Governors of Bethlem Royal*
Hospital [1985] A.C. 871 should be applied to the facts of this case. The
judge appears to have been persuaded to find a distinction between
advice given in a "therapeutic" and a "non-therapeutic" context. Such a
distinction is wholly unwarranted and artificial. The general duty of the E
doctors treating the plaintiff is, in the words of Lord Diplock at p. 893,
"not subject to dissection into a number of component parts to which
different criteria of what satisfy the duty of care apply." I entirely agree
with the careful analysis made by Lloyd L.J. in his judgment.

I feel it right to add that in this case it was unfortunate that the
judge was not able to hear evidence from the general practitioner, who
clearly played an important and relevant role in the story. F

> *Appeal allowed.*
> *Costs of defendants against plaintiff*
>   *in court below not to be enforced*
>   *without order of court.*
> *Costs of appeal against the legal aid* G
>   *fund of The Law Society, not to*
>   *be proceeded with without granting*
>   *The Law Society opportunity to*
>   *make representations.*
> *Leave to appeal refused.*

15
16

17

Solicitors: Hempsons; Pritchard Englefield & Tobin. H

---

15. Order. 16. Costs order.
17. No appeal to House of Lords allowed.

BIBLIOGRAPHY OF FURTHER READING

In addition to the materials specifically cited, the following are of general relevant to the matters discussed in the various chapters.

Chapter 1

H. L. A. Hart, *The Concept of Law*.
Dennis Lloyd, *The Idea of Law*.
Edwin M. Schur, *Law and Society*.
M. D. A. Freeman, *The Legal Structure*.
G. Sawyer, *Law in Society*.
Karl Llewellyn, *The Bramble Bush*.
Robert S. Summers, *Law: Its Nature, Functions and Limits* (2nd ed.).
E. A. Hoebel, *The Law of Primitive Man*
R. Dworkin, *Taking Rights Seriously* and *Law's Empire*.
J. Raz, "Legal Principles and the Limits of Law" 81 Yale L.J. 823 (1972).
S. Roberts, *Order and Dispute*.

Chapter 2

Robert S. Summers, *The Technique Element in Law"*, 59 California L.R. 733 (1971); *Law: Its Nature, Functions and Limits* (2nd ed.).

Chapter 3

Smith and Bailey, *The Modern English Legal System*.
J. A. Jolowicz (ed.), *The Division and Classification of the Law*.

Chapter 4

Bishin and Stone, *Law, Language and Ethics*.
Walter Probert, *Law, Language and Communication*.

Chapter 5

Thibaut and Walker, *Procedural Justice: a Psychological Analysis*.

Chapter 6
D. Lloyd, "Reason and Logic in the Law" (1948) 64 L.Q.R. 468.
A. G. Guest, "Logic in the Law" in *Oxford Essays in Jurisprudence* ed. Guest), p. 176.
Edward Levi, *Introduction to Legal Reasoning.*

Chapters 7 & 8
See materials under Chapter 6.
Sir Carleton Allen, *Law in the Making.*
Sir Rupert Cross, *Precedent in English Law.*
R. W. M. Dias, *Jurisprudence.*
Julius Stone, *Legal Systems and Lawyers' Reasonings.*
William Twining and David Miers, *How to do Things with Rules* (2nd ed.).

Chapters 9 & 10
S. A. Walkland, *The Legislative Process in Great Britain.*
D. Miers and A. Page, *Legislation.*
Twining and Miers, *How to do Things with Rules* (2nd Ed.).
F. Bennion, *Statute Law.*
H. L. A. Hart, *The Concept of Law.*
Sir Carleton Allen, *Law in the Making.*
The Law Commissions' Report in Interpretation of Statutes (Law Com. 21) and see the literature listed there.
J. H. Farrar, *Law Reform and the Law Commission.*
Maxwell on the Interpretation of Statutes.
Craies, Statute Law.
The Report of the Committee on the Preparation of Legislation
Cross: Statutory Interpretation (2nd ed.), Bell and Engle.

Chapter 11
Glanville Williams (ed.), *The Reform of the Law*, Chap. 1.
G. Gardiner and A. Martin (ed.), *Law Reform Now*, Chap. 1.
J. H. Farrar, *Law Reform and the Law Commission*, Chap. 5, and the materials there cited.

Chapter 12
O. Hood Phillips, *First Book of English Law.*
Sir W. Holdsworth, *Some Makers of English Law.*

D. L. Carey Miller, "Legal Writings as a Source of English Law" (1975) 8 C.I.L.S.A. 236.

Chapter 13
D. Lasok and J. W. Bridge, *Law and Institutions of the European Communities.*
K. Lipstein, *The Law of the EEC.*

Chapter 14
W. Friedmann, *Law in a Changing Society.*
Stuart S. Nagel (ed.), *Law and Social Change.*

Chapter 15
Henry W. Ehrmann, *Comparative Legal Cultures.*
M. B. Hooker, *Legal Pluralism.*

Chapter 16
Aristotle, *Ethics.*
R. W. M. Dias, *Jurisprudence.*
P. Stein and J. Shand, *Legal Values in Western Society.*
L. Fuller, *The Morality of Law.*
R. S. Summers, "Evaluating and Improving Legal Processes—A Plea for Process values," 60 Cornell L.R. 1 (1974).

NAME INDEX

SUBJECT INDEX

333